Praise for *Bound Up: On Ki*

"Honest, informative, and often hilarious, *Bound Up* brilliantly renders all the complexities that come with being an American Jew. In exploring her identity through the lens of Nazi kink, Fridman invites readers to investigate the complexities of Judaism, power, and personal identity in ways both daring and profound. With honesty and insight, Fridman's unique perspective pushes the boundaries of understanding desire and the enduring legacies of the past."

—Joey Soloway, director and producer of *Transparent*

"Fridman is my favorite type of writer: one whose fascination with a subject is so profound and acutely felt and rigorously investigated that after reading her work I come out obsessed with the topic. I will be thinking about her completely original (and erotic!) exploration of Jewish history in *Bound Up* for years."

—Bess Kalb, author of *Nobody Will Tell You This but Me*

"'I've promised myself I'll say words I've been taught not to, to uncover what they conceal,' Leora Fridman writes in her revelatory book, *Bound Up*, and she does just that, exploring kink as it relates to intergenerational Jewish trauma, disability, and merely trying to exist as a woman in the twenty-first century. In her thoughtful exploration of her own story, Fridman tells a wider tale of power, grace, and survival, and readers will be grateful to benefit from her bravery."

—Lynn Melnick, author of *I've Had to Think Up a Way to Survive*

"Hot, smart, and intimate, this book kept me spellbound and turned on, provoked by Leora Fridman's intricate thinking about unthinkable things. I would follow her anywhere she pleases, in all her nimble explorations and fascinations."

—Dori Midnight, liturgist

BOUND UP

BOUND UP

On Kink, Power, and Belonging

Leora Fridman

WAYNE STATE UNIVERSITY PRESS
DETROIT

ISBN 9780814351598 (paperback)
ISBN 9780814351604 (e-book)

Library of Congress Control Number: 2024931984

Cover art by Chelsea Granger. Used by permission of the artist. Cover design by Ashley Muehlbauer.

Grateful acknowledgment is made to the Bertha M. and Hyman Herman Endowed Memorial Fund and the Wayne State University Endowment Fund for the generous support of the publication of this volume.

Wayne State University Press rests on Waawiyaataanong, also referred to as Detroit, the ancestral and contemporary homeland of the Three Fires Confederacy. These sovereign lands were granted by the Ojibwe, Odawa, Potawatomi, and Wyandot Nations, in 1807, through the Treaty of Detroit. Wayne State University Press affirms Indigenous sovereignty and honors all tribes with a connection to Detroit. With our Native neighbors, the press works to advance educational equity and promote a better future for the earth and all people.

Wayne State University Press
Leonard N. Simons Building
4809 Woodward Avenue
Detroit, Michigan 48201-1309

Visit us online at wsupress.wayne.edu.

for the ancestors who couldn't have imagined

I want to sharpen my pride on what strengthens me,
my witness on what haunts me.
—Eli Claire, *Exile and Pride*

Language is what eases the pain of living with other people,
language is what makes the wounds come open again.
—Anne Carson, *Plainwater: Essays and Poetry*

Contents

On Beasting

Like many a nice Jewish girl, I begin in Hebrew class. Dana would sit on one side of me and Michael on the other. Dana and I would pass scribbles of stick figures with boobs. Michael would peer over my shoulder and smile faintly, his pencil perfectly still over his orange notebook, a notebook more beautifully designed than any paper product I'd ever seen. Michael and I hardly spoke, though a heat hovered between us.

"But he'd never like me," I'd say to Dana, "he's so *blond*." Which he was, and blue eyed, and German. Dana and I laughed, "your Aryan crush," she said.

I was otherwise mostly around people who looked very much like me. I was nineteen on a study abroad program in Israel/Palestine made up of both American and German students. On one of the few times that I tried to initiate conversation with Michael, I asked him why he'd come to Israel. He looked down at the floor. "Have you ever heard of philosemitism?" he asked. He told me that he was very interested in Jewish culture and people. "You have a depth of history that fascinates me." Only then did he look up from his thick lashes, as if seeking my approval.

"See," Dana hissed later. "He's *fascinated* by you." We darted away to my room. "It's just because I'm so dark and hairy," I rolled my eyes, "I'm a foreign creature." I watched him from my balcony in the blocky gray Brutalist dorms as he played soccer on the lawn. He smiled mostly at the ground.

Fascination: it's an odd word. Evoking what it means to fixate, to draw attention unto and hold tight. Derived from late sixteenth-century Latin: *fascinum*, witchcraft, *fascinare*, to cast a spell. In its origins, fascination indicates a power over someone. The person fascinated cannot be blamed for being drawn to the fascinate-*or*. Michael couldn't be blamed for his fascination with Jews, then—it was something in us that cast this fascination over him. I watched his body move limber across the grass, lit up by the glaring spotlights over the dorm yard, unburdened by responsibility.

Before I met Michael, I felt white. I felt absorbed by American culture. But place me against a German, and I didn't feel assimilated at all. He was the one entitled to observe me, and I was the one under the microscope of cultural stereotype. I was fascinating to him because I was outside of his whiteness, dominance—I would not yet have said "supremacy."

Israel was the place I was supposed to feel belonging and protection. Throughout my childhood I had been trained to believe that I wouldn't quite belong anywhere but here. Here, I would find shelter. The more I learned about the Occupation and about the establishment of the State of Israel, the more these convictions would begin to deteriorate, but I hadn't quite gotten there yet. Maybe this was an opening act—to travel to my "homeland" and meet Michael, a boy with whom I felt much more exposed, bared, visibly ethnically marked, much less protected than in the United States. The site of return did not enfold me. When the right (white?) person came along, they could see right through it.

A few days after Michael got home to Germany, he emailed me. "I'm sorry I was too shy to talk with you," he wrote, "but I think you are so sexy." I read the email over and over to make sure it wasn't a joke or mistranslation. "The Aryan likes me," I breathed to Dana, shaking my head in shock.

Eventually I wrote back: "How could a stud like you be shy?" I made sure to type a winky face after. (This was in ancient times, before emoji.) I'd never used the word "stud" before, and I could feel myself step behind the force of it. The word insulated me some. Michael replied a few hours later that he was confused by the word "stud"—"I can't find this in my dictionaries," he wrote, "do you think I am like a horse?" I explained the connotation, and he let it lie.

As our emails unfolded, I noticed this tendency to let things lie—to accept a compliment without comment, or not respond minutely to every single question I asked. A kind of restraint he had that I couldn't relate to. He abstained from drilling down as far as possible into the other. I *always* asked, always drilled, didn't let anything drop.

"What about Judaism do you respect so much?" I wrote. "Why don't you like your own German culture, do you think?" Sometimes my questions came out of genuine curiosity, but I was also suspicious. Something else was under there, and I wanted to expose it.

"But why is Israel interesting to you?" I asked. I didn't trust his first answer, that he found the Hebrew language beautiful. I asked again, "*why* do you think it's beautiful to you?" Interrogating, hoping to reveal what he didn't want to admit to himself. The more I knew, the more I could guess what he might be thinking, and the more I could prepare myself for his reactions.

We kept up those emails for about six months, letters in which he gave me charmingly a-grammatical descriptions of his small town in Germany, and I expounded on identity politics, historical trauma, pop music, and how I planned to become a feral backpacker with wild dreadlocks. (I was nineteen.)

"But please never ruin your beautiful hair with making dreadlocks," Michael wrote back, "this would be a big shame." I grew flushed reading this, aware of the consistency of his gaze. He had continued to look, engage, imagine what I might look like now or later. His fascination—something in me drew his notice. And of all things, for it to be my curly hair, the most visibly Jewish thing about me. When anxious I would twist my curls between my fingers and clots of hair would collect around my knuckles. I would try to get rid of these quickly, dropping the knots into the loose sleeve of my jacket or down behind a friend's couch.

"We have to keep our Jewish hair under control, sweetheart," a camp counselor once said to me. She taught me to comb my hair while it was still soaking wet so that my hair's natural frizz would cling as closely to the ringlets as possible, contain itself in the spiraling form that other people marveled at.

As long as I've been aware that other people can see me, I've been aware of my hair. I don't meet anyone without them asking or saying or wondering something about my curls. They're the part of my body I most know exists in public, and so I curate them. I spend more on haircuts than I do on any other kind of appointment. I don't broadcast how much my hair products cost. My hair is the part of me people note, and so I invest in it.

Once, I visited a Jewish summer camp in upstate New York where there is a rule that no one can say anything about anyone else's body. It's called the "no body talk," rule,[1] and it is their way of heading off body image issues in young kids, sheltering them from hypervigilance.

It was pleasant, at first, to be inside of that rule, to escape the constancy of physical catalog. But I also resented it. Camp counselors stated that we should focus on "wisdom" and "Jewish values," and I noticed some concern in me about this harsh divide between the physical and the wise, a concern from old stereotypes about Jews and intellect, nerds who never exercise or stand in the sunlight. I thought of how Nazis themselves held that part of the problem with Jews was their unbalanced emphasis on the mind over body, that the Third Reich would return German culture to a soundly embodied state. Any return to the body has its conditions, and controls.

The "no body talk" rule was meant to keep kids from ruminating about their bodies, but it made me think about my body even more, and not pleasantly so. The minute someone tells me to stay away from something, I assume there's something wrong with that thing. In this case, I assumed there must be something wrong with my body, an assumption that I can't say is new to me. As early as I can remember I've been tugging pants up to cover my belly, smushing my breasts back into the bra, especially on the right side, where one breast is just slightly larger than the other, a common human reality that bras are not designed to accommodate, and so of course we assume it's the breasts that are wrong, not the shapes of the cup.

These are very minor labors, but they have set me up to remember that my own body needs to work to belong. I remember scraping my knee in a playground and being told not to cry, to move on, to put on a happy face. Later, I remember smearing concealer underneath my adolescent eyes in an attempt to mask my exhaustion, my sleeplessness, the eruptions of pain that were already keeping me awake while other teenagers slept off their growth spurts. I learned that makeup could mask my pallor, even my skin tone, smooth over the unpleasant.

"No body talk" assumes that if we don't talk about it, the talk won't continue internally. My body is mostly approved of by the prevailing gendered norms, but it all feels precarious. I am polite, I smile, I am slim, and when it all works, I enjoy the approval it gains me. "What a sweetheart," I remember hearing my job interviewers say as a glass door swished closed behind me. It was the early spring before I graduated from college, and I knew I'd succeeded at playing a young-lady-early-adult. I had complied with what my interviewers believed a sweetheart to look like and act like; I had asked them endless questions about themselves, was modest about my own achievements while remembering every detail from the last few issues of their magazine. I had used eyeliner and mascara to make my eyes look wide open as a newborn fawn, my cheeks miraculously flushed by an imaginary few moments of late afternoon sun, my waist defined as that of a thin young person who has not been pregnant, my freckled light-skinned arms foal-like, just toned enough to carry boxes of files from one end of the office to the other without threatening anyone of any gender with my strength.

I do not suffer active mistreatment or shaming most of the time, as many other people do, and their experience is an aggressively harmful one distinct from what I am describing here. I am rewarded when I have the capacity to meet normative standards, and yet the body talk does not stop. It preoccupies me, hangs out in my brain such that I can remember and critique exactly what I wore to a job interview fifteen years ago when I sure would rather have that brain space for something else. My questions now come from within conformity; if even the body that almost succeeds is interminably hounded and distracted by these standards, why do I continue to try?

The more I think about Michael, the more I want to think about Nazis. Up until now I have been bored of this topic. I learned more than my share about it in school, in synagogue, in youth group—I can't think of many Jewish occasions in my life that haven't at least touched on the Holocaust. The writer and critic Philip Lopate describes how often American Jews "name-check" the Holocaust as a specific and noncomparable moment in history, one that we are not allowed to compare to other horrors or tragedies.[2] This Holocaust name-checking reminds us that we are separate. What excited me when I met Michael is that the history of the Holocaust might link me to someone who wasn't Jewish, as opposed to set me apart from them. When I met Michael, and when I sensed the prospect of touching Michael, the history was animated. My skin—that which encases me—it prickled, came alive with possible contact. It was the first time this history became substance that I could engage in relationship, to build relationship instead of cutting me off, instead of making me feel necessarily isolated and endangered.

I was educated to believe that you should know your shit before you challenge it, study the classical forms before you break them. So when I begin thinking about Michael in this way, I read. I avoid the polemics I know well about how the Holocaust cannot be universalized or made into a metaphor. I begin with Susan Sontag's 1975 essay, "Fascinating Fascism," which examines the appeal of Nazi imagery. What I find most useful is how Sontag thinks about photographs of Nazi regalia and the ways they balance a sense of erotic risk with an equal amount of control. "The fascist ideal is to transform sexual energy into a 'spiritual' force, for the benefit of community," Sontag writes.[3]

The idea is to infuse the erotic in cultural objects, and thus control it on an individual level. The Third Reich wanted to return its citizens to a "healthy" sense of embodiment, but to channel any impulsivity of the body toward the needs and objectives of the state. I can imagine that here "body talk" would be allowed, because it benefits the state to organize bodies by their strengths and weaknesses.

Sontag goes on: "The erotic is always present as a temptation, with the most admirable response being an heroic repression of the sexual impulse."[4] The mind meets the body, acknowledges its needs, but only acts on them in regimented ways.

"Why has Nazi Germany, which was a sexually repressive society, become erotic?" Sontag asks. I think of my quick leap to call Michael my Aryan. In a way, this naming makes him benign. I see what he could have been—or what other people might categorize him as. By calling him by this term, I nullify its power over me, especially in the context of two people who might touch, who might examine and judge and consider the strengths and weaknesses of each other's bodies.

"Making love, how the body acts, is a counterpart or antidote to what has been done to it," writes the poet Elizabeth Alexander.[5] "What has been done to" me is not an immediate trauma or the blunt force of lived experience of state repression. It's inheritance of story, the odd mixture of Jewish pride encased in other people's hatred. It's what makes me feel only tenuously white, what I begin to understand as the haunting of fresh absorption into a governing culture.

I don't remember a time before I knew about the Holocaust or about pogroms. I don't remember a single visit to my grandmother's house without a story about someone who was murdered for being Jewish, always accompanied by a certain sideways glance, a look back over a shoulder toward nothing—or, not nothing, but what moved over there in my grandmother's memory, and what moves now in mine. Always looking over the shoulder and tensing the back. If this movement, this tension or gripping of the shoulders is "how the body acts" already, sex is bound to have some shadows, too.

"I'm looking for my Nazi kink," I begin to say to my friends, only half joking. Sex begins from what my body already knows. My "body talk" is instinctively negative because that's the talk I've fed it most often. My body talks—and acts—like my people are under threat. I feel as though I've been training for threat my whole life. It does not then feel like a leap to turn purposefully toward situations of performative, spectacular danger.

I begin digging deep in dark parts of the internet, looking at things outside of my, uh, usual taste. I google "Nazi love story," "Nazi sex." Quickly I become familiar with the mouthful of a term "Nazisploitation," which refers to sexploitation films fantasizing Nazi sex crimes. On YouTube you can find snippets of the worst, kitschy ones, like *Surf Nazis Must Die*, or *The Beast in Heat*, in which a Nazi doctor creates a half-human half-beast with a libido so high that he "requires" his keepers bring him an endless stream of prisoners to rape. I look back over my shoulder when I'm watching this one, partly to avert my eyes from the most gruesome scenes, and partly to make sure no one is catching me taking in such terrible content. But I don't stop. *The Beast* is just funny and gross, and I fast-forward through most of it, but other films I watch in full, noticing my eyes straining open, looking for something that will actually surprise me.

As someone known for my adamant prohibition on violent, horror, or scary movies, it's bizarre to find myself staring into the screen at *Ilsa, the She-Wolf of the SS* while she carves into someone's skin. I find marks inside my own palms from my fingernails pressing down so hard. Or: here I am watching Lena's hand wobble as she wields her gun in the face of Anselm Rossberg, the ex-Auschwitz guard she's stalking in *Winter Hunt*. I cringe when Max, a former concentration camp guard, shoves his former prisoner Lucia to the floor as they reenact their wartime interactions in *The Night Porter*. I don't feel much in my body, but I note a growing sense of companionship as I make my way through these films. A sense that I'm not alone in looking in this direction, that others too feel the compulsion to melodramatically recreate.

I'm looking for something in these films, even as I cover my eyes every other scene. I lie in bed at night replaying scenes in my mind, imagining uniformed men looming above me in the dark. I sit up at three in the morning and swallow another sleeping pill. I need to rest so that I can wake in a few hours and convince others that I'm a normal functioning human, not a haunted obsessive. These parts of me compete. One leg jerks involuntarily as I try to fall asleep.

When I travel to Germany for work as an adult, I reach out to Michael to see if he wants to meet. It's been years since our emails tapered off, when I'd returned to the United States and gotten busy with other things, other people I could see and meet in person regularly. I wonder if the same email address will work. But he responds right away and says that yes, he'd love to come see me—in fact he will be coming to Berlin for work, for a conference on animal rights. It turns out he is now a spokesperson for a German animal welfare organization. When I google him, the first page of results are statements he's made to the press about a gorilla that ran away from the zoo.

When we meet, it is in the neighborhood where I am staying. We are somewhere I know better than he does, even though I have only lived here a few weeks, but I have been to this bar before and I suggest it. I try not to be early, hoping to be the one to get to gracefully sweep into the room with the wind behind me, but he gets lost on the way and is late and so I settle into a corner table and try not to watch the door.

When he walks into the bar, he looks directly at me so I know it is him, even though his hair color is a little different and his frame thinned out. He walks quickly to my corner, eyes on me and nothing else, as if he doesn't need to see the edges of the tables or chairs in order to cross the room.

"Hello," he says, smiling, and sits down without removing his coat.

"It's you," he says. I laugh. It's not my favorite of my laughs, a harsh one, a high one.

"It's me," I say. "Is it you?" I feel a flutter of panic, realizing that perhaps I will need to make an effort at conversation. Will we know where to go or how to begin? He leans his forearms onto the table. His jacket, open, hangs away from his chest. I gesture to the bartender so that they will approach.

"So," I start, "I did google you. It seems like you are very dedicated to animals?" It is a habit of mine, to disarm with a direct question to avoid small talk that will make me feel boring. Sometimes people are taken by this habit, how it invites them to also reveal something quickly, but others are thrown, needing more time to ease in.

8

Michael nods now, his chin lowering several times to his chest as if taking in the topic very seriously. I can't tell yet how this is going. I try again. "So, animals are important to you? Or is it just your job?" I hope this will give him a choice of a few avenues he could choose in how to respond.

"It's my job." He speaks softly. "But I do think they are important." He tells me in simple language that we must care for other species if we care for the earth. It occurs to me that his English might be rusty. His formality could be that—a language barrier—or just a slow adjustment to what I've asked of him.

The bartender arrives, and Michael points to my beer, asking for the same. Thus far, I am the one leading us. It's new for me, this leading. I feel more comfortable being told where we'll go, but tonight is an edge, or a ledge I walk out on and test for whether I can stand.

"Why are animals important to you personally?" I ask. "Tell me about that. It's not something I grew up with." I wasn't raised with pets, and I am usually afraid of them way before I find them cute. I don't take easily to their licking or their little nips. Other people always need to explain their thing with pets to me and seem vaguely disgruntled when I don't instinctively relate.

"We should be kind with beasts," he tells me, pauses. I wonder if this explains his gentleness with me. I think of my thick lips as I sip my beer. I watch his almost frail shoulders as he shifts in his seat, and above them the few strands of gray in his blond hair, a kind of elegance I've always been in awe of. I've been enjoying getting older and realizing I am attracted to some qualities that mark a person as aging. Michael seems to take some caution with his body, as if perhaps it has been injured on its way through the years. He takes off the jacket, finally. Something feels more at ease about him then, a bit more adjusted. He sighs and gives me a small smile.

"It's you," he says again. I think he is encouraging me to slow down, not rush forward in the conversation, but I rush because I'm not sure I want him to scan my face so closely. I wonder if I look old, if I've slipped out of the set of characteristics that he was attracted to back then. We all know it's easier for men to be old and still considered hot. I feel my thighs spread wide, my feet not quite touching the floor and so my legs tense, dangling. One thing about asking questions is it turns the gaze away from myself.

9

"I'm curious if you remember our emails," I say, knowing of course that he will. But I want to hear him affirm it. He shifts back into his seat and grips the table with both hands, and I realize suddenly that he might be nervous, too.

"I remember not just our emails," he says. It's a thicker tone of voice, and he is blushing. Something goes softer in me. "I remember sitting next to you and not being able to speak," he says. It's a little much, a little soon, a little cheesy or overwhelming. I don't know how to respond, so I pull my hair in front of my face and giggle. I hope that in retrospect this will be funny. Or maybe cute?

Michael observes me for a minute. His gaze is more serious than I expect. "But you never even looked in my direction. Back then." I see that there are dark arcs under his eyes. So much time has passed since we were teenagers, and so much life that hasn't been said.

I reach for his hand. Someone had to. "Michael, here's the thing." I lean forward and bring my other hand to my arm, stroke the brown hairs below my elbow so that he looks there too. Something sparks between us now that we are both eyeing my surface.

"I'm so dark and hairy, and you're so light," I say. It's not a tactful thing to say, not particularly flirtatious, at least not in the senses I've known so far. But I'm a stranger here, and so being weird carries less threat. I feel as though I'm spotlit, but a little less worried about catching my better angles. The beam is so bright it highlights what I wouldn't have chosen to say.

"I don't know, I'm not like you," I add, "I never thought you'd be into me." Michael looks confused.

"But that's silly," he tells me, "People are often attracted to opposites." He brings his fingers also to my arm. His thumb is a thumb I do not know. Where he moves it, the hairs on my arm rise.

"Sure," I say, "but I didn't know if you'd be attracted or repelled." I think for a minute. It is baffling having a body that people react to differently in different contexts. I assume a lot and know so little about what Michael thinks makes a hot person.

"I figured that where you came from, there was a very different version of beauty," I say. "I look nothing like it." Is this clear enough?

He scrunches up his face. "I think you are more clever than that," he says. His fingers tighten around my arm, as if reminding me of their presence. I have not forgotten, but I'm not sure how to feel them. The point of pressure where his thumb presses into my muscle like he is straining to hold on. I try to concentrate on his words though his touch is distracting, pulling something out of me that feels less orderly. It could be attraction or dread.

"I don't know you that well," Michael says, "but my impression is that you know these things are complicated."

I rush to reply. "Yes, yes, of course they are complicated," I say. I feel a little impatient with the abstraction, though I understand he wants to remind me that I am smart. I look at him and try to move something in the conversation closer. "I never assume people will be attracted me," I say. "It seems like a safer way to go."

"I can understand that," he says, but I don't know if he really understands or just feels that he does because we are in physical contact. "You are modest." It's not what I meant. The way Michael speaks to me, it sounds more like he *wants* to understand my words than like he does. He is inching his fingers up my forearm and now his finger is settling into a groove inside my elbow. He presses it there. I do not move. The pressure reassures me. The touch has gone on long enough that I believe he really wants to be here. I look at him for an extended moment, unsure of what to say, rare for me. He nods back, only once, and something locks in between us.

Around us, other people murmur in German. I look down at our table and then back up again at his face, feeling like I am in a movie about long-lost lovers meeting again. An inevitability settles over me, and with it a stillness, a quieting at the center of my chest. I realize we are definitely going to kiss, and there's very little I could do to ruin it.

We talk more first—about the past and also now—but touch is the best part of the time we share. Eventually we walk out of the bar and along the *kanal* and it is bitterly cold. We do silly things like I read the names of the boats aloud and he corrects my German pronunciation, and then I shudder in the wind, and he uses the excuse to wrap me in his arms.

I sense the role I am playing but it doesn't bore me. It feels like a familiar game. I lift my face away from his shoulder and there is his mouth, ready to kiss me. It is easy between our lips, parts of a body that know what they are looking to find. Our body heat dissipates quickly in the cold, and so I press my mouth harder to his, less romantic than insistent. He moves his face away, just slightly.

"We kissed," he whispers. Something that was missing, now slid into place where it was destined to go. I put my mouth against his cheek and smile so that he can feel it in the dark. "We did," I say. I shiver involuntarily, and he holds me more firmly. "I like that," I say. I say it into his ear. I wish for everything to be crystal clear between us.

"Come with me," I say, moving away to grasp his hand and turn toward the road. He doesn't understand at first, pulling me back to him, but I am wanting to go in a direction, efficient. "Let's go," I say. He understands eventually, and I bring him back to my apartment.

Later, in bed, he rubs me in long swaths down my back like he is calming a nervous animal. I sigh.

"I'm like a kitten," I say.

"No. You are like a woman," he says. He touches my cheek as if looking for closeness, but it's not what I want from him now. I have steered for so much of this evening, in the bar, from the *kanal* to here, and now I want him to step into something, to let me feel soft and pliable beneath his hands. I want to try on being a creature.

I turn my face to the pillow and return his hand to the small of my back. I need a moment not facing him to think. Several times tonight, he has recognized my body but not my words. I want him to play with me in speech as well as he seems to engage with my body language, but he does not pick up the words where I place them. We don't seem to be able to agree on where "kitten" goes, or "hair."

The only way to get him to play with me the way I want, it seems, is to communicate it without language, to let him touch me—feel me—like the animals he works so hard to protect. I want to be the beast and him the gentle tamer. It seems it's too much for him to acknowledge this, so I won't force him. I haven't found a way for us to talk and understand each other well, but we can communicate in other modes. I moan softly as Michael brings his hand to my sacrum and then scratches me with three fingers all the way up my spine. He cups the base of my skull and I release a full sigh. He stays in my bed several more hours, but until "goodnight," I say no more.

The next day I am reading Hannah Arendt and waiting for Michael to text, knowing now I am playing another kind of game. I keep one eye on the phone and one eye on my book. "Power corresponds to the human ability not just to act, but to act in concert," Arendt writes.[6] I read her as permission. What I'm doing with Michael is "in concert," I hope. An action of one body causing a response in another, and a power—there is more I can do if we do it together.

I give in and I text him first. By many standards, I shouldn't. I shouldn't come on too strong, and I'm worried I'll push him away, so I make sure everything I say hands a bit more power over to him.

"Sorry if I was a little creepy last night," I start.

"I'm sorry for digging things up that maybe should've stayed in our past." I duck under the apology and wait for him to lure me out again. Still nothing.

And so, an hour later. "Thanks for letting me be your little Jewish fling." A harder push, an experiment in crossing another line.

Nothing.

He must be very busy.

Before Michael, I never wanted anyone to call me "little." Even though I literally am, barely five feet three if I've been doing a ton of yoga. I'm regularly mistaken for a teenager. When I get "little lady" on the street it feels condescending. But something happens with Michael that makes me invite this word, and not just the smallness but everything else that might come with it: an anticipation of being designated submissive, an invitation toward what I fantasize may be in his mind.

I do not think I am weak or monstrous, but I do think I am perceived as such. The gender I was assigned at birth contributes to this; the weakly feminine. My ethnicity backs me up with its own stereotypes and tropes. I attempt to comply, to regulate my figure and behavior in order to please, but I am always encountering new failures.

A human body simply can't function without flaws and slowness, and my own has its specific versions of these. I've experienced chronic fatigue and gynecological pain since I was twelve, and I was diagnosed with endometriosis in my early thirties, underdoing my first excision surgery soon after that. I'd been extraordinarily tired for years, and the diagnosis and surgery were a huge relief, giving some rationale for all the time I'd spent on the couch, unable to work due to physical pain and resulting brain fog. I'd been ashamed of my periods of incapacitation for so long. Once I was diagnosed, I could lead with an explanation of my chronic illness and occasionality disability so that others would be prepared and ask less of me when I was having a flare-up.

When I'm sick, I cannot regulate my body as much. It flickers, moving in and out of its capacity to conform. Though I would not have wished sickness on myself, this flicker does empower me in some ways: it lets me test the parameters of what makes me likeable and how I am perceived. When I am sick, I cannot stand up ballerina-straight, let alone suck in my belly. When I stop trying to obey physical norms because I have no choice, I look around and find that I am not immediately socially rejected, which while it may sound histrionic, feels accurate. I have not been abandoned by my friends because I had to cancel our plans or could not muster a smile. I have not fallen through the earth into a dark hole, left for dead. Instead, I have invited my friends into new ways of interacting with me: texting memes, sending voice notes, lying next to one another with our eyes closed and feet up to mediate the pain.

When I explain my illness, I set accurate expectations so I will be less likely to disappoint. I name my weakness as protection, and I name it similarly with Michael, a possibility of revulsion before he can have his own reaction. Instead of staying a pathetic pining woman waiting by the phone, I step into this act and own it. I stare at the dark screen and feel the drama of someone else's power, my legs and back stiff with cramping. Or are they just stiff from standing by and waiting for him?

I imagine what I might have done to disgust Michael, why he does not respond. He will not do this to me. I will do this to myself. "The villainy you teach me, I will execute, and it shall go hard but I will better the instruction."[7] Yes, that's Shylock, in the speech in *The Merchant of Venice* in which he is begging for his life. Because what proves you deserve to live more than your capacity to star in the role they taught you to play?

"I was a woman of appetites, a growling beast. I was a person." This is Melissa Broder, in her novel *Milk Fed*, in which the narrator controls her own body and then, through a queer romance, dramatically releases this control and finds a new relationship to herself.[8] I think of Broder's line when I feel the urge to take things too far. Broder moves from woman to person through the invocation of the beast. When I act the beast, when I allow my appetites to growl, gender restricts my body a little bit less.

I imagine Michael in a conference room, receiving my texts and rolling his eyes, looking back up at the other suits in his meeting, much more important things to do. I imagine he will confess to a friend that he slept with a woman who was obsessed with identity and obsessed with him, that she was maybe fun in bed but definitely "too much." He will find my dark hairs in the folds of his shirt and hurry to pull them from the cloth. They will cling, coarse and thick and gloomy.

I hesitate. Can I fantasize about this? I am treading hazardous territory, as Hannah Arendt herself also did, exposing herself to vitriol for so-called victim-blaming. In her famed coverage of Adolf Eichmann's trial, Arendt was not afraid to point out the participation of Jews under Nazi rule in carrying out the organized eradication of their own people. Arendt stated many times that she was not implying that Jews were to be held responsible for their own suffering. But she also did not turn away from entanglement, the reality of Jewish Councils who played into the parts designed for them to (theoretically) avoid their own personal suffering.

Arendt focused on Eichmann's banality, unwilling to see him as a terrifying monster and unwilling to side with the prevailing Zionist narrative. Many Jews and Zionist critics trounced her for this complexity, calling her cold, unempathetic, and a "self-hating Jewess."[9]

I don't think Arendt was self-hating, but I do think she was willing to concentrate on the behavior of individual humans when other people wanted her to consider only groups. It wouldn't have been termed *identity politics* at the time, but it was essentially that. Jews were the victims in the Eichmann trial and any complication of this categorization interrupted the narrative. Arendt was no stranger to looking Nazis in the face on a personal level: she famously studied under and then had an affair with Martin Heidegger, who sympathized with Nazis for much of his career.

Heidegger was thirty-five and Arendt seventeen when they first became lovers, and so it's not difficult to imagine why she had trouble taking him off a pedestal. She once referred to him as "the hidden king [who] reigned in the realm of thinking" and called her feelings for him *"Eine starre Hingegebenheit an ein Einziges"* or "An unbending devotion to a unique man." I can understand the appeal here—even if it might seem demeaning, organizing one's life and thinking around one person can be settling, consolidating. Arendt devoted herself to him. Through this devotion she gained intellectual lineage and eventually developed what she defined as her own philosophy. Heidegger was a lightning rod who forced her to decide where she stood.

Heidegger began to publicly support the Nazi Party in 1933. When Arendt asked him to reject National Socialism, Heidegger refused but assured her that his feelings for her were unchanged.[10] Though Arendt struggled over years with Heidegger's politics, she continued their on-again, off-again affair, even defending him publicly as a fallible if innocent man swept up in a political milieu. It's tough to reconcile these choices of Arendt's. It's not what you want your heroes to do—stay in a relationship with someone who espouses hate. But it fits, in a certain sense: Like Arendt's stance on Jews who collaborated with Nazis, she did not look away from Heidegger's moral failures but also did not abandon him for them.

I can't make the leap and say that Arendt was somehow perversely *into* Heidegger's Nazism, because nothing in their correspondence points to this being the case. I have no evidence that Arendt was necessarily being kinky about this. But given how dedicated she was to reasoning through moral choices, she has to have developed her own logic, her own justifications for this relationship. It seems most likely to me that what she was doing was actively thinking through moral failure, including via relationship, including the human, including even her own body. Perhaps staying in relationship with Heidegger was the way to get to do that—to discern the ethics most intimately. Arendt was a relational thinker: she believed in working to comprehend the incomprehensible, and she believed in doing so in conversation with other thinkers, with other opinions as they emerged. She refused to push away that which terrified her.

I read Arendt while I wait for Michael to text back, and her thinking goads me on. By today's standards, Arendt's relationship with Heidegger might be called sexually exploitative, given the power imbalance. But it seems that Arendt was conscious of this dynamic and pushed into and through it until she was able to gain the kind of peerly respect she desired between them.

I push Michael. I am trying to outsmart him before he even hints at anything that could feel exploitative. "Your little Jewish fling," I text and I smile to myself, feeling crafty, as if I am a step ahead of him on a path we both know, but only I am willing to point the way. The scorned woman, the Jew whose sexual energy overwhelms the proper man, the wild seductress who will never find a husband that way. I control it because I get to think through this without being hurt. I trace stereotype and performance, where we each come from and how this colors our roles and our relations, what my body reconstitutes when it receives approval or rejection.

It's dangerous, this way of thinking. I risk annoying him or offending him, I risk stereotyping, I risk blaming myself for any hurt or danger on the horizon. But something ignites in me with Michael that I both haven't known before and seem to have known forever. The obviousness of our difference makes me less afraid. I point at what has already occurred historically and ask that we move together in a manner that acknowledges these occurrences. Other people's bodies have moved in these dynamics, and a courage opens in me when I place myself plainly among them.

I'll tell you so you don't have to do it yourself: When you google "Nazi kink" or "Nazi fetish," one of the first things that comes up is a letter to the American sex advice columnist Dan Savage. A woman has written to him asking if, as a Jew, it's OK for her to ask her Christian German lover to role-play a Nazi during sex. She tells Savage not to worry, that she is not suicidal, nor does she want her partner to literally murder her. "[I'm] just your garden-variety self-hating Jew," she writes. To respond to her letter, Savage calls in Mark Oppenheimer, a Jewish writer, because, Savage says, he needs the support of a Jew to answer this question. Oppenheimer responds that he isn't worried about the kink and encourages the writer to talk it through with her partner. He *is* worried, though, about her calling herself a "self-hating Jew," and how uncomfortable she seems with her identity. He recommends most of all that she work on that part.

Savage is very careful with shame. Elsewhere, in another column, he responds to a gay man who enjoys being "abused" by straight men in bed, meaning he enjoys role-playing being humiliated for being gay. The gay man is writing in to make sure Savage thinks this is OK. Savage approves and compares this kink to any other kink that plays on existing oppressive power dynamics, including, he says, Jews with Nazis.

"Basically, you have to build a firewall between your fantasies and your self-esteem," he writes. "A submissive who can enjoy his fantasies without being shredded by them is in control, not being controlled—regardless of how things might appear to a casual or misinformed observer."[11]

This reassures me, reassures me enough to read more, watch more. It might look like I'm poking a wound up late at night with Leni Riefenstahl, the German actress and film director who is famous for producing Nazi propaganda. In *Triumph of the Will*, I watch crowds roar while Hitler speaks of purification. In *The Victory of Faith*, I let the stiffly marching soldiers stomp a rhythm that I already know in my bones.

It doesn't hurt me to watch these. I skip through the films and pause when I want to. I shrink the YouTube window until it's tiny and I feel swollen with possibility. It's not unlike being turned on with no release. I am gathering material that I have the sense will pull me toward something, attract me toward something I don't yet know, people I don't know yet, parts of myself, even, too.

I close the door to my room and sit on the floor with my back against it, as if anticipating a person who will come to capture me and take me away. I don't feel scared. I'm acting the bit I'm supposed to. In a way I've been sitting like this for years. Like many American Jews, I grew up on a steady diet of young-adult Holocaust novels in which little girls hid in closets and forests. (At least all the ones I was given involved girls.) Quivering bodies crawled into corners and hoped not to be acted on, waited and prayed to be saved. The erotics of the captivity are easy to see now, but back then all I knew was that I was obsessed with these books. *Number the Stars, The Devil's Arithmetic, The Upstairs Room*. I devoured them indiscriminately, and for years they were the material of my every nightmare. These books shaped so much about what I know about power, and where to look for it—in what direction. If, as Arendt defines it, power corresponds to "acting in concert," then these books also defined for me what it means to act with others. When I come across power, I have this story to fall back on: the frightened Jew-beast hiding in the dark and waiting to be moved around.

But it's not a contemporary story, or at least not the one I live now. As a white assimilated Jew growing up in the United States, I was not oppressed, not hidden, not demeaned. It's relatively new, historically, that I was not—and my Jewish education wouldn't let me forget this. The comparatively new assimilation of some Jews into whiteness in the United States means that my parents and grandparents remember being not just excluded but persecuted.

The logic of whiteness is contextual and shifting, and so it makes sense that we don't understand exactly when and why we came to belong. "Race is inherently fluid, nuanced and irrational and there is much to learn by probing and interrogating how Jews of European descent are racialized today."[12] I read this in "Understanding Antisemitism," a 2017 publication by Jews for Racial Economic Justice (JFREJ) that gathers a wide range of academic sources to catch us up to what anti-Semitism has meant in the past and means now. I love the way this paper combines the nuanced with the numerical; on the following page a chart arranges income distribution by religious group so as to statistically dispute the myth that Jews control global wealth. These numbers clarify the historical realities of Jews even as these realities are manipulated by the molten, churning logics of race and racial capitalism. Because these two cannot be separated.

"For centuries the targeting and scapegoating of Jews—either by individuals or societal systems—has had the effect of confusing non-Jews (and sometimes Jews as well) about the true nature of systemic oppression."[13] It's validating to be told there's a reason I'm confused. Anti-Semitism historically worked to shroud and protect the prevailing economic systems.[14] Jews were positioned to do the dirty work—meaning, at different moments in European colonization, lending money, tending bars, or meting out salaries so that, should workers become unhappy, the Jews could be blamed instead of the ruling class. We are the ones you can see and access, what historians describe as the buffer role, middle agent, or "middleman minority," roles that "hide and enable the mechanics of capitalist exploitation and systemic racism."[15]

While Jews were legally granted some white privilege in the United States as early as the 1705 Virginia Slave Codes, our whiteness remained shifty until the latter half of the twentieth century, when most American institutions stopped excluding Jews.[16] The more white we became, the more access we had to professional advancement, particularly into roles like teachers, doctors, and lawyers—middle agent roles. "In big cities, these professionals are often the face of systemic racism and class oppression. . . . Neither the professionals in middle agent roles, nor their poor, working-class and POC clients are actually empowered to change the system," the JFREJ report states. "This focuses anger about racism on Jews."[17]

How cyclical, how familiar it sounds. To look at assimilation this way is to understand it not as any achievement of said model minority, but a very clever tactical placement. As Aurora Levins Morales writes: "The goal is not to crush us, it's to have us available for crushing."[18] Here I sit in the dark with my screen, feeling available for the crush.

More than a lived experience of oppression, what lives in me is that sequence of availability and blame. I know that while many Jews are safe now, this safety is dependent on whether we are currently in favor with the economic forces that have granted us their permission to acquire financial security. Let me be specific: By the time I was born, my family had accumulated enough wealth to buy a big house with a yard in front and back, to send me to some of those fabled Jewish summer camps, and to get me through college without loans. I had the freedom to choose writing and teaching as my careers even knowing they were not the most lucrative, because I have a safety net. If I were to lose my jobs or capacity to work, my family has enough financial resource to back me up.

I feel concerned writing these words; concerned that they will be twisted to imply that I am that legendary moneyed Jew they love to hate. But my individual class privilege feels important to point out in the hopes of understanding that the problem is not Jews. There are bigger problems of which anti-Semitism is a symptom. "Antisemitism frames the function of capitalism as a problem of human or communal mischief rather than as intrinsic to capitalism itself," I read in the JFREJ report, "Capitalism isn't oppressive because Jews are ruining it; capitalism is oppressive because capitalism is oppressive."[19]

There are so many things I'm afraid to say, questions I'm afraid to ask, and it's not because I'm your "garden-variety" anxious Jew, but because I'm a white-identified Jew living under racial capitalism. Materially, I am very secure, and yet my body has not caught up to this reality. It remains concerned with what guidelines it needs to follow to stay in the position that's been laid out for me, wary of inquiries that might boot me out of the lap of power. This lap, this crotch, this fertile pelvic bowl. I jab at it because I want to see what it's made of, what it makes, and what it delivers. The systems underneath, the same systems that restrict my behavior by duping me into the idea that only they can keep me safe.

I test the limits of this safety when I watch Nazi films, when I revisit young adult Holocaust novels, or when I pull Michael's face closer, demanding he see me the way I tell him to. I used to want to keep the lights low or the gaze on someone else we all could agree was hot. This time, I invite Michael to observe where I am not white enough or not femme enough, because somewhere something glimmers at me, suggesting that *enough* isn't paying off. Michael looks out from a body I have been instructed could hurt me, but the more I test him, the stronger I feel, the more I wonder how many gauche gestures I could make, perhaps even how many mistakes. "How vulgar," I whisper to myself imperiously, the word puffing out my mouth, thickening my tongue, performing both judger and judged.

Dark Night of
the Species

I inherited insomnia from my father. It found me early, so that even as a teenager I never slept in. I would wake at any hour at the slightest provocation, the slightest scratch of the tree at my window or creak of floorboards in our old house as someone shuffled to the bathroom. I would breathe in quickly, startled, and sniff at the air a few times to affirm that I was in fact alive. Then my whole body would tense awake, my skin prickling and my hope for sleep vanished, no matter what time of night or how tired I might be. I'd try to fall back to sleep, but my mind would begin to spin immediately with whatever it could find: an upcoming test, a slightly off interaction I'd had with a friend, the way I'd heard my parents hissing to one another as I fell asleep, the video of Rodney King being beaten I'd seen on the news. Everything urgent, nothing somnolent.

Eventually I'd give up and go down to the kitchen, where often my father would be sitting with the newspaper, sometimes one light on or sometimes a flashlight, depending how early it was. He'd make me a coffee in silence, and I'd take the comics page. It was a peaceful scene. One insomniac knows not to ask another what happened. Because anything could have happened and also nothing. The answer is: *I was lying there, thinking.*

My sleeplessness has only gotten worse as I've gotten older and have more things to worry about and prepare. The only route to insomniac serenity is acceptance, waiting out the hours until other people will be up, finding something (anything) to do with that time.

In this waiting time, I've made many of my worst choices. Numbed with fatigue, I've taken drugs I'd never consider in the warmth of the day. Under cover of early morning darkness, I've stared into screens and delved into topics I should know better than to explore. What's usually off-limits is predictable. It's a combination of old boyfriends' wives' Instagram feeds and YouTube videos of Nazi gas chambers. Things my mind knows to stay away from once exposed to light. But in the dark, the internet unravels before me.

In one such desperate moment, I happened on *The Furred Reich* by Len Gilbert. The book is an erotic novel created for and by furries—people who dress up as animals, often for sexual purposes. In the strange cross-jumbling that happens between kink and costume play ("cosplay" for short), some furries have come to identify also with World War II reenactment and dress up as both furry animals and Nazis. One notorious furry who goes by the name "Foxler Nightfire" wears a red, white, and black armband over his fur suit. Emblazoned on the armband is a paw emblem that closely resembles the Nazi insignia, and Nightfire poses in front of swastikas and Nazi-looking flags in his bedroom. He is one of a group of people who identify themselves as "alt-furry."

It is from this world that *The Furred Reich* arises. In this novel, written by a self-identified alt-furry white supremacist, the main characters are soldiers fighting in World War II who get magically transported to a world of speaking animals with whom they have a variety of soldierly and sexual adventures. It's just the sort of thing I can't stop reading, and I can't wait to tell people about it in the morning when they wake. I read for company, for surprise. The text takes me to worlds I didn't know existed, traces affinities and alliances between people I don't know and wouldn't likely take the time to acquaint myself with if I met them in person.

I read to observe these figures from a safe distance. I read alone. I read *The Furred Reich* and other foul content, my better judgment lost along with my capacity to sleep. I read prison rape erotica and I watch films in which characters dressed up as concentration camp prisoners are penetrated by multiple guards and then shot. I keep one eye squinted closed and the volume turned way down. My muscles are clenched and trembling, but I feel compelled toward these things nonetheless, to seek out what haunts me. I can't quite read my own body, and years of seeing doctors for chronic and invisible illness have taught me that without someone else's reflections, I can't know what's going on inside me. Am I vitamin deficient or hyperthyroid? Am I interested or fixated? Am I attracted, or just steeling myself? Attraction and fear overlap, and this enthralls me, a new combination of feeling.

Alone with my screen, I am free to dive further than anyone would recommend who loves me. My friends are mostly liberated people, liberated at least from some of the most normative boundaries around sexuality. Most of them are queer, some kinky, many nonmonogamous. Many of us have been talking for years about the evils of shame, how important it is that we accept anyone for what they like, who they like, and where they like it.

There's this edge, though, around fascists. Even with Andy, my therapist friend who is always telling me that "all coping mechanisms are legitimate" and "trauma survivors sometimes need to reenact." Even she doesn't like it when I make a joke about being a stubbly Jew.

"Sweetheart, don't shame yourself for your body hair," she wiggles her head from side to side, not quite a shake, "even as a joke."

"Why not as a joke?" I ask her, "The ideas are in me, so I should let them come out." I imagine sweat surfacing at my pores.

"Language matters," she says, "you, especially, would know this." She means that because I'm a writer, I should know the power of verbalizing, how language re-cements.

"But it's funny to me," I tell her, "It's funny because I might be stubbly, but I'm also other things. It's fine for me to admit it." I'm trying it on as I say it aloud, and it feels true. It might even be helpful, this small admission. When my body conforms to gendered standards, it conceals the work it takes to shave—literally, to remove hair from the body, but also symbolically, to shave oneself into the shapes demanded as femininity. Maybe it can help in a very small way for me to make the effort visible.

"Have you ever shaved the top of your foot?" I ask Andy. "I started doing it when I was twelve. Even before my pits." As I speak, I open my arms wide, allowing. Andy glances from one of my palms to the other, as if double-checking what's inside.

"I have enough people in my life who tell me I'm pretty or smart," I smile and shrug, wanting her to join me in some levity. "I'm okay." Who, exactly, am I proving this too?

"Well, yes," she says, "I'm glad you have those people." It feels dull to me, a reassurance I don't need. I'm not looking for affirmation. I'm looking for my limits, something kink hints that I might be able to do with care. But when I tell Andy about *The Furred Reich* she screws up her face. The usually sympathetic therapist eyes are narrowed, blinking quickly.

"I just don't know why you would go there," she says, "I'm not sure that can do you any good." She sounds sad for me, concerned. "Sometimes we need to protect ourselves a little," she says, "with boundaries." That old line, *boundaries*. That old "we," the accumulated cultural knowledge that knows best. I'm pushing up against it as I push up against what I've heard for years about boundaries. The idea that it's up to each of us to defend our own time or our security, that if we don't hold our borderlines someone else might come tumbling in.

Andy shakes her head. "I wish you didn't feel you had to do this, sweetheart," she says. It sounds saccharine. Andy is trying to be nice, but it's a crystallized niceness.

"I hope you'll get this out of your system," she says. She wants this to be something therapeutic I touch into and then get over, though right now it feels like a whole new country in which I want to make my life, a whole new set of rules for citizenship and forms I learn to fill out. I want to understand what happens when I fit in *there*.

Yes, I'm fitting into something gross, evil, and for many people something unpleasant to hear about. With Andy, I learn that I'm crossing a line of what healing is supposed to look like. I'm not supposed to be curious about what fascists fantasize about, or what fascists might be like in bed. My friend wants to take care of me, but it feels frail, fearful. I think she is worried about not letting "their" values pour into "ours," that somehow if I watch or read about Nazis having sex I might slip and land in their corner.

I'm coming to realize that perhaps I feel the opposite—strong enough to cover myself in a mud that will cause me to slip. I have enough white (and thin, relatively able-bodied) privilege for this to feel feasible, like it will not destroy me. Even if it endangers me some, I will have more security to return to once I've looked into the shadows. The Jewish writer and activist Melanie Kaye/Kantrowitz writes incisively about how she understands this tendency as an aspect of American Jewish culture, a difference she notes from how others deal in information.

"Even one's body is barely one's own," Kaye/Kantrowitz reports, "A friend says, you return from the toilet, and everyone wants to know, did you go? The nosiness characteristic of Jewish culture relates both to responsibility and to danger: if you constantly monitor information, you may be able to ward off disaster."[1]

Here I'm wondering less about whether I took a shit and more about whether someone took a shit on me, we could say. I feel relaxed when I say the worst thing I could imagine being said. If I preempt it, it won't ever catch me by surprise. But not only that. It's a defensive move, yes, but one that allows for defense while the unpredictable is happening. I "ward off disaster," as Kaye/ Kantrowitz says, but also I cast a spell on now. *Fascinare* in the Latin. A spell that draws attention. I'm fascinated by now, by the reality that disaster not only happened, and not only may happen again, but is still happening, too. Under different conditions, with different players in different positions in place.

I go toward the furries for something contemporary, and something distinct from austere, dissociated repetition. It's not "never again," that very well-intentioned but monotonous phrase Jews use when we promise to prevent future genocides. This phrase confirms genocide in our past and in our potential future, inculcating a narrative of injury and defense while concurrently blocking out what could be happening now—the reality that the vilest of human cruelties demand our attention in this very moment. We—I—have been coded into these cruelties by my arrangement in whiteness.

Instead of "never again," I'm looking for something like *now, again*. I know how to look back and venerate, and how to panic about the future. I want to understand what my body is enacting in this moment; what I'm doing to people and what they are doing to me. Michael and I had an impact on each other. These impacts were both informed by and separate from the political histories that imprint what we each find attractive.

"Now, again." When I speak it over to myself, I sound like a stage director commanding that a scene needs more practice. "Now, again." Playing roles, I begin from sex, because that's where this emerged for me. But there's that saying attributed to Oscar Wilde: "Everything is about sex, except sex, which is about power." When I speak "now, again," I invite the possibility that I too may be implicated in power—that Jews, in my case, may be implicated.

I attended my first white antiracist allies meeting in 2010 in Oakland, California, in the wake of Oscar Grant's murder by BART police officer Johannes Mehserle. I remember my own desire to mark myself as Jewish and not just white at this meeting. I also remember the simultaneous sense that my whiteness was more relevant to the issue of racist policing than my Jewishness. My whiteness held more power, more usefulness to the struggle, more capacity to reach the sources of oppression, including the mindset in which white people believe that racist policing is a necessary protective mechanism.

I am more Jewish in Berlin, and then more white again when I go home to Oakland, occupying dramatically different positions in relationship to state repression and resistance. It is scary to shift the positions I believed I occupied on the spectrum of victim-to-oppressor. I was born into an owning class family in which we both work to survive and accrue wealth based on the earnings of others, benefiting from underpaid labor and racist laws and lending histories. Though Jewish whiteness in the United States is recent, my lived experience resides inside of that recent time. It is frightening to understand that while my ancestors were victims, my body can enact white supremacy now. In the fact of "now, again," the version I was given of my history will not hold. It is true of the past, but it cannot remain intact if I want to relate in the present.

The Furred Reich is not for everyone. Obvious political issues aside, as a book it's largely boring and poorly written. It takes me a good forty pages to grasp the relationships between different characters and scenes. I find it almost impossible to relate to the characters with whom I am supposed to empathize, namely, the Nazi soldiers presented as hapless sufferers.

I read constantly for my work and have gotten in the habit of putting most books down when they are this bad, not having time to waste on their pages. But *The Furred Reich* gets me out of this habit, out of many habits, you could say. I am motivated to keep reading because something is breaking down in me about good and bad, evil and virtuous. *The Furred Reich* is not trying to be good, not by the standards of literature or of contemporary American leftists. The book is so obviously soaked in evil that it reflects back to me the racialized and gendered norms I least want to concede.

In the scene that sticks with me most, Hans, a German soldier battling Russians in the trenches, wanders from the battlefield into "Oasis," where two female-gendered animals who somehow also speak English find him wounded, nurse him back to health, and—naturally—offer to de-virginize him with a casual threesome. It's a bizarre if predictable male fantasy—to be taken from battle against one's will (no shame incurred) and then cared for by beings who dress one's wounds, stroke one's cock, and leave coins in one's helmet on their way out so that one can buy bread. *The Furred Reich*'s protomasculine characters want babying. They just want things to be easy.

> Kairah's ears flicked and she reached forward to run her fingers through Hans' hair, probably out of sympathy. "We'll stay with you until we are confident you are fine."[2]

I almost feel sympathy for the narrator because his bare desire to be parented is so clear. It feels more honest than the men I've known who pretend they're looking for an equal, but once over at my apartment respond best to being coddled. I think of a man years ago in San Francisco who pouted when I disagreed with his views on gentrification and only agreed to shift his mood when I apologized, made him tea, and massaged his shoulders. "I'm sorry I stressed you out," I said, "let's relax now."

It's all there in *The Furred Reich*.

> "You need to rest," she explained, hands dunked into a bucket of water with a damp rag, which she rinsed out and placed along Hans' forehead and back of his neck. He blinked as peaceful, damp darkness covered his blue eyes.[3]

Hans is innocent and bumbling as he receives the more expert sexual advances of one of the animal-women. They are simultaneously gentle and wild.

> He couldn't help but be intensely curious about what he would soon get to see. Hans had never even seen a woman naked before, but Kairah wasn't really human.[4]

It's easy to be a *lady in the streets but the freak in the bed* when you're not really human.

> Up her inner thighs and belly was a bright white fur which covered modest breasts crowned by pink nipples probably similar to those of a German girl.[5]

The trappings of human-ness are close enough to "a German girl" (here, representing an idealized form), while the white fur serves to make the body further innocent, outside of the constraints that might otherwise interfere (ethically, socially) with the "simplicity" of Hans's desire.

> A former virgin, Hans could only try his best. He was no longer nervous, and felt as if he could step out of his own shoes for Kairah.[6]

Not just the animal, but the human too can step out of their usual stance. This sexual interaction—already out of space and time because Hans believes he is dreaming—is also free of social responsibility.

I find myself eager to consume and understand this book, downloading the epub file and converting it to pdf to make it easier to scroll, scanning through its pages for the sexy bits and the World War II references. But *The Furred Reich* is so predictable that I lose patience quickly when close reading. I become less interested in the book than in the culture it belies. Furry culture, as I've come to understand it, is struck through with a desire to be soft and unseen—to be cloaked in a kind of beast-form that makes one impenetrable to complex cultural and human interaction. Furries are cuddly and larger-than-life, accessible, touch-able, and still distant. This is something I can understand: the desire to be both intimate and immune.

I can understand, too, the longing to be free of social responsibility. I've spent years monitoring my own speech to make sure it seems as fair as possible, as considerate as possible to all audiences, trying to avoid the inevitable mistakes. These are the politics of my moment, yes—the fear of getting something wrong and being "cancelled"—but my behavior is enhanced by the anxiety of historic Jewish precarity in relationship to state power. If I'm perfect in my politics, I imagine, perhaps I will be allowed to stay. A small slipup, though, and I might be blamed for everything. As we understand from the history of anti-Semitism, the more assimilated Jews are, the more we are implicated in the oppressive economic and racialized systems of power. There's only so long we can play both sides before both sides will notice and we become yet again the proverbial scapegoat, a nonhuman figure that holds a sanctified level of blame, exorbitantly ridiculous in its rejection from the community.

Alt-furry tricksters know how to use ridicule to their advantage. Just as the soldiers in *The Furred Reich* get to escape the war for the care of servile beasts who need nothing from them, when alt-furries are cornered by journalists or others trying to get to the heart of who they are or what they believe, they tend to retreat into the fluffy: cosplay, irony, a softness that no one can interrogate. In her piece examining "the truth about Nazi furries and the alt-right," Amelia Tait quotes Foxler Nightfire defending those who dress up as Nazis. "They're very interested in World War Two history and they like to re-enact," Nightfire writes, "They're just kinda cosplay in attitude, but when people look at it they don't see that."[7] *Kinda cosplay* is the retreat I mean—a costuming that does not require the wearer acknowledge their position in surrounding systems.

I am tired already of pointing this out, taking screenshots that I will send to friends in the morning with a long line of eyeroll emoji. Pointing out invisible structures is a habit I have, an action I repeat, though I usually only do it in contexts I know well. With my uncles who don't notice all the women are doing dishes, with my parents donating to climate change activism while investing in Exxon because the return on investment is high. I'm jealous of *kinda cosplay*, of play that experiences itself as untainted. The more I read about alt-furries, the more I feel the need to look. What am I keeping invisible? What am I skipping over to make my own narrative persuasive?

Many have attacked Nightfire for his Nazi-appearing armband and for the hateful and racist comments he's reportedly made online. Though he denies that the Nazi armband is meant to represent hateful views, he says, he is not willing to stop wearing it because "it's so ingrained in my character, my fursona." This fursona also complicates his views on race. When Tait asks him directly whether he hates Black people, Nightfire states:

> Their two parts to that one, in my normal day life not at all. . . . But in my per-
> sonal sexual life "I don't like any race," which means I wouldn't sleep with black
> man. Now my boyfriend is mix black/asian. I sleep with him just fine, when I was
> young I use to be anti-gay. So why the change? It's because he not a "human"; to
> me when I look at him. He a blue wolf.[8]

The blue wolf escapes into a forest that magically scrapes him and his partner clean of racialized experience.

In my Googling, I find a photo of Nightfire and the blue wolf with their arms around each other in what appears to be a hot tub. Both wear furry costumes from the shoulders up but display human skin below and into the water. The blue wolf is significantly slighter than Nightfire and appears nearly childlike in Nightfire's beefier arms. I find myself feeling maternal, worrying already whether Nightfire is abusive and controlling of the smaller man. I stare at the photo, trying to get a sense of their dynamic, but their glassy furry eyes give me nothing.

This is the spookiest photo of Nightfire I find. It doesn't include any references to Nazi uniforms, but it's creepy because it appears in a vacuum, the air of the situation sucked clean out, nothing left but joking. I stare at the photo and my hands begin to sweat. I remember breathing this kind of vacuum-air into my own body, in hot tubs in high school with boys who snapped the strap of my bathing suit or made comments about the shape of my butt. If I would call them on it, they'd raise their hands in surrender. "Jeez, just kidding! Girl can't take a joke."

In another photo tweeted from Nightfire's account, the two men hold each other in a mountain canyon, furry heads on, fully clothed now though Nightfire's bare human hands grip the blue furry wrist of his partner. In another tweet, Nightfire writes, "Nah I got fucked good by a black man in blue wolf fursuit lol" with a picture of the two of them in full costume. His narrative has some serious holes, I guess. Here it clearly isn't true that Nightfire experiences his partner as nonraced. But the "lol" casts everything to the wind.

In her article, Tait interviews another alt-furry who goes by the name of Qu Qu. "You can't easily tell how many layers of irony we are on," Qu Qu, says. He continues:

> This is by design, and you will start to see more and more political movements which bury themselves beneath layers of irony and yet still manage to get things done. I can assure you though; we are on more layers than just five or six right now, my dude.[9]

So many layers that slip through my hands. I would love to have a sense of humor. I want there to be space for everyone's sense of humor or kink or sexual preference. But I can only want this if there's a social sphere for us to share, if there's a texture to reality on which we can agree. With the alt-furries I don't have this shared reality. I don't mean that I need us to be the same: we all come from different experiences of race, oppression, gender, and power dynamics. But sociality becomes possible when we make a nod toward these, instead of blanking them out or assuming we can know the textures of others' lived experience.

With the alt-furries, everything is ironic and so there is no social, no care. Reading them, I have to stop and question: Is it ever safe to reveal aspects of myself, knowing that disclosure may not get us closer, and it may even be used against me? I want to be slippery, too, but not to escape. I want to interact with hate and not be crushed by its menacing load. By laughing, kissing, exchanging body fluids: can I move hatred through my body so that it can be released?

I do, because I write. A book is not a social exchange, much as I might wish it to be. I want to care, but that's not what I do here. Here I write how I see, even as it may alienate or be misinterpreted along the way. I peer at my screen in the dark and shudder. The pdf of *The Furred Reich* seems to pulse in front of my exhausted eyeballs. It is late, and no one is around to confirm the world I think I know. I have to figure out how to write and possibly be wrong.

In the late afternoon in Oakland now it is sunny and I have been with other people all day, in present time, and I feel able to go back into reading again. I sit down with my third cup of coffee and smirk, because the final chapter of *The Furred Reich* is literally titled "Pure Again."

In this chapter, the war seems to be over for its main characters. Hans is happily mated with a snow leopardess whose life he has saved, but who experienced a voice box injury that means she may never speak again. (No nagging girlfriend.) As the scene closes, humans and wolves raise a toast to Hans's heroism.[10]

Qu Qu's "layers of irony and yet still manage to get things done," echoes again. The playfulness of *The Furred Reich* doesn't prevent it from leaving its mark. I close my computer and I feel slimy, coated by it. Like in the Nickelodeon game shows of my childhood, someone has thrown a bucket of goo over me. It's their goo that they assume should go over my body, not because I consented to it, but because those are the rules of their game.

The alt-furries rework seemingly every stereotype while refusing to admit the harm these stereotypes do and have done. They help themselves to the content or the tropes of history without the impacts or the trauma. In this way they serve as an important reminder that there's only so much I can understand without other people. I can look at Nazi porn in the dark by myself, but until I run these ideas by and with other humans, they risk getting stuck in a solipsistic loop.

I slink over to the couch and lie on my back, mentally reviewing the events of the prior day because that sometimes works to calm me. There was a tiny tiff with my partner. I wonder whether I smoothed it over enough to earn his affection: the thought flashes across my brain just before I can stop it. It feels like a reflex, though I feel stupid for letting it in. Something like the animal in me, the one who absorbs social mores and isn't quite controlled enough to eject them fully.

It was a small fight. I was angry that he hadn't taken care of something he'd been saying for weeks he would.

"Do I just have to do it myself?" I rolled my eyes. "Sometimes you just aren't a strong leader." What I meant was that I wished he had done a task sooner, moving forward the repairs on our house instead of waiting for me to notice they needed to be done and bring it up.

"You need to learn to take charge," I snarled, as if this was something I had mastered. He looked shocked and turned away. "I need a little space," he said.

I knew my comment would hurt, which is why I said it, and if I had been a bit less under-slept, I would have realized I shouldn't have lashed out, wouldn't have let it leave my mouth.

"I'm sorry," I said, a few minutes later, tapping on the door of his home office, "that was dumb. I didn't think it through." My partner runs a company, and runs it well, generously balancing the giving of direction with letting other people's voices be heard. It was unfair of me to generalize and mean of me to point my arrow at that spot.

"You know better than that," he said, weakly, almost pleadingly. "You know how to articulate what you need. Just say what you mean." For years he and I have worked on how to fight *well*, as our couple's therapist would say: by moving quickly to the core needs at hand, and away from the surface frustrations, the desires to be right or to win.

"You're right," I said, "I'm sorry, I know better, and what I said wasn't true." I could see his posture relax at that, his shoulders lower, and I knew it was time to move toward him from the doorway, to sit down on the floor below his desk chair and reach up to touch his knee. "Let's be on the same team, OK?" I took his hand. Our team against the team of impulse, of lashing out with phrases and feelings that aren't really us, at our core.

"It's stupid shit that lives in me," I said to him later on the couch, my fingers up his shirt, twisting in the soft hairs of his chest. "It's this momentary need to tear you down to get what I want." I brought my hand to the back of his hand and scratched my nails very lightly there, playacting a claw, and we both smiled.

"I know," he said, his hand reaching over to still mine, "we're all working against patterns that aren't our own." It's as if what I've done floats up out of my body and away from us, out the window, no longer belonging to me. The impulse to hurt is base, and so forgivable, separate from what makes me me.

I'll try not to do this again, and maybe, over years, I'll get better at it. But much of the time it's a kind of inevitable circling of behaviors. Enact, absolve, repeat. The clawed animal rises up inside me, wants temporarily to be cruel and hurt someone, and then the animal instinct falls away. If something is animal-istic, at least it comes off as not my fault, not something I need to integrate into my understanding of who I am. It could almost be role-play if it had been agreed on beforehand. I mess up, and then the mess up gets ascribed to a role, a beast who I'm not.

Many people I love love their pets, and they are always trying to get me to bond with them.

"Just look into his eyes," they coo, "he loves you so much!" I stare at the dog, who to me just looks hungry, whose yellowy drool falls to the carpet.

"You guys already love each other," my friend yelps, and I nod because it seems to make her happy when I am close to an animal she loves. It seems like the ability to get along with pets proves something to people about how human I am, and I don't want to fail this one. I rub the animal and try not to judge it for the smell that fills this home. I mimic how other people move around these beings, gentle and babying. Their relationship to one another seems to happen across the body of an animal, and I don't want to seem anti-social or unwilling to participate. Out of the corner of my eye, I watch for my friend's reaction.

Neither of my parents were big on animals, so we didn't have pets growing up, and when we would visit friends or family who had them my parents would let me cower behind their legs and ask the owner politely to put Lassie or Simba in its crate.

"Animals aren't meant to be in the house," my father would shake his head, "it's disgusting." He meant this about the pee stain on my aunt and uncle's couch, or about the pile of kitty litter reeking in the kitchen.

"The animal would do better outside." He'd point to the squirrels in the tree that no one had to clean up after. Maybe this is where it got confusing: he pointed to the two together, and the difference between beast and pet collapsed in my mind. To this day, I am suspicious of people who differentiate between them. It seems slippery, arbitrary. I watch for the rules as an outsider. My friend's dog is not a wolf, and so it matters how I touch it. My friend's cat is not a tiger and so it matters if I can relate to its stretches or try to guess what it is thinking.

In his 1977 essay "Why Look at Animals?" John Berger describes how the animal became a figure of spectacle. Of the human gazing at the animal, Berger writes:

> He is always looking across ignorance and fear. And so, when he is *being seen* by the animal, he is being seen as his surroundings are seen by him. His recognition of this is what makes the look of the animal familiar. And yet the animal is distinct, and can never be confused with man. Thus, a power is ascribed to the animal, comparable with human power but never coinciding with it. The animal has secrets which, unlike the secrets of caves, mountains, seas, are specifically addressed to man.[11]

Though etched with dated gendered language, Berger's thoughts ring in me, especially on those days when I hang out with a pet and try to get into it. I especially appreciate Berger's description of the essentializing of difference. The animal, Berger argues, has become where we place our grasp of our own knowledge—we project onto them how much we believe we understand.

The fact that they can observe us has lost all significance. They are the objects of our ever-extending knowledge. What we know about them is an index for our power, and thus an index of what separates us from them. The more we know, the further away they are.

In the animal we hide the secret and unknown. The image of the animal swallows everything we feed it. The animal can't speak—at least not human language—so we can pretend it consents to be this hiding place for us.

It makes sense, then, that fascists would find the animal such a great place to hide. It makes sense that they could obscure themselves there and not have to take responsibility for any of their behaviors. Tait can interview these Furries to her heart's content, press them in every way possible, but in the position of animal they will continue to back away and mirror only what she projects on them.

"The animal has been emptied of experience and secrets, and this new invented 'innocence' begins to provoke in man a kind of nostalgia," writes Berger. "According to this view of nature, the life of a wild animal becomes an ideal, an ideal internalized as a feeling surrounding a repressed desire." We place everything we can't own on the animal, and then we wish we could have it. I let myself off the hook for being mean by comparing myself to an animal, and long for the ways that being an animal would keep me innocent, absolved.

Alt-furries take this a step further. In *The Furred Reich*, furry bodies beg the human for whatever he most wants to give them. By mating with these inno-cents, the human is affirmed in his own rightness—his own near-divinity—by a body he experiences first and foremost as a mirror. Then, by dressing up as one of these innocents, he reflects the mirror back to catch only light. I wonder what would happen if I could similarly wrap myself in the beastly body and so allow everything to be okay that is otherwise intolerable. To follow their example in one but not in every way.

I learn from Berger that the animal holds everything we can't speak with, can't understand. Which is why I go digging there, for the enigma in the animal role.

Alt-furries love talking about how attacked they are, particularly by Leftists, though also by white supremacists and the alt-right. So much about what they spout repels me. It sounds ridiculous when they say they are fighting against "systemic species-ist oppression"—but it's also so bombastic that something rises in it that I can relate to, something about blame and blamelessness. I too have wanted to be the innocent victim. It takes so much work to be a functioning adult. I can see the appeal of being excused from responsibility. I can see the appeal of never having to explain myself but being deserving of love and consideration, nonetheless. I wonder it in writing, also: can I share fragments of a story and still interest a reader in thinking with me, even if I don't give everything I am?

I ask not because I'm feeling cagey, but because I want to know what it takes for a person to care. My fear is that it takes hurt, as I've learned from victim narratives. I fear that in order to matter, I have to be hurt enough. I have to be visibly damaged, so that someone can peer into the wound and decide it is worthy. That I myself am worthy, too.

In *Conflict Is Not Abuse*, the writer Sarah Schulman describes these criteria as a "punitive standard in which people are made desperate, yet ineligible, for compassion." The standard is "punitive" because if we're not wounded enough, we are then punished by lack of love, lack of mattering to other people.

In her book, Schulman looks at contemporary American disputes mediated by police. She uses these disputes to show how policing has become our most public display of attention. If something really matters or is really threatened, most Americans call the cops. We operate punitively. Schulman describes how we come to believe that only those who can claim they've been abused and mistreated deserve help, whereas those of us in more "normal" states of distress, illness, or pain must fend for ourselves in capitalism's creaky machines of health care, communication, and compassion.

I have lived with chronic pain for most of my life, and I fended for myself until I couldn't. The more open I have become about my own conditions, the more friends I make who also identify as chronically ill or disabled, and the more time I spend with them, the more I begin to understand that sickness and difficulty accessing the tools we need to survive are habitual human experiences—none of us escapes life without experiencing sickness or access issues at least once. From what researchers call the social model of disability, I have learned that this is not the fault of the human who has a problem and needs to be fixed, as held by the so-called medical model of disability. We are not impaired. Rather, the social world is impaired because it is not appropriately meeting our needs.

I have found this model a great comfort over years now of chronic pain preventing me from performing at perfectionist levels. When family members have struggled with grave illness, I have found considerable relief in noticing the social and environmental factors that contribute to their suffering, as opposed to blaming them for not being able to get out of bed, or avoid addiction, or complete a four-year college degree.

What I haven't figured out yet is the deservingness piece, the piece that intersects with hierarchies of suffering, victim Olympics, and Schulman's arguments about punitive codes. Very rarely do I consider it okay for me to ask for help, even once I have medical diagnoses. This is, to some extent, because of the privileges I hold. I come from a family who has always had enough money to pay for medical bills, and so I hesitate to tell others how angry I am about the neglectful practices of my medical insurance, my required MRIs that cost thousands of dollars, the stressors my family suffers when supporting a family member through alcohol withdrawal. The stressors don't seem sufficient because I have so much other privilege. Shrouding all this is a belief that I have to be in pure utter need if I desire care.

"This concept, of having to earn the right to have pain acknowledged, is predicated on a need to enforce that one party is entirely righteous and without mistake," Schulman writes, "while the other is the Specter, the residual holder of all evil."[12] What if I do not want to be either? I want to live somewhere in between, somewhere that acknowledges complicity, mistake, and reparation. If I don't make a choice to be either righteous or evil, I am left wanting care, craving care, and willing to do a whole range of strange and performative twists to fall into caring arms. This scares me because I see one possible result of this position in the alt-furries. They twist themselves toward stereotypes of the maternal or the child or the beast to be loved, and in the depth of their craving ignore all the associated harm.

Role-play and BDSM dramatize both this harm and craving, but it's not necessarily some complex scene requiring a furry costume or a dungeon, ropes, and elaborate consent rules. It plays out on the level of the vanilla and everyday. Over and over as an adult woman I have had to prove that I can use a hammer and nail, that I can drive a car, prove, prove, prove that I'm not the weak female I'm assumed to be. I hiss at my partner that I worked all weekend cleaning our home and cooking, infuriated that he doesn't immediately see all this labor. In

part I am trying to prove that I have done enough to deserve care and kindness, to deserve to stop working for the day. What could happen if I tried less
hard to prove it? What would happen if I played more into the passive or submissive narratives designed for me—not to permanently obey these categories,
but to point out how simultaneously tempting and ungainly they are, how very
much like role-play?

I don't find the role-play partner I'm looking for right away. Maybe it's a tall
order, or maybe it's a combination of too many desires, impossible for one person to meet. Michael was my starting point, but he does not want to verbalize
or play what I crave.

When he finally texts me back after our night together, it is many days later,
and the charge between us is difficult to remember or restart. He is polite, and
it is nothing like I want him to be.

"It was wonderful to connect again." He dodges my apologies and comments
about Jewishness entirely. "How is your work? Did you meet your deadline?" I
am bored by these questions, reaching for something else.

"Did you make your train home?" I ask.

"I did. I was late, but so was the train."

"I thought German trains were always perfectly punctual," I text. I do not know
if he gets the connotation of my stereotyping German efficiency, how they packed
Jews into the cattle cars with their careful timing and record-keeping to match.

"Definitely not always," he texts. Um, OK. It falls flat, and I don't know what
else to try. I am about to put the phone down for the night when he sends an
animated GIF of two dogs snuggling.

"I wish to do this with you right now." They are both small dogs, maybe
puppies, and one licks the other's face. This is his way of trying.

Michael is not going to bite. He doesn't want to engage with me about our
German-Jewish dynamics, about what is or isn't ugly in what our bodies carry.
It's my thing, not his. I want him to name context he doesn't want named. He
prefers instead to leave it at cute and physical, leave it at two soft bodies as
indecipherable and simple as puppies.

But I guess we're even: I projected something onto him that wasn't his thing,
and he did the same to me. I fold my laptop closed and promise myself to take

at least a few days away from both him and from alt-furries. I look one more time at my phone, where the puppies from Michael wiggle creepily. I feel more honest now, clearer on where we stand. We know each other so little that he thinks I'd be into a puppy GIF.

I pushed Michael enough to know that we are not well matched to role-play. But the pushing is taking me somewhere that I like, somewhere I can imagine things about him and about me, and try them on in my own head, even if I don't have his consent or willingness to try them together. Michael took me somewhere I can think toward and against. I don't know how I feel about yet, but still I can keep speaking.

"Do you ever feel Jewish when you're having sex?" Leah and I are on the phone and so I have asked her maybe more directly than I would if we were facing each other. She is a writer whose politics I trust and whose courage I admire. Together we've formed many reading and discussion groups over the years, a practice we learned from post-Occupy activists in Oakland reiterating forms of democratic and political education. When I approach a complex text, writing project, or even personal confrontation, I tend to fall back on this relational form of learning. Like the political reading groups, I turn to my friends to best negotiate a shared present moment, a political position with which I'm not sure how to interact.

With my Nazi kink explorations, I choose carefully. I don't go right to a group. Individual conversations with friends seem to meet the intimacy of the subject matter better, more immediately.

"I don't exactly think about my body as Jewish," Leah says into my ear, after a pause. "Is my body Jewish?"

"Maybe only when I name it that way," I say. "When I point at things on my body and call them Jewish." I tell her about Michael, how I wanted him to see me as beastly.

"Do you mean hate sex?" Leah asks.

"Not exactly," I say, "I don't really want him to hate me."

"Maybe I'm too vanilla," Leah says, "but I don't get it." She recommends I call Amelia, a mutual friend who is a direct descendent of Holocaust survivors and has written more directly about her inheritance.

"Are you talking about the *The Night Porter*?" Amelia asks right away. "That movie scares the shit out of me." Amelia has a growl of a voice.

"Because it's violent?" I ask. The film includes flashbacks to concentration camp scenes as well as a present-time relationship that borders on the abusive, depending on how you read it.

"No," Amelia speaks impressively quickly always, like she already knows her opinions on everything. "Because I think it turns me on, and I don't think I'm OK with that."

"Is it the Nazis?" I ask.

"Not like the Sontag," Amelia says, assuming without asking that I've read the fascism essay. She is a committed academic and trained to set forth her mastery of subject matter. "I don't think uniforms are hot," she says, "even if I should."

I jump in, "there's no *should* here," I say, "just wanting to think with you about how we react." I can feel my teacher or facilitator persona coming on, wanting to draw out Amelia but gently, not forcing.

"Do you actually like that movie?" Amelia presses. She is more confrontational than most of my friends, and it is a different experience talking with her than with people who jump to agreement and empathy. There is something pleasant about how she presses me because it contrasts with my own orientation.

I shrug even though she can't see me. "I admire it," I say carefully, "but all reactions are fair."

"But you obviously think it's worth considering," she says.

"It helps me think through what I feel," I say, "that's what I hope a lot of art can do."

"Like Levinas says." Amelia stops, again assuming what I know. I could pretend, but I don't bother.

"I don't know what you mean," I tell her. "Do you want to tell me what of his to read?" It's interesting to me to notice that I'm not afraid in these conversations of not knowing enough or seeming too sensitive in my approach. It's that teacher training kicking in. If I'm here to help us expand on a subject, I have little to prove.

"It's good you're thinking about this," Amelia says before we hang up. I can't see her face, so I can't tell if she means it. I wish for a moment that this phone conversation was a negotiated scene, that we were play partners and so we could pause to contract the fine points of what we're willing to sort through, what words we want to use, where our experiences differ. But it's not—Amelia and I are fairly new friends, and we haven't formally agreed on how we relate. In the absence of a set structure, I offer words about which I am conflicted and hope to hear what others think.

"If conflicted people were expected and encouraged to produce complex understandings of their relationships, then people could be expected to negotiate," Schulman writes, "instead of having to justify their pain through inflated charges of victimization." I'm looking for another way to scaffold relationship. Even as I center the Holocaust—that moment in history so commonly used to trump any other trump card—I crave not to inflate or defend. I turn toward what we have used to justify ourselves and try to disentangle. An untidy process, as any "complex understanding" begins.

Most people I love don't like that *Conflict* book of Schulman's. Many people I respect politically don't approve of Schulman because they say she pathologizes trauma, overgeneralizes, criticizes trigger warnings too harshly, gaslights survivors, and sides with abusers. Some of these critiques ring true for me, and some are a stretch or a generalization themselves. But it is precisely to Schulman's point, how these critiques take shape. They ask Schulman to be either flawless or evil—and if evil, she must be shut out. Even though I don't agree with every tone or every sentence in Schulman, I still want to be in dialogue with her thinking. It is the path that Michael sends me down, mucky exchanges with real humans, some of whom are annoyed, correct me, or redirect me to talk with someone else who knows better than I do.

Every time I pick up the phone for one of these conversations, I feel excited, my body thrilling and attentive when someone tells me to try harder, to be careful with how I am reading Audre Lorde, for example, because it was not written exactly for me, and the subjugation Lorde describes is not the same as that of my ancestors. "Thank you," I say, genuinely grateful for a friend close enough to point out weaknesses and flaws. If it's possible that I get to be wrong, how much more do I get to be? How else do we get to be together?

Fascinatrix

I am trying to tell my friends about *The Sound of Music*. My friends are not understanding because they are German. I am in Germany again, years later, and again I find myself talking about something it is hard for other people to see. It's lighter this time: I have made new friends over my time here, and many moments go by when we are not speaking of genocide but instead of the art we are making, of our scrambled digitized brains, of what we miss from the 1970s and 1980s. Tonight over beers we are talking about childhood movies. They know most of the American ones, but when I mention *The Sound of Music* they shake their heads.

First, I try giving a summary of the plot.

"It's a musical, but also about the rise of fascism," I say, "and how song can triumph over differences." It sounds hackneyed and corny as it comes out of my mouth, so I try to make it more personal. I try to explain how I was twelve and chubby and slumped against the couch in New England, but also, through the movie, could inhabit the body of a lithe blond nun flouncing through the green hills in the sunshine. The way she spun her skirt and I spun with her until we were both dizzy, the way I rewound the videocassette to watch her hair lift gently up one centimeter in the wind and then settle perfectly back down into place in her short bob.

"It's about her character being messy but perfect that way?" I say weakly. I can tell it's not going over well. My friend Emma breaks the awkward silence. "What about *The Little Mermaid?*" Everyone begins to nod. It is clear they all want to talk about something else.

I've never had to explain *The Sound of Music* before, because most Americans feel and know it in their own bones the minute that I bring it up. *I have confidence in confidence in ME!* That magical feeling when we hear the songs in our heads together. Together, we arch our backs into exaggerated upright posture. We fling our arms out to the sides and laugh, and then we set down the topic, known territory that surges beneath us.

I suppose a dramatization of social constraints and freedoms in Austria before World War II has different implications to German vs. American audiences. Less playful to them, I guess. Less easy to make it fun.

I watched *The Sound of Music* again when I knew I was coming back to Germany. Yes, I am aware it takes place in Austria, but I watched it because it was my earliest context for Germans and German history. Plus, I'll take any excuse for research that means mouthing songs I can't remember not knowing. The movie is so recognizable it's like swimming through my own body. I watch what I already know to approach what I don't.

I am in Germany this time to write an essay about several contemporary artists based in Berlin who make work about power and illness and disability.[1] First, I interview Inga Zimprich about her work with Julia Bonn on the Feminist Healthcare Research Group,[2] and then Zimprich introduces me to the British artist RA Walden, a compatriot in the Sickness Affinity Group (SAG) collective. SAG "investigates accessibility as both a topic and curatorial method" and seeks to offer "a supportive environment for fragility and wellbeing" in which sick and disabled bodies are centered.[3]

The politics of SAG are radical for Berlin for a few reasons. To begin with, the members are forthcoming about their needs to sleep and eat—which maybe sounds normal, but to acknowledge these needs as part of group processes goes way beyond the usual accessibility norms of most art spaces. SAG's members do not assume anyone's capacity to stay up all night at a club, or, more broadly, to move at a frenzied pace. The first SAG meeting I attend is held at Walden's apartment partly because Walden is not currently well enough to leave their home. Within two emails, the meeting gets moved to their living room, where we gather on chairs and carpet and introduce ourselves with names, pronouns, self-identified disabilities and creative practices.

"I'm Zora," says the person to my left in a British accent. English is the working language for the group. Zora wobbles their head from left to right as they begin to list. "White, queer, sick." I enjoy watching them move. They close their eyes and the wobble moves into their shoulders and spine. "I work in video, sound, performance." I forget for a moment if this a performance itself. "I'm working on the same thing still, burlesque stuff centering disabled bodies, a lot of it's gross." A giggle from the group, and Zora's eyes open again. They look at me—the one person they haven't met before—as if they are checking my level of amusement.

"I use porn a lot," they say, maintaining eye contact with me. I smile without effort, glad to be checked on in this way. *Cool*, I mouth. I don't say it aloud because we're not supposed to cross-talk while others speak. "A lot of samples," Zora says, turning back to the center of the circle. It's unclear for a moment if they mean video samples or samples for medical tests, or both. I feel at home in this blurriness, and then Zora turns to their left. "Next?"

After the meeting is officially over, a few of us linger at Walden's kitchen table. "The kettle is there," Walden gestures, their voice nearly a whisper. "The tea is in the top drawer."

Walden is not mobile today, and so they direct us to find our way around the narrow space. Zora puts three white mugs on the table, and then hands me their phone, where something is playing. "Here's some of my work," they say, "it's hard for me to describe it." It's so rare these days for someone to hand you their whole phone, the container for so much banal and intimate information. I hold it lightly, with just my fingertips, as if that will prevent me from trespassing.

On the screen is a video collage made from GIF porn. A blue-green octopus arm waves in the background, and in the foreground a human face, partially obscured, is licking a foot.

"I love how weird this tongue looks on this heel," I say, turning their phone screen back to them, "it almost becomes part of it." *Weird* is so nonspecific, but it seems like Zora gets it, and we've already exchanged stories about times when our brain fog is too intense to find the intelligent vocabulary that we would like to be able to recall and use when discussing the art we love. I've already told them about the time after excision surgery when I crouched over the toilet for three hours, unable to shit, moaning nonsense language and imagining I was giving birth to an alien species.

In this kitchen I'm in a place where body talk is standard, where sick bodies are standard, where healing is nonlinear and the crass belongs. Zora tells me how they try to overlap the erotic with the gross because these are both equally parts of their life.

"I wake up in the morning feeling like crap," Zora smiles, and picks at the peeling surface of the table.

"I like to wake up and ask myself, what forces are working on you today?" They tell me they ask others this question too, to begin interactions by being transparent about what is pressing on the person already. It's not "how are you." It's less annoying because it's asking for a specific answer, not a vague glancing off.

"What's working on you today?" They say now. They push a cup of tea toward me across the table. When they ask, I look out through the cloudy, cracked pane of the window and feel the weight of my own body in the chair. This body traveled three flights upstairs to attend this meeting, and its hips and knee joints ache.

"What's working on me?" A cat jumps into my lap, and instead of petting it I move my hands off my thighs and onto the table.

"I think it's the Germans," I say. I look out the window at more bricks. "I'm not used to being around them, and I'm always self-conscious about what they think I'm doing here." Zora nods. They are from rural England, though they've lived here longer than I have so probably, I imagine, have been able to let the history go. I wish I could let it go—I wish Berlin could be just the richness of artist community I've found here, or even just the antigentrification struggles I've come to learn about, or just conversations about sexual freedom for disabled people and how we can put that on stage. But everything gets colored, colored in, shaded by the rest.

"I'm feeling Jewish," I say to Zora, and take a sip of my tea. It tastes muddy and sour. "I wish I could be anything else." I didn't come to Berlin intending to write about the Holocaust, but when asked for context what else is there to say.

"I didn't come to Germany to be so Jewish," I groan later to my friend Ellie over FaceTime. I don't want to be that guy. I'm cozy in the small cave-like room where I'm staying at an artist residency in Neukölln. My room just fits a single bed and a desk. Barely any natural light filters through, and when I'm in there I can't quite tell what time of day it is. I've always been a morning person, but in this room I sleep most of the day and get up only when my phone beeps at me that it's time to get ready for the night. I stumble out of the room and must cross the communal kitchen to get to the bathroom to wash my face. I clutch a raggedy towel and a tube of mascara in my hand and hope to see no one, but when I open my door another artist at the residency is standing at the kitchen counter boiling an egg.

"Where are you off to tonight?" he asks.

"Oh, just a play," I tell him, "I'm going to a play." He is an American painter, also passing through, and we have been inviting each other along to things, but I don't want company for this outing. I turn my back to him but don't want to seem rude, so I leave the door open as I stand at the bathroom mirror and open my mascara.

"I'm writing about it," I say, which is true. I lean over the sink into the scratched mirror and bring the mascara wand to my lashes. I don't mention what it's about.

The musical *Stella* started showing at the Neuköllner Oper Berlin in 2016, but still critics continue to call it "anti-musical" material. The musical is based on the true story of Stella Goldschlag, a notoriously beautiful and seductive Jewish Gestapo agent who helped round up other Jews in Berlin during World War II. As she tells her father, she's "not much of a Jew" anyway. She has no interest in Jewish traditions and considers Jews old-fashioned, restrictive, bookish, and annoying. Stella is the ultimate self-hating Jew, a blue-eyed blond who only reads as Jewish when the identity is forced on her by the rise of the Nazi party.

The subtitle of the musical is "the Blond Ghost of Kurfürstendamm," a title given to Stella by Jews running from her roundups during the war. Stella's blond hair is central to the narrative. In one key moment in the story, Stella and her mother evade a Nazi roundup of Jews at the factory where they work. When confronted by a guard who asks for their identity cards to prove that they are not Jewish, Stella dramatically unfurls her headscarf and demands, "Is this what a Jew looks like?"

The scene is dramatized to the point of kitsch in the show. The screens surrounding the upper floor of the two-story set display a zoomed-in image of blond curls tossing in the wind, multiplied over in a grandiose gesture much like those opening scenes in *The Sound of Music*, the lush and endless hills.

On the basis of her hair performance, the guard allows Stella and her mother to go free. Stella evades identification as a Jew several times, primarily by choosing not to wear the required yellow star. This ruse fails her when she is arrested in connection to the falsified (non-Jewish) identity papers she carries. Nazi police torture Stella in pursuit of the forger of her papers, and she agrees to work for them. Her job eventually expands in scope, and Stella—along with her boyfriend Rolf, also a blond Jew—becomes a full-blown "catcher," searching Berlin for Jews (many of whom she knows from childhood) and making sure they are rounded up and transported as the Nazis wish.

In the days after I see the musical, I want to talk to everyone about it, but I don't. My American friends have heard enough about the Holocaust, and if I bring it up again, I will be that neurotic, consumed beyond reason by my particular genocide when there is so much else to worry about. The line is so thin between smart and obsessive. I wish I could remember who taught me about this line.

Instead of talking about the musical, I read. It's my way of conversing with other people while trying to avoid harm. Not a true conversation, but when I read into a topic I'm wondering about, I get to think it through without potentially hurting anyone. It's preparation for the in-person conversation, preparation to engage and respond.

Through Oakland's interlibrary loan, I find an old copy of Peter Wyden's memoir about his life as Stella's childhood friend and his adult search for the truth behind her story. The plastic book jacket crinkles in my hands, and it doesn't seem like anyone has taken out this book in years. It's not the easiest read: Wyden's narrative is lurching and often sentimental, but I press on. I find I have a kind of patience for Wyden's slow recounting of his grade-school crush on Stella. He is mystified by her, and I am charmed by this cloud of mystery. She glows in front of him, and he tries to draw up the courage to approach.

I know that feeling. There's something pleasant about being the dorky dark kid watching as the gorgeous person moves, tracking how they act in the world as if I could grasp it, while sure that I can't. From this position, I can see what "forces" are acting on me, to recall Zora's question. I recognize the tropes of whiteness, and they rationalize why I am where I am.

Wyden tracks Stella both to appreciate her beauty and to comprehend her moral failures. He spends the entire book trying to understand, looking backward and forward in time, trying to explain her choices. Lacking much systemic analysis, he comes up short.

Though he doesn't find the excuse he's wanting, I like that Wyden tries anyway. His bumbling feels a little like what I am doing trying to understand my own body in Germany. History is pinned on to me and I feel I must respond, though I feel caught in something hackneyed, out-of-date. Instead of echoing the old story, I go to the play, I meet friends, I speak with the artists about disability and kink. I try to pull the history forward into this moment, watching how it is altered and confounded along the way.

In *The Generation of Postmemory*, scholar Marianne Hirsch argues that descendants of the traumatized continue to remember trauma and catastrophe through multiplied images, narratives, and behaviors.

"Postmemorial work," she writes, "strives to *reactivate* and *re-embody* more distant political and cultural memorial structures by reinvesting them with resonant individual and familial forms of mediation and aesthetic expression."[4] The musical about Stella relies on this mediation. It does show us the famous rows of shoes to indicate those gassed at concentration camps and it does flash archival clips of Nazi-occupied Berlin on the set's multiple screens as the live-acted Stella plays out her "catcher" part below.

What is different is that live bodies move among these notorious scenes, mediating what they mean now. Far too many times, I have sat through a Holocaust documentary or a Holocaust literature panel at an academic conference and felt bored to tears, even angry. Angry because of the insistent and yet limited repetition of what we should remember, what it exactly means, and what images have already been selected to represent this memory and meaning. It's done already, and so all we are allowed to do is reenact and repeat.

Because I can't escape this repetition, I work with it as material. It's not new that the Holocaust should be material to artists and writers, but for the repetition itself to instruct the work—that could be something different. That the frustration with the stiffness of memorial structure—that this very mechanical repetition be "reactivated," as Hirsch would say. Maybe this can make it more pliable, applicable to now.

Instead of insisting only on memory, the musical takes Stella out of her historical setting and into our contemporary one. Though the musical does name-check familiar images, it reinvests them with humor, with song, with live aesthetic expression that occurs next to the familiar memorialization. It interferes, reanimates, and so does not commit us only to the static, the dead. It commits instead to the magnetism of being influenced and disrupted by one another.

In his memoir, Wyden skitters between his dismay at Stella's role in the decimation of Berlin's Jewry and his desire to place her inside forces beyond her control. He recalls Stella at seven years old, already possessed of a kind of glittery womanhood from which he couldn't look away. He remembers being a little boy walking behind her after choir practice, in awe of her shape and charisma. I close my eyes and imagine that I am walking along with him, staring at Stella's hips swaying, hair swinging. Her womanhood fills the scene.

"In traumatic histories, gender can be invisible or hyper visible; it can make trauma unbearable or it can serve as a fetish that helps to shield us from its effects," Hirsch writes.[5] Stella's gender serves this way for Wyden, and for the musical. Her beauty shifts the camera away from the issue of Jewishness toward sex and attraction. This complicates who holds the power. When I'm thinking about sex, I'm thinking less about horror. If I spend time examining why Stella is so beguiling to people, I can demonstrate to myself that Nazis are not the only people who can dominate, not the only form of control. Yes, Nazi-cultivated forces still work on me. They affect the way I understand myself. But they don't force me into a corner—or, if they do, I can bounce from it, deflect.

I think this is perhaps the "shield" Hirsch describes, a coping mechanism for trauma that deflects the calcified Jewish story of inevitable trauma. To be this shield, Stella's body has to be caricatured, larger than life. Stella's femininity is so exaggerated in the stories about her that it focuses me from state violence and genocide toward interpersonal altercations, alterations—how one body alters another in real time.

In the musical, men are constantly falling down. They sink or trip to the ground many times in dance numbers throughout the show. They're graceful about it, because they are actors and dancers, and the action is comedic because the political and the violent are incorporated within the scaffold of seduction. As an audience member, I get to contemplate falling. I contemplate not only the old images of Jewish bodies shot and falling over into pits. The pits are there, but in the background.

In the foreground, someone swoons for Stella, and I get to think about how a body can stand in the way of what another body wants to do. How a body can push another body over without touching it at all. What it means to fall for someone, to have someone fall for me. I think of the first time I realized someone was attracted to me, when the gossip at summer camp got around that someone wanted to kiss me, and how impossible that felt, how slowly it dawned on me that my body wasn't ugly to everyone. I remember staring into the foggy scrap of glass in the bathroom of my bunk, trying to assign new meaning to what I saw there. These eyes, this hair, that lip. Something about these parts could make someone want to get closer to me.

I could stare forever and never understand this fully. When you're the object you're not supposed to understand.

Though I am not descended directly from people who survived the Holocaust, I have many extended family members who were killed by Nazis and many family members of friends. My great-grandparents on all sides escaped mass murder and forced military conscription. I have been awash always in this history and its explanations and evidence, and along with this awareness comes that fear of too-muchness, the sense that other people are monitoring my Jewishness and that if I am too Jewish, I will be disciplined back into my place.

Almost every family story I remember contains a grain of self-consciousness. One example: My great-grandfather was proud to open a dental practice in the Centro Histórico of Mexico City even though he spoke with a strong immigrant accent. He ended up there because he was fleeing Poland during the period when the United States was closed to Jewish immigration, and refugees chose the next country down. Among his non-Jewish neighbors in the Centro, my great-grandfather's practice was known as the "German dentistry," even though he wasn't German. But he let that word spread because, unlike Jewishness it was an acceptable kind of foreignness that brought with it little danger.

In the stories I remember being told, what other people know of us is a matter of life and death. Perhaps this explains some of my fixations in the mirror, my monitoring of what other people know of my whereabouts, my assessment of what others see. It gets specific when I scan someone's face with each word that I use to describe this book as I begin to write it.

"It's not really about Jewishness," I say. As if a drop too far would put me out of favor with the powers that be, powers that are not defined but are always there, heavily armed and shouting *Jude*. In my imagination, it slips that quickly to that place. And it gets specific when I can't invite a mild white painter-bro with me to the musical in Berlin because I can't guess how he'll feel about it. The peril is obviously minimal, but the urge to assess is immense, out of proportion with any actual danger.

The urge has served me well as a student and as a writer. I consider meticulously what forms people expect from a poem, an essay, an academic talk. Rarely do I replicate these forms exactly, but I always think about how I am failing, which standards I am not living up to. I make sure to come into the room—the classroom, the bar, the magazine—with a reason why I do or do not perform what is expected. The fragmented essay: I have a million reasons for that. The travel to Germany: I am aware of how many American Jews have already enacted parts of this story, returning to places like Germany and Poland to reclaim, to find their roots, and I am happy to explain to everyone who will listen which parts of this I reproduce.

It's people-pleasing, most of it. It's a desire to fit in to the existing fabric, to say that I know what already exists and here is where I slot in. I don't have a better word for this than assimilation. Sure, I hold on to my Jewishness, but I do everything I can to explain that action. I assimilate by weaving, hoping no one will feel threatened by difference or surprise.

No one taught me explicitly to assimilate. I cannot think of a single talk when a family member sat me down and told me to be watchful or to make sure I checked what others wanted first. And yet it filtered through.

When I sit down to write about the musical, I begin from this assimilating behavior. Even though my role is supposed to be as a writer, someone with opinions on the work, someone able to describe it to others. When I am writing about a time in history in which Jews were targets, I notice even more strongly the need to monitor judgments. I go looking for levels of interpretation. So much has been passed on without being explicitly stated that I long for the exact words people do use. What have other people said about Stella? On Goodreads I find this:

STELLA: ONE WOMAN'S TRUE TALE OF EVIL, BETRAYAL AND SURVIVAL IN HITLER'S GERMANY BY PETER WYDEN

The story of Stella Goldschlag, whom Wyden knew as a child, and who later became notorious as a "catcher" in wartime Berlin, hunting down hundreds of hidden Jews for the Nazis. A harrowing chronicle of Stella's agonizing choice, her three murder trials, her reclusive existence, and the trauma inherited by her illegitimate daughter in Israel.[6]

JULIE RATED IT "REALLY LIKED IT"

With all that I have known and have read about the war, I gained a new perspective through this book. I didn't always like the style, because sometimes it felt choppy, or I wanted more information, I was fascinated and couldn't put this down.[7]

JULIE COHEN ADDED IT

This book, more than any other I've read, gives a clear and fascinating picture of what it was like to be a German in pre–World War II Germany, and more particularly, what it was like to be Jewish during this time and have such terrible choices to make.[8]

It's that word again: "fascinated," "fascinating." Someone is looking at Stella and can't look away. I am looking at Stella and can't look away. I want to be hyperverbal, to understand what's at the root of this word. I begin to track *fascination*. Maybe if I follow this word far enough, I will be able to explain why I look, justify why I watch.

Linguists largely agree that the English verb *to fascinate* comes from that Latin noun *fascinum* and the verb *fascinare*, meaning to use the power of the *fascinus*, a sacred ancient Roman image of an erect phallus that was said to have been a symbol of the welfare of the Roman state and more generally of masculine power.

Suddenly the *fascinus* is everywhere. I don't understand how I couldn't have seen it before. Ceramic and bronze phalluses with wings fill my screen, page after page of erect cocks pointing upward, sometimes with loops to connect them to pendants, sometimes with tiny legs underneath them or female figures riding above the erection as if it were a horse. Sometimes two erections sprout one from the other in opposite directions. They are freestanding sculptures, sometimes pictured in museum vitrines, sometimes being sold as replicas on eBay. They are mostly small, usually the size of a quarter and at most the size of my hand, but occasionally larger when they are carved into the rock walls of ancient Roman buildings.

I laugh first, so quickly it is mostly a snort. I keep reading.

The original meaning of the verb *fascinare* was to use the power of this phallus to practice magic, bewitch, or enchant. I'm intrigued by the unusual pairing of the word "bewitch" with a phallus, something so commonly gendered masculine. The witch is usually gendered female, sometimes especially old and sometimes especially young, but not usually in between.

Merriam-Webster tells us[9] that the one doing the bewitching attracts or delights as if by magic. The witch compels in ways that can't be explained by logic. To fascinate means to mess up how things were supposed to go. There I was, minding my own business, and along came Michael. Along came Stella.

I read this back against what I know so far: If Stella is a *fasci*-nating woman, then that means she uses the power of the phallus to bewitch. There's almost a gender-flipping quality here. Stella's hyperfemininity enchants those with phalluses, yes. But to say that she fascinates means that she also makes use of a phallus of her own, of this symbol of masculinity. Maybe it means that she messes with gender, too, even with her melodramatically fluffy skirts, even with her theatrically blond curls. Her performance of gender makes funny that which is supposed to be unyielding.

Scholars explain that the *fascinus* is powerful not only because the erect phallus implies virility and potential reproductive power (that forward thrust) but specifically because the obscenity of this image generates "emotion, shame, or laughter that diverts the evil eye."[10] I guess I'm behaving correctly, then, giggling to myself at the tiny stone phalluses and imagining squeezing them between my finger and thumb. I guess the *fascinus* is doing what it's meant to do. It's funny first, even if within this humor is a flavor of shame.

The ridiculousness of the phallus is distraction, and this is its force. The phallus pulls the evil eye away from something ("look over here!") and toward its own dangling strangeness. Instead of demonstrating force, this phallus demonstrates deflection and deviation. It's a queer diversion of masculine strength. I use "queer" here in the sense that opposes the heteronormative binary of penis + vagina, active + passive, maybe even dominant + submissive. The *fascinus* captures one's attention and plays with it, lifts it high above the realm of ends and means. It exploits that attention for protection, distraction, and armor.

I tell friends I am researching the *fascinus* because it lightens the mood. "It's all these tiny cocks trying to protect themselves!" They are hilarious because they are so small.

"If you look at a double-headed cock," I say, "even fascism becomes funny." Fascinated and powerless before Stella's legs and hair and eyes, even Nazis become ridiculous.

Who is evil here, and who is the evil eye that this whole system of amulets was set up to protect against? The *fascinum* shows up to protect someone from too strong of a gaze. Pliny the Elder writes that the *fascinum* "was suspended under the chariots of military field commanders (*imperatorum*) at their triumphal processions, whom it defends as a remedy against envy (*medicus invidiae*)."[11] *Invidia*, translated as envy, also means "looking upon." The evil eye gazes on something to curse it, so the suspended *fascinum* captures this gaze and rebounds the curse back toward its origin.

I watch Stella's musical and feel more Jewish than ever, giving in to this identity as I go along, captured. The fascination of the story rebounds the history back on my body. The choice left to me is what to do with this body I am bound within. How do I move in it? What of it do I want others to see?

The *fascinum* directly attacks the way we see and look. Daniel Oden writes of a figure of a fascinum on a Roman mosaic that "depicts a phallus ejaculating into a disembodied eye."[12] Craig Arthur Williams describes a terra-cotta figurine dated to first-century BCE in which we see "two little phallus-men sawing an eyeball in half, thus visually evoking the power of the phallus over the evil eye." Well, that's incredible. Phalluses fight back against that which threatens to see them.

"The humorous touch is notable," Williams continues, "and recalls the earthy humor on the subject of penises, especially large ones, that pervades the textual tradition."[13]

I am thinking of teenage girls squirming at the topic of penises, even those adult heterosexual cis-women who, smirking, say they are disgusted by the shape, the curvature, the smell of a cock. I have always been confused by this derision, and a little contemptuous of its stance. I've blamed it on the way too many heterosexual people hesitate to sexualize the masculine body, leaving the role of the object to the feminine. It has bothered me, this distinction, this unwillingness to make the penis an object of beauty. But the *fascinum* adds a new layer. Maybe this squirming is the roots of the *fascinum* acting up, doing something queer and magical. The "humorous touch" belittles, and so challenges the power dynamic of the male gaze. Maybe that smirk is more radical than I realized. If the penis is silly, its dominance can begin to slip aside.

Daringly silly, the Stella musical encourages a kind of brassiness from its opening scenes. It's bold and gaudy. The first musical numbers are about Stella's dream to become a jazz singer. We get elaborately choreographed Broadway-style dance numbers in which men in suits chant about how Stella will *be a star*. They toss her into the air. The lightheartedness of the opening scene layers the campy with the historical. It destabilizes what exactly is real and sets the stage for the increasing and churning instability of ethical ground under Nazi rule.

Cameras and live recording are vital to the production. We see the opening dance number not only in its animate form but also captured on film from above and projected onto the screens above the set. We experience the choreography from multiple angles. From above, we see Stella twirl in the arms of men over a piece of paper that covers the floor of the set and is literally reinscribed through the show: with her name, the word *überlebe* (to survive), and, later on in the musical, with other symbols and detritus from the set and its costumes (Jewish stars, spattered blood).

The musical numbers read more as spectacle than as narrative, and the show moves back and forth in time between childhood fantasy, wartime scheming, and Sella's postwar legal trials to blur our sense of what's occurring in the present. This brisk layering of realities and the use of live camera projections lends an illusory air to everything, along with the jolly tone.

See under: at one point in the play, the character of Adolf Eichmann sings a musical number in which Eichmann jauntily recounts being asked by the führer to engineer additional solutions to the Jewish problem. The line between historical reality and dark humor drifts toward ridicule as Eichmann marches across the stage.

This line has been literally produced before. In Mel Brooks's *The Producers*, we famously watch an audience take offense to a musical about Hitler. On the opening night of *Springtime for Hitler*, the camera pans across the shocked faces during its opening scene as the audience members begin to murmur their disgust and stand up to leave. The scene turns when the actor playing Hitler is so utterly goofy that the audience relaxes and experiences *Springtime for Hitler* to be a satire. If it's a satire, the audience can sit through it, tolerate it. Because they do, the play succeeds (contrary to the producers' intentions for it).

"Thirty-seven years after Brooks declared war on taste and propriety, 'The Producers' has lost its power to shock or offend, but it's retained its ability to amuse," writes Nathan Rabin of the 2005 musical adaptation.[14] In *Stella*'s version of this amusement, Eichmann sings a droll waltz and holds open a leather binder detailing, we can assume, his "solution." I watch him gesture toward the binder and I keep checking to see if I am offended by this lighthearted portrayal of a man in charge of such horrific details. But because the musical is so campy, I am not.

It's the magic spell of mockery. At first, when Stella can evade identification as a Jew, her beauty makes mockery of Nazi presumptions and regulations. Later in the story, when she uses her same capacities to manipulate and round people up, she ridicules the communal ties purported to bind Jewish people, and of Jewishness itself. Her beauty makes a parody of her many husbands, the men who are drawn toward her and so depart from their erstwhile designs.

In *Notes on "Camp,"* Susan Sontag concludes that camp is apolitical, but *Stella* advances a campy politics. In the musical, role play opens possibilities for a subject that was previously stuck, static. *Stella* resists comfort in norms. The show is campy because it demonstrates these norms as jittery, impermanent. It's a camp that defends me from a singular narrative of what it means to be a Jew: the dead kind.

In enjoying *Stella*, I am not enjoying the idea of Jews dying, nor am I yearning for or identifying with this death. Camp, as Sontag defines it, means knowing that one is playing a role. In a campy politics, humor allows me to see the part I enact and decide what to do with it. A Jew, a woman, a person meeting a past lover, an American living temporarily in Europe. Stella helps me step into these places and see that I am stepping.

I grew up in the 1980s and 1990s in New England. Most Jews I knew lived in the suburbs, though my mother would point out the abandoned crumbling synagogues in the neighborhoods that in the 1990s we still called "the inner city." Jews didn't live there anymore. Most Jews had moved out to places like Newton and Brookline or even Belmont, where I grew up. Places where affluence and whiteness and being permitted by the government to accumulate wealth meant that they could buy larger and larger houses in quiet green neighborhoods with school systems known to churn out high-achieving college-going students.

There was no anti-Semitic violence in these neighborhoods, though when it occurred—far away, in other counties and states—we attended rallies in protest in which we sang in Hebrew and swelled with pride as police minded the barricades around us peacefully. I grew up inside of Zionism, and it would be many years before I would even begin to understand the colonial violence and displacement these Hebrew songs conjured up. Back then, we Jews were entirely the innocents with two safe homes—one on the Mediterranean Sea, and one here, in New England. There were no Stellas within our ranks turning us over to the military. I grew up as a white person who assumed the police would protect me, not round me up.

What there was, though, was a system of beauty and money, and how money could get you closer to fitting in. I knew preteens who were getting their hair professionally straightened in fifth grade and whose parents bought them expensive-enough clothes to make even a prepubescent body look elegant. I remember weeping with my mother in Filene's Basement trying on dresses to wear to my Bat Mitzvah: "everything looks so lumpy." I stared at my body in the giant mirror, the zipper half up the side, the tulle jetting out horizontally from my partially formed waist. My mother stood back and looked at me helplessly.

"This one's just not right for you," she said, "let's get it off." And the zipper sticking and locking in the cheap material, so my mom had to say, "breathe in" and I sucked everything back that I could, terrified to rip the dress.

"Come on, honey. If we rip it, they'll make us pay for it." The threat of authority hung there, a specter of my own body's wrongness. My family had enough money that if we'd had to pay for a ripped dress, it wouldn't have ruined us, but the stakes felt nightmarish as I sweated and sucked it in. It haunted me, the idea of some kind of official who would arrive and punish me for just how wrong my body was.

It seemed to me at the time that all the other girls got their dresses at more expensive stores, stores where they offered free tailoring with any dress. The price of a dress at those boutiques was something like a designer wedding dress already. At Bethany's Bat Mitzvah I stared up at her stiff blue skirt suit, the way the skirt just brushed her hips, the shirt tucked in, the boat neckline a perfect half-moon that only just exposed her collarbone.

"Your outfit is amazing," I mumbled to her afterward in the receiving line, when she stood at the entrance to the party flanked by her parents and shook everyone's hand. "Oh, thank you," she dipped her head, "it's a Jackie O style." The prepubescent girls I knew tried to be Jackie O at their Bat Mitzvahs. They were the ones I looked up to, not the shtetl Jews from the movies we were raised on or stories about tenements and street peddlers in Brooklyn. The girls I grew up with were fully prepared to imitate what they knew about the ruling class.

And yet my own body wasn't there yet, or my parents didn't spend the money to purchase something that would make my body comply, or both. I told my mother about Bethany's skirt suit and she rolled her eyes. "It sounds kind of Christian," she said. If you spent enough money, you could be almost Christian.

I'm uncomfortable here, bringing up money again. There's plenty that has been said about Jews and money: restricting it, spending it, managing it. But I've promised myself I'll say words I've been taught not to, to uncover what they conceal. The Jews I knew did not ruthlessly accumulate wealth in the way anti-Semites claim we do. To be ruthless would mean it lacked without compassion, feeling no regret or pity, no *rue*, no sorrow or remorse.

But *rue* was everywhere amid the Jews I knew. Remorse, regret, concern about how one's actions would affect another's. The Jewishness I have lived in involves an obsessive concern with what others experience and project on us, and how these projections are then exaggerated by anti-Semitic tropes. The relationship to wealth and ownership that I experienced is far from ruthless, full of trepidation. It is overdeveloped in response to the very idea that someone would think us merciless or unfeeling. To defend ourselves from this stereotype, some of us conform. To Jackie O, to paying to look white, to changing the prayers we said in synagogue to use Christian words like "clergy" and "hallowed," to have organs installed in our Reform synagogues. Maybe then Christians would recognize the sound of our worship as something sacred.

Every year my father complained about the organ music on Yom Kippur. "It just isn't Jewish anymore," he grumbled.

"I don't mind," my mother shrugged, "I think it's nice." Standing between them with a prayer book in my hands, I knew you could feel either way, but what I most knew was that something was being slipped over our heads, something that made us *nice*. If there's one skill I acquired from being an awkward preteen complaining about clothes, it was access to shiftiness, the evasive. The perfect assimilated body was out of my reach, but I could touch it, stroke it, know that occasionally I might fit in.

But there was another choice, too—to not try. To be grumpy about the organ, to wear a cheap dress and not be allowed yet to shave the hair coming in dark on my legs. To fit in was not a stable sanctuary. I could see it from halfway in, and I could see the work it took to keep you there.

On the occasions when I've tried role-play in the bedroom, I find it more comfortable than vanilla sex. You get to know exactly what you are doing, which words are allowed, and which aren't, what exactly a person wants from your interaction. There's less guessing, and so less likelihood of getting it wrong.

My partner and I switch. I am the stern one, or he is. When we first begin trying this, it is many years into our relationship, and it is difficult, because we are used to the traditional trappings of "making love," intending to be sweet, wanting to be kind, looking into each other's eyes. When we start role-playing, we agree on a safe word, the word one of us will say if we want to stop. *Pineapple*. But when my partner presses my wrists above my head for the first time, he winces, eases back, and doubts himself. He doesn't wait for me to "pineapple."

"You sure you're OK?" He asks.

"I'm great," I say, rearranging my face from passive to warm and reassuring.

"I promise I'll let you know if I'm not. Stay in it for now," I say, and push my wrists up against his hands so that he will lean in with more of his weight.

He learns eventually to trust the role more, and not to ruin it with questions. When you're in a role, you shouldn't break character unless you're in danger—or the other person is—because breaking ruins it. You're in a groove, a known way of how to interact, and if you break out you will have to reset it and invent again.

In Germany, I feel my position in a groove. An identity in which I am placed, both comfortable and uncomfortable, but unbroken. I feel captured by Jewishness, like I cannot choose to step in and out of it as I sometimes can my whiteness in the United States. In Germany, I cannot take my identity on and off, and this has something to do with how much someone else needs me to keep this identity on. The German Jewish writer Max Czollek calls this "the German theater of memory,"[15] drawing on the work of sociologist Y. Michal Bodemann. In this theater, Jews have designated parts that we did not sign up for. We cannot quit them because Germans need us to stay in place to feel secure in their processing of genocide as past. They look at us and they can't stop looking, or there is great threat to their security if they do.

In *Sex and Terror*, the French writer Pascal Quignard writes: "The *fascinus* arrests the gaze, to the point that it cannot detach itself from it."[16]

A German woman stares at my *hamsa* necklace and asks if she can touch the little hand. I nod, and as she pulls it slightly toward her, it strains against the back of my neck. I watch her fingers turn it over and it looks as if the object has become hers now. She rubs the copper between her forefinger and thumb. Together we look at her fingers on the shape.

Quignard describes how the phallic totem was supposed to pull the gaze unto itself, to capture an eye so it could not wander around and curse something else, cause anything else to be *fascinated* or controlled. Working in Germany, I feel concentrated. I focus easily on my work, and I do not feel confused about what I am doing here, as I am a neat peg in a hole, a rare feeling of being correct.

Fascination distills me. To distill means to condense a liquid, to make it more strongly itself by vaporizing it and then collecting its vaporized essence. "What forces are working on you today?" I recall Zora's question, and how I answered first that it was "the Germans," as if they were oppressing me, making me less able to be myself. But what their presence does, I realize now, and more exactly, is boil away unnecessary layers of defense and hesitation, condensing my desire. I want to look evil in the face and prove that I can survive it. From this body, from this moment in history, in this context of American Jewish life, I am safe enough to survive.

Quignard traces the word *fascinum* to the Latin *fasces*, a term for sticks tied together as a bundle. Italian political unions (*fasci*) used as their symbol the Roman image of *fascio littorio*, meaning sticks tied together around an axe. This bundle had been traditionally used by the Roman civic magistrate for violent punishment, and to them represented unified strength. Not a single, fragile stick, but a collection difficult to break. A fitting image for the unions, who passed along the term and implications of the *fascio* as some worker's organizations leaned toward and later became what we refer to today as "fascists."

The *fascio littorio* is roped together beautifully, precisely, and in the images that I look over you can't see the knots. The bundle looks more woven than tied. It reminds me of the pride with which rope bondage practitioners wrap their rope, the way a bondage top lovingly gathers the knots in their hands. I picture a bondage bottom relaxing against the rope, trusting that the top knows how to make it hold.

For years before I let someone put knots across me, I watched to understand what other people did. In Berlin's KitKat Club there is always a lot to look at, and it's fine to just watch if you want to. If that's what you're into. The first time I went to KitKat, it took me a long time to see anything but the person hanging from the ceiling. There were flashing colored lights and dancing and people having sex in the corners and a pool filled with rubber floaties and naked people, but what my eyes wanted to look at most was the rope bottom hanging over the club's biggest dance floor. The person hung suspended from one metal harness on the ceiling, the knots at their thighs and chest pulling up and the rest of them hanging down, feet dangling toward the floor, spine limp, head tilted back and closed. Their chest and belly were bisected in neatly knotted rows, the flesh warping up around the rope like clay. One hand was tied to one foot, so they formed a messy arch or sometimes, in the strobe lights, a rainbow.

It took me a while to get close enough to see the details. I picked my way through the packed dance floor, half pretending to dance, waving my hips. More people seemed invested in the music than in the person hanging, or maybe, I thought to myself, it was more respectful to ignore people when they hung. Within a few feet of the hanging person, a space cleared out and I stepped into it, only to realize why it was empty. The floor was wet, dangerous for dancing, covered in some kind of liquid, maybe multiple kinds, mixed. Sweat dribbled from the hanging person's face and toes and arms.

The person hung there, very still. The rope swayed slightly, but the person had gone completely slack, yielded fully to the rope's hold. I watched a bead of sweat as it moved from their forehead into their short brown hair and then fell to the floor, lit for a second by a green light behind it. I don't know how long I stood there watching, my heart pounding. Not even this person's toe twitched. This person seemed to hold the most power I could imagine, the way they hung relaxed. They conceded to what enclosed them and used this to perform something public, with others.

Months later when I read about *fascio* I think of that person again. Rope bundles together and creates a strength that wasn't there before. A new kind of strength that is also about giving in, not trying to resist something more powerful than your own body. The *fascio littorio* pulls things together, gathering weakness unto unified power. The stick is overtaken by what it becomes.

I'm not the only one who is so taken with Stella that I can't stop writing about her. The non-Jewish German writer Takis Würger's eponymous novel was released in German in 2019, and then a year later in English translation. The book is mostly a romance and has been trounced by critics for its fictionalization of Stella's story into a "Nazi story for dummies" or "Holocaust kitsch." I can't dispute these critiques, but the book's flamboyance is also what keeps a reader inside it.

From the Goodreads reviews of Würger's novel:

STARDUST SEEKER RATED IT "REALLY LIKED IT"
Beckoning and exciting in spite of everything![17]

AIYANAURORA RATED IT "WAS SOMETHING AMAZING"
I have never read such an authentic book about World War II. It is very interesting and because it is so well written it is easy and fast to read.

"Beckoning." That magic spell again. "Authentic." The kitsch spins across the trauma and ropes the reader in.[18]

SCHERZKEKS RATED IT "WAS AMAZING"

First of all: I would like to congratulate the publisher for the beautiful design of the cover. A great metallic effect, which shimmers black, silver or gold depending on the viewing angle. I do not want to write anything about the contents of the book for fear of revealing too much.[19]

LESELISSI RATED IT "LIKED IT"

What a story!

What a woman! Fierce!

Of course I could not resist it, and immediately googled Stella Goldschlag.[20]

Stella's heirs have lodged legal disputes against Hanser Verlag, the publisher of Würger's novel, as well as against the Neuköllner Oper, where the musical was performed. The managers of Stella's estate demanded the musical cease performances and the novel be pulled from shelves, saying that Stella expressly wished that her life not "be taken out of context and distorted."

But this very distortion lies at the heart of the telling and retelling of Stella's story. Stella distorts. She distorts how she is seen, manipulating her own image, and manipulating the experience of other people whose gaze falls on her. The fascinatrix, Stella stops people on their way to their own intents and pulls them somewhere else, somewhere radically disorienting. She wraps us up. She tops us, deciding on our behalf what we will do and who we will be in the public eye.

Stella doesn't make me feel stronger in my own values, or in my fantasy that I'd be able to resist violent fascism that like that of the Nazis. If anything, I feel more aware of the reality that I too could give in, be captured or turn sides. But she makes me feel stronger in a different way, in a subby way, to use the language of kink. Especially because I am looking back on her from the future, from this point in time—she makes me aware of the choices that I do and don't have. She presents the possibility of play to confront the most disturbing things I could imagine occurring, the things that have occurred to people in my bloodline, people who look like me.

There are moments when I want to go limp in a partner's arms. There are moments when I want to be yelled at, when I want to hear the worst insults, so that I can see that language fill the air and know that I have lived through it. These moments are especially important because I am living with quite a bit more agency than the Jews Stella rounded up on the Kurfürstendamm. What I can do from here is let these terrors exist without letting them be my entire identity, knowing as I do that today many American Jews have financial and social capital, and many are not bearing the worst brunt today of genocide and racism and state violence.

My way may not be everyone's, just like my kink is not everyone's. I wish we could make a contract that I'd stop writing when my reader stops feeling okay, but I can't reach you like that. I turn my gaze where it's okay for *me* to play.

"How do you know if it's working?" It's a question someone asked at an erotic hypnosis workshop I attended on a whim. The workshop was led by a man with a thick Israeli accent who went by the name of Dr. Eyal, a lofty title of compulsory authority. Unclear what kind of doctor. I couldn't tell if the name was a joke, and erotic hypnosis didn't work on me, at least hasn't yet.

Dr. Eyal insisted it takes a lot of practice. He smiled a charitable smile, first at the participant asking the question, and then out at the rest of us, his audience. I wanted to know, too, when it would work, or what it was supposed to feel like. I hadn't dropped into a trance or fallen asleep at my partner's command.

"You'll only know it works from your partner," Dr. Eyal said. "You have to be open to feedback. There's no failure, only feedback." This was one of his favorite phrases to share at introductory workshops, he told us, because so many of us were afraid to try. Like any catchphrase, it made me suspicious, but he moved on, guided us through the instructions for "hypnotic bondage," in which one partner hypnotizes the other into not being able to move.

"Now bring your awareness back to the folding chair beneath you," my partner commanded at the end of our trial run. "Open your eyes." His gaze on mine was hopeful, but I knew I'd disappoint him.

"Did it work?"

"Not . . . really?" I tilted my head to one side, cushioning the prospect. An earlier me might have pretended I'd been hypnotized just to please him, but I didn't bother this time.

"I liked *imagining* you could freeze me?" I told him. "Even if I didn't feel much?" The rise at the end of my sentences, uptalking. I could hear it in my own voice, and I knew I wasn't supposed to do that if I wanted to sound strong. But it felt useful, here, to perform a small amount of that gendered cushioning, pretending it was a question when it was not.

My partner let out a breath then that I wondered if he'd been holding the whole exercise. His shoulders dropped markedly and filled out the sleeves of his flannel shirt. I grinned and reached across to where his right thigh met his knee, squeezing, encouraging more release.

"I didn't think it was working either," he said. He didn't seem too let down, actually—more reassured that our experiences aligned. "Probably good enough?" He uptalked a little, too, I noticed. I liked that echo of insecurity between us.

On Diasporic Speech

When Jenny posts about fascination it is not about a starlet, or a fascist. It's about plants. Jenny posts a picture of a long strip of crumpled flower running across the top of a gray-green cactus, and in her caption explains that this is a mutation called *fascination*, in which the plant develops its flower in a wavy horizontal line instead of blooming bolt upright on one single point.

I pounce. It ends up being a slippage, my misreading: the plant mutation is actually called *fasciation*, no "n" in that second syllable. But the word still has its roots in the prefix that I love.

I hear the prefix because I have been waiting for it. *Fasci* is a home I've made for myself, to the extent that even when I am swiping or scrolling I have its structures in the back of my mind. I am surprised not to have encountered this plant word sooner. Fasciation, I read, literally translates to "banding or bundling,"[1] or "the act of binding up,"[2] the same way "fascism" came from the Italian for a bundle of sticks, this bundling now applied to flower petals.

Fasciation can occur because of a shift of hormones in the plant's cells, because of genetic mutation, or because bacteria or damage on the growing tip of the plant causes the plant to shift the course of its growth. When plants develop this mutation, their flower forms a cylinder. Fasciated flowers often look flattened, like long ribbons, undulated folds. In some cases, these folded flower heads are prized and bred intentionally, as in the case of the cockscomb celosia. Most sources say the cockscomb got its name because it looks like the top of a rooster's head, but my sense of humor knows better than that. *Fasci* is heaven for dick jokes, and I'm not decent enough to resist.

*   *   *

I look up from my phone and leave my sublet apartment for the day. I am headed for the archives at the Jewish Museum in Berlin, where I am ostensibly on a research grant to look for examples of Jewish humor in the face of trauma, for when and how the traumatized turn stereotype back on themselves comically, for what reclamation means. I'm looking for my roots, intellectually. How is what I'm thinking about built on what's been thought before?

In the archives I try to feel professional, legitimate. Even as I flip through cartoons exaggerating Jewish noses and phalluses, even as I bring my own lunch in a messy set of takeout containers wrapped in reused plastic bags. I spread out my writing materials on the long white tables and read. By midmorning I am already worried that my meal is leaking into my backpack, so I take an early lunch break. I decide to sit and eat it in the Garden of Diaspora, the courtyard positioned right in the middle of the W. Michael Blumenthal Academy, the building in which the archives are held.

In the introductory text for the Diaspora Garden, I read that the garden was designed to represent the Jewish diaspora and includes plants "with a special connection to Jewish life or Jewish personalities," plants in various stages of "seeding, rooting, growing, and wilting," and plants in a "'diaspora' process in the sense of dispersion." The plants sit in beds on "floating plateaus," or wooden platforms that to me appear rather makeshift, reflecting, the pamphlet reads, "aspects of life in the Diaspora."

I crouch in a corner because there are no chairs, but suddenly I want to know every word about this space. I pull up the Diaspora Garden's audio guide on my phone and poke in my earbuds. I hear that the garden evokes "literally the dispersion of people who have left their traditional home."[3] I look up at the plants suspended from the ceiling. "Traditional home" under which tradition? I am uncomfortable in my crouch. I turn to open my containers of sauerkraut and hummus and place them on the wooden floor next to me along with my half-melted compostable fork and the scrap of paper towel I brought along.

"The plants come from different climate zones and have to adapt to their new unfamiliar environment," I hear. My ears are sweating around the earbuds. I stand, dizzy, and take a slow stroll around.

From the looks of it, it doesn't appear that "adapting" is going well. The garden's plants look scraggly, underwatered, and crawling from their beds toward the floor. The audio guide pauses for a moment and I can hear my own feet creaking on the wooden planks I walk across. I do not like it here, even with the abundant air, natural light, and potentially charming climbing vines. I return to my corner and wonder for a moment if I'm allowed to eat in here. It isn't, after all, a public park—it's an exhibit in the center of a building with lots of rules about how and where to touch things. I feel grimy and concerned. I take a few hurried bites and worry about the smells emanating from my containers, even though no one is in here with me. It is very quiet. In the background of the audio guide recording, I hear birdsong, but I do not hear that sound in the garden itself. Nothing lives in here but the plants in their beds. And those seem barely living. I stare. The plants look back at me, inert, comatose in their limp sprawl. They have nothing to tell me. They let the audio guide speak for them, the professional curation of their existence.

I feel a rising nausea, not sure whether it's about how quickly I'm eating, this place, or my illness flaring up. My endometriosis triggers are multiple and varied, from alcohol to lack of sleep and "stress," so it's hard for me to know what to blame. Or when I will be well. I rarely plan to meet people in public for lunch meetings, because the middle of the day is a time when I get weak for reasons I can't track.

I wrap my containers back up and, dazed, make my way toward the exit. Near the doors I pass a pile of thick black bags with drainage holes, which I recognize from information in the audio guide: these are intended for children to take small plants from the garden home with them so that the garden is "continually in the process of dispersion." The intention seems to be to make a new environment for the plants. One that is still and emphatically defined by being far from home.

The Wandering Jew trope has plagued us since at least the thirteenth century. The earliest versions of it trace to a pissed-off Jesus: In the High Medieval legend, poor Jesus was dragging along his cross and tried to stop to rest and drink, but a miserly Jew refused to share his water and resting place.[4] Jesus cursed the Jew with eternal life without rest until the apocalypse, that is, until Jesus's Second Coming.

It's a confusing curse. Eternal life might at first sound appealing. Some versions of the legend indicate that the Wandering Jew was granted immortality because he was in fact one of Jesus's favorite disciples.[5] This lends an element of affection to the curse, an affection not irrelevant to the curatorial choices I see in the Diaspora Garden. The garden presents a kind of awe or respect for the nerve and determination required to wander to the ends of the earth.

By the time I learn about the Wandering Jew trope, the curse is veiled—I have to look for it, investigate in books (also held, I should note, in the Blumenthal Academy's collection) about religious history and mythology of the Middle Ages. But when I understand the curse better, a lot of philosemitism makes more sense. Underlying any awe is a logic that we *deserve* this diasporic position, that it was predetermined by something ungenerous in us.

It's important to remember that the Wandering Jew is not an idea Jews made up to explain ourselves. It's a story other dominant cultures recited to assign us our place.

I walk out of the garden and into the academy's bunker-like bathroom. I have taken shelter so many times in public bathrooms when pain comes over me that I consider a wide flat sink a place of comfort and relief. I lean over a faucet, splash cold water on my face, and stare into a mirror until my nausea subsides.

The Diaspora Garden makes me feel ill when it seems to dissolve me, to dissolve us. It is one dying version of a story, yet another place in Berlin where I am labeled a victim. It makes me nauseous after years of being a white person in the United States during a few crucial years of antiracist activism, years in which I have attended meetings in living rooms and warehouses to talk about how to counteract racist policing and how to work on our own internalized racism and root it out, how to offer reparations for the way we benefit from whiteness. It makes me nauseous because I understand that the Wandering Jew story is there to control us, to pass down the idea that we deserve our migration and refugee patterns.

But the more I read, the more this story cracks. We fled when others wanted us to go. We came to believe that we were always moving because we were all always under threat, but this was also a white, European story. Jews in the Middle East and North Africa, Central Asia, and the Balkans lived relatively peacefully for a long period before European colonization, not regularly persecuted for their Jewishness as European Jews were more methodically.[6]

"This history disproves narratives that assert universal persecution as the permanent condition of Jews in the world," I read in the JFREJ "Understanding Antisemitism" report. "The histories of Mizrahi and Sephardi Jews throw a beautiful wrench into attempts . . . to manipulate Jewish fear by universalizing Ashkenazi historical trauma."[7] There is no universal explanation for why Jews live in many different nation-states, and I'm suspicious of any story that attempts to function that way. Such stories are political projects that serve the culture that created them. The State of Israel uses such a story to dictate the inevitability and unquestionable necessity of a militarized Jewish state, forcefully possessing and commanding land at horrific human costs. In the Diaspora Garden, this same story shores up the place of Jews in German relationships to the state's murderous history. If Jews are peacefully diasporic, then murder is in the past, further from the public eye. We are useful to Germans as long as we stay in our lane.

I cannot stand in the Diaspora Garden because it traps me there. More dying, more of the same, the rerun of emaciated bodies in a ditch. And after the ditch, the survivors spreading out across the world, the propaganda of the Statue of Liberty welcoming them with open arms, the pickle carts and delis of the Lower East Side. Or the survivors planting trees in the desert of colonial Palestine on an allegedly blank canvas of erased Arab villages. Or that ridiculous earworm of a song *Wherever You Go, There's Always Someone Jewish* that I was taught as a kid that lists places where Jews can be found:

> Some Jews live in tents, and some live in pagodas,
> And some Jews pay rent, 'cause the city's not free.
> Some Jews live on farms in the hills of Minnesota,
> And some Jews wear no shoes, and live by the sea.

I know every word of this song and the catchy tune that leads us back to the chorus: "You're never alone when you say you're a Jew / So when you're not home, and you're somewhere kind of newish / The odds are, don't look far— 'cause they're Jewish, too." Jews are all around, the song teaches us. We're all across the globe. It name-checks places and experiences in a vacuum, the way the garden vacuums out why or how or the nuances of its myths.

I am living in Oakland, now, which is not where I was born, which is also not where my parents were born. But my birth in Boston or my living in Oakland are not diasporic in the same sense of the garden. I was not pushed: I chose. The Garden of Diaspora catches in my throat because it does not acknowledge my ability to choose. Yes, other Jews have been victims, but I am not. I want a live relationship to the roles I've inherited, not one so clearly engraved for the sake of political control.

I am lucky to have models for redefining a flourishing life. For years, I have been writing about how chronic illness both radicalizes a body and makes it patient. Shored up by the company of other sick and disabled artists, I feel less a victim and more an inventor of other ways to inhabit being. I draw on the ethics of disability justice when I enter the archives as an artist-researcher, poking around in the books with my associative logic, validating this as another way to learn, not lesser than more systematic methodologies. I make plans with friends that are accessible to us both, shifting our meeting place from a lake on the edge of Berlin to a café near a friend's house where she can bring her wheelchair. I do not pity either of us but marvel at our creativity in determining the best plan.

"Crip Ecologies links the fragility of the body to the fragility of our ecosystems, exploring the vulnerability of both," writes RA Walden.[8] Walden writes about a project in which they collect and preserve objects like seed pods and flower stems to emphasize how rarely they go to interact with the outside world, and thus how valuable these objects become to them. I love Walden's "vulnerability of both" because it is so different from the garden: instead of bracketing one experience as defined by suffering, Walden yokes an individual sick body to ecosystems so as to expand the concept of fragility beyond the human and draw awareness to ecological concerns.

My body is fragile, sometimes, yes, but this reality can expand me instead of trap and restrict. When I require care, I become less individual, less independent. But I'm no longer sure that that word "independent" is the one I most want to use to signal maturity, achievement, or healing. I turn the language of victimhood back on itself, fold and fold it again, churning. Victimhood moves, and I want to be awake enough to move with it. Yes, I know fascism is rising again, in Germany too. All the *more* reason to stay awake and not frozen in one place, one determination of identity and reaction.

What we used to say about ourselves does not fit forever. A friend tells me about how when she visits her parents, her mother overfills the fridge and force-feeds her, "you know," she says, "like our Jewish mothers do." But my own mother does not have these same food patterns. Or someone assumes I won't eat bacon though my family has never observed Jewish dietary laws, or another friend complains about how she's just started dating someone but "our Jewish parents always ask if he's a doctor or a lawyer," when I've personally never felt this kind of pressure from my own family to date someone with a certain profession. My parents have equally welcomed a musician, a poet, and now, a developer of solar energy projects—who is also a musician who likes to read and cook and bake bread.

I name these qualities or habits of a person I love and I sense how hollow they are, how little they describe the feeling of being close to them. Categories can give us a starting place, but they fail to bring lived experience closer. I nod to these categories to concede that we use them, not expecting them to predict much.

In *Ways of Seeing*, John Berger notes that "when we 'see' a landscape we situate ourselves in it."[9] He writes primarily of 2D artwork, but I see the exhibition of the Diaspora Garden this way, forcibly so. It exhibits diaspora as a story specific to Jewishness—and thus to me—in a blanket fashion. I feel pinned to the wall as some of the vines in the garden have been pinned to lengths of rope in an attempt to lead the plants toward the ceiling, though they twist away from the guidelines and yellow where their roots protrude from the dirt.

Later, I ask my friend Berivan about the garden. Berivan used to work for the Blumenthal Academy leading programs, and we've already rolled our eyes together about how the building's renowned architecture isn't built for actual humans to work inside. I ask Berivan if it's on purpose that the garden is on the messy side. It's won many prizes for landscape architecture, and I want to assume thoughtful intent. Berivan laughs.

"Definitely not," she says, "it's just that no one is taking care of it." She tells me that the garden has been semiabandoned as museum staff move on to other priorities. Maybe other forms of monumentation are considered more effective now. But, Berivan explains, she did plenty of time in that garden during her time working at the academy. During one work event, she tells me, she used the garden to explain to colleagues the interreligious and varied symbolic history of the plants included. Berivan begins listing off to me the seven biblical species featured in the garden: the fig, the olive, the date, pomegranate, grape, barley, and wheat.

I am very amused by the fact that I am standing in an apartment in a Turkish neighborhood in Berlin with my Kurdish German friend, listening to a list of plants I learned in Hebrew school. I remember sitting in plastic synagogue chairs at a long table around a blue and white plate of these same fruits, twelve of us feasting on one single bruised but preciously imported fig.

"I learned about these plants like they were from far away," I tell Berivan. "They were exotic to us, too." Berivan is about to finish her thesis on Kurdish genocide, repression, and diaspora, and I do not need to lecture her about the mythologies of original landscape, but I say it still, verbalizing to make sure it all gets across.

"The minute you begin talking about plants, you are also talking geography." I shake my head and can't stop shaking it. In the Diaspora Garden, nation-states are not named as the origins of each plant, but most of those present originate in the Middle East. These plants reference a place, a ground, an ecology of dirt, but in the bright courtyard they do not touch the German outdoors, the native soil. They are root bound in their containers, held there for the sake of keeping the exhibition intact. They imply an indigeneity—one that is interrupted, held constructed in air—but tied even in this interruption to a single place of origin. What upsets me is the sense of exception here: the story that the Jewish diaspora is exceptionally dispersed, continually and expositively so, assuming that all *other* peoples are rooted on solid, constant ground.

I tell Berivan about the first day I worked in the archives in the Blumenthal Academy, how I walked into the stacks and felt tears spring to my eyes, my body sagging against the steadiness of a corrugated metal shelf.

"I felt like I'd arrived," I say, "where I belonged." I hid there against that shelf for a while, turning away from the librarians at the long desk, hoping they'd think my weeping was just deep concentration on the volumes of collections about Jewish ethics. I tell Berivan I didn't know then if my tears were a feeling of belonging in a library, or belonging in a Jewish institution, or the legitimacy and validity I felt working in the archives, in such contrast with the usual tenuous professionalism of a freelance writer.

"But I literally cried," I tell her, "Longing so hard to be home."

Berivan pulls me in for a hug then, and I am surprised by its velocity.

"We know home is bullshit," she says softly, and I can feel her wide smile as she breathes out close to my ear, "people have been moving always. Our home is with our people." She pulls away, strokes my hair, and laughs. We laugh together at how basic it all sounds.

"I mean, I don't want to be one of those rootless cosmopolitans—" she gestures into the rainy Berlin street, "who don't give a shit because they don't believe in home." No, it isn't that. Not to be cosmopolitan, roving the great cosmos without ties or obligations. Not to deny trauma, but also not to force home to grow suspended from the state.

It's true I don't feel entirely at home in the United States, growing up as I did with one parent who isn't from here, and conditioned as I am Jewishly to always have one foot out. I know nothing about the towns in Poland or Ukraine that my ancestors called home. Nor do I feel at home in Israel, after years of traveling there to investigate my connection to it, learning gradually about the vicious details of the Occupation, and slowly, excruciatingly disengaging from the belief that that land belongs to me. I feel sometimes at home in Mexico City, speaking the slangy Spanish my father raised me with, always dumping cinnamon in my coffee and hot chocolate, tolerating brisket only if soaked with salsa, cilantro, and lime. I don't feel always at home in Berlin, but I feel flashes of it in moments like my friendship with Berivan, who on paper is different from me but in practice understands my questions intimately. These flashes are the homes I believe in, and the fact that they are flashes do not invalidate them as such.

"The beauty as well as the terrible trouble of diaspora is that it has no original point," says poet and theorist Fred Moten. "We mistake it and we reduce it when we think about it in terms of origin."[10] He speaks of Black diaspora, describing the locations designated as Black origins as "places of innumerable gathering and differentiation," and marking Black sociality as "where those differences were cared for." I hesitate to reference Moten's work given its centering of Blackness, and I do not want to imply that Jewish and Black diasporas are the same. They have evolved from different genocides and colonizations. That said, these two diasporas coexist along a contemporary understanding of whiteness, and I want to learn from Black thinkers who have much more practice than I do slipping out from forced and carceral diasporic molds.

In conversation with the white Jewish artist Gregg Bordowitz, Moten considers the motifs of Black and Jewish diasporas as linked through the investigation of diaspora itself. He describes the possible freedoms available through difference—as opposed to restriction inside of an identity forced on a person.[11] Moten jokes about the links between Black and Jewish diasporas, but the joke maintains the difference, so that the conversation can take place in a way that, I venture, could "care" for difference, as Moten might say, as opposed to requiring it to correspond in order for discussion to continue.

"We mistake it and we reduce it when we think about it in terms of origin." Moten treats diaspora like a figure which or who can be mistaken, almost a person misunderstood or misrecognized, taken for someone else. I sense care too, in the way he uses the verb "reduce"—wishing to give diaspora the full extent of the space it takes up as an object, as a sovereign subject, not wanting to diminish it to something within the limits we already grasp.

In my experience, most humans are baffled by care, even if we want it. To be cared for means to be taken in with others, washed through by what others offer us, be it medicine, time, love, talk. I am thinking now specifically about language, and about how being sick has required me to accept terms I wouldn't have chosen for my own body. At the same time, this acceptance has offered me a more animated understanding of self.

I think back to Walden's "Crip Ecologies" project, which builds on a tradition of disability politics that reclaims the term "crip" from its use as an insult. Walden identifies themselves as crip, as sick, as flushed with the words that others have used to injure in the past. When they use these words, they place themselves in a new home in which their crip-ness defines not an alienation but their robust sense of belonging—with others, and with the more-than-human.

I want to come home in this way. I crouch in the garden looking for my own body, listening for the sounds of my own breath. "I mean having a body in the world is not to have a body in truth," writes Anne Boyer, "it's to have a body in history."[12] Boyer writes this in a book about having cancer that becomes a book about capitalism, about how medicine participates in the brutal regulation of bodies even as it claims to heal. Boyer uses the techniques of a poet here, repeating a phrase and swapping out a crucial noun: world, truth, history. Boyer's language enacts the layering of self, environment, and nonlinear time. These plait and cannot be disentangled.

"To have a body in history." I lie down at night in Berlin and listen to phrases whisper through my mind: *fascism, fascination, fascinum, fascinare.* I place myself in the country and let words in another language embrace my consciousness, integrate with what I want to consider. An inverted or backward diaspora, looking for the origin of words more than of persons. I locate myself in speech and wait for it to show me where I am.

I won't ever know if I'm rambling rightly if I refuse to play exactly the cursed Wandering Jew atoning for my crimes. I'm sure that somewhere in my wanders I won't successfully be absorbed into the surrounding culture, won't please. My relationship with home will never be a complete story—not because it is uniquely outstandingly diasporic, but because I participate in a story that continues to tell.

"The boon of language is that *potentially* it is complete," writes John Berger, "it has the potentiality of holding with words the totality of human experience. Everything that has occurred and everything that may occur." I have been well, I have been white, I have been a normatively attractive cis-gender woman. I have been ill, I have been wrong, I have thrown up for reasons I couldn't track down. Language can't contain the totality, and yet, with reclaimed words like crip and sick, it theoretically attempts. "[Language] even allows space for the unspeakable," Berger continues. "In this sense one can say of language that it is potentially the only human home, the only dwelling place that cannot be hostile to men."[13]

Reading Berger, I come home to a text where I can rest. I can rest because the text does not claim to be able to say everything (or say everything correctly) but holds the attempt. I hug Berivan, a person I've only known a few months, and she may be the one, in this moment, who knows me best. I watch another of Zora's toe-porn gifts, mesmerized and satisfied, as though I might never need to see another form of sex again. I pursue my home in the *fasci* root that stretches across dialects and genocides and people and time, a moving target that admits history and evolves, unlandscaped, incomplete.

Monumental

I first hear Nas use the term "Person of Color" when she is speaking in quick German to her partner, Jens. They are having a side conversation in front of me, and she knows I don't understand German, but I recognize her clear enunciation of the letters "POC," and ask her about it when she and Jens both turn back to the table.

"It came from Audre Lorde," she smiles. Lorde spent time in Berlin in the 1980s and early 1990s and is said to have catalyzed German understanding of whiteness as well as Afro-German identity.

"We still use her words because we don't have better ones," Nas says. "People don't know what terms to use for race here. The words in German come from the Nazis, and we don't want to use those." I don't know what exactly those words would be. I think vaguely of eugenics and the measured circumference of a skull.

"Germans usually use a word which literally means *migrants* to describe people of color. As in, I am a *migrant* even though I was born in this country, just because of my racial background." Nas was born in Germany, but is of Lebanese descent, and her parents emigrated from Syria. She arches one eyebrow and gives me a knowing smile, though I'm not sure, exactly, what she knows. The smile is something about how we are sitting on the same side of a booth in this bar in Berlin, how we both have olive skin and dark hair pouring over our shoulders, how we can't help but full-body cackle when we laugh, and Germans turn to look.

Jens sits across the table gazing into his mostly empty beer mug. He is tall, blond, and light-skinned, and hunches over the square table with its oblong green banker's lamp. I've been trying to include him in our conversation, but he seems used to listening, and does not meet my eyes. I get an immediate sense of his deference to Nas and thus to me, since I am the object of her interest. The bulk of the talk passes between Nas and me, with Jens in the background leaving space.

Nas asks me where I'm from, and I tell her first about Boston, that I was born in a cold city where my family did not seem to feel completely at ease, that my father came from Mexico City to Massachusetts for school. There he met my mother, who was from the Northeast but hated the snow and sunk into herself in the depth of winter or fled somewhere seasonally for sun. Nas maintains close eye contact, nodding, so I go on.

"They liked it well enough there, but it didn't feel like our place," I say, "I grew up speaking Spanish and some Hebrew." I shrug, "So, they were always talking about a lot of other places we were from, like Poland or Lithuania or Russia or Israel. Almost anywhere else."

"Are your people from *here*?" she interjects, and I shake my head.

"Not exactly, though some people think one of my family's last names traces them to a city in Germany," I say. My grandmother on my father's side carries the name Mintz, which some Germans will tell you indicates that they used to live in the city of Mainz. My family disputes this. If they inhabited Germany at some point, they've been too many places since.

I have extended family everywhere. In every country I've visited there is a distant cousin to reach out to, or at the very least a family friend. That is, every country but this one. Here I've had to make my own friends.

"I wish I spoke German," I tell Nas, "My family speaks a lot of languages, but that one wasn't encouraged. My *abuela* in Mexico City speaks at least seven languages." I begin to count on my fingers. "Yiddish, Polish, French, Spanish, English . . ."

"Why so many?" Nas asks.

"Well, because they had to," I say, then notice this is something I've been taught to repeat, an old narrative about coping, living on the margins in case we had to move on. Is that even true? I am abruptly embarrassed by this rote story, the slick, signaling way I've parroted it. I know better, or at least have read better.

"If we only view the margin as a sign, marking the donation of pain and deprivation, then a certain hopeless and despair, a deep nihilism penetrates in a destructive way the very ground of our being," writes bell hooks. "It is there in that space of collective despair that one's creativity, one's imagination is at risk."[1] To me, bell hooks is a paragon of relational resistance, of positing how we engage with one another as a vital site for intervention in structural habits. I want to suspend hooks's named nihilism, to be even just a little more creative, to hear, now, about someone else instead of something I've regurgitated.

I turn to Jens and wave my hand under his face as if to wake him up from his quiet stance over the beer.

"Where are *you* from originally?" I ask.

Nas snorts before Jens can even look up. "He's not from anywhere!" she says. "He is the most German German. I call him my White Bread." I look at him to check if this a joke. He barely moves. I am growing desperate to hear him speak for himself.

"But where did you grow up?"

He looks up then, finally, first at her and then at me, and mumbles the name of a small city in West Germany.

"Has your family been in Germany for a long time?" I ask. Again Nas makes a scornful sound under her breath, and this time Jens smiles too.

"I'm just German," he says. He reaches across the table and takes Nas's hand between two of his. They exchange a glance I can't read. I look back and forth between them.

"I guess—in Oakland we always say where we're from, like—" I'm so used to a world in which to say you are *just white* is a sign of ignorance, complicity with the erasure that whiteness performs. I keep trying. "I guess I'm still curious about how you think about your ancestry—" It's not something I usually have to explain. "—Or the culture you identify with?"

"Oh, culture—" Jens comes alive a bit more, tapping the surface of the table. "Punk culture is really important to me." He plays bass in a punk band, he tells me, and the radical leftist politics of punk culture have formed him since he was young. "Those are my people," he says, and shrugs. I don't feel satisfied.

"But is that, like, how you identify?" They both roll their eyes. They tell me I am being "so American," assuming everyone comes from somewhere else.

"Identity politics." Nas waves down the server and orders us some tequila. "It's what your people drink!" She tells me that she visited Mexico City last year and felt more belonging with the culture there than she does here in Germany.

"You know, it's not always about the nation-state," she says. We move on. Nas tells me about her master's research into how North African refugee communities maintain cultural practices once they arrive in Berlin. She grasps my shoulder, "very much like the Jews," she says.

I'm interested, and, I'll admit, feeling comfy here in this subject matter. But something nags in me. I'm curious about who gets to participate at this table, and how Jens lurks on the other side of the table with no history at all.

Later they both walk me home in the chilly Kreuzberg wind, and I try to ask Jens more questions about his band and hometown. I feel uncomfortable about having spoken so much while knowing so little about him. Jens begins to speak about how punk squats resist gentrification. He tells me about the politics his band addresses in their songs. But Nas cuts him off.

"Punks don't really know what they're talking about, and more importantly they don't know how to dance." She shuffles across the wet cobblestones, arms rigid at her sides. Jens bristles at this and begins to explain something about hardcore music and the body, but Nas grabs my hand and physically turns me away.

"Don't listen to him. He doesn't know anything." It's so theatrical that I don't expect him to take it seriously, but he stops speaking and pulls up his hood. She points a finger like she's sending a child to time-out.

"You're done," she says to him. She swats the butt of his jeans, then links arms with me and ushers me up ahead of him. He seems slightly annoyed but walks obediently a bit behind us the rest of the way home.

Back in Oakland, I recount this conversation to my friend Anat, and she points out that it sounds like an S&M relationship. I resist at first. I tell Anat it's not something Nas and Jens have formally agreed on. Neither of them says the word "reparations," though it seems to me that something like this is at work. Anat nods.

"So, they have an *unconscious* S&M relationship." This does describe the way these two people assign each other parts. What makes me uneasy is the unconscious part. Chosen power dynamics and consensual kink, I am into. When one body is absented without agreement, I'm not sure how much this repairs.

It's not an entirely unusual pattern, nor the first time I've watched a German person absent themselves. Germany is so often held up as a model for reparations due to the number of memorials and museums it has dealing with the genocides of World War II, and due to its efforts to prioritize the history of the Holocaust in grade-school education. (Jens corrects me about the name of a concentration camp, and, when I am surprised by his certainty: "You don't understand. In school we learn about the Holocaust *every single year.*")

There is much to be commended about this memorialization, but it also blanks people out. Over and over in Berlin when I voice that I am Jewish, white Germans stiffen in front of me and begin to offer an immediate deference to my opinions, refraining from sharing about themselves. In the face of this polite groveling, I yank harder to make conversation, offering risqué jokes and asking more personal questions. It rarely works.

Berlin is notorious for being a place without taboos, especially when it comes to sex and gender, and for having long encouraged the creative freedoms of artists and weirdos of all stripes. But I sense the edges of its taboos around race, less as fear than as absence. German bodies step back from the scene. To make space for the voices of others, or to take cover behind their memorials and their massive concrete slabs?

Something clearly hurts there. Something is not healed. It pricks enough to make a body jump back. I try to understand this behavior through what I am familiar with. I remember the times when I stiffen or feel the need to absent myself because I am scared of what will come next. I think of the times in Oakland when I sat at meetings at the Anti Police-Terror Project, a Black-led coalition. I remember that first time I watched a Black woman break into tears, screaming about the murder of her nephew and her brother within the same few months. The horror that had been inflicted on this woman's life and community was not mine and yet I was implicated. I sat back in my seat, immobilized. I didn't have a script yet for my place in this situation, and without that script, I froze. I remember the only thing I could feel was the plastic and metal hinge of the chair against my lower back. I could barely understand what the woman was yelling, and my gaze on the room grew fuzzy and dim.

"We've all seen white women act like corpses around women of color," writes Melanie Kaye/Kantrowitz, "so afraid of doing the wrong thing: meaning, anything natural, treating a person like a person." I find it especially helpful to read Kaye/Kantrowitz's analysis, given that she is a white Jewish woman who continuously reassessed how she participated in movements for racial justice.

She continues, "For guilt is a freeze emotion: you can't think, you can't feel, you can only knee-jerk. This is the infantilizing function of guilt: you lose faith in your own responses because the risk of their being wrong is more than you can handle."[2]

These days we call this "white fragility," the incapacity to act compounded with the immobilizing fear of being anything but completely perfect. I've experienced this many times, and I'm sure I will again, even as I work to pause my body on its way to freezing up or panicking for lack of a perfect response, because there is no perfect response—there is only "treating a person like a person," as Kaye/Kantrowitz writes. Which is never a perfect act, only a responsive one.

It's also helpful here to remember the historical "middle agent" positioning of Jews, specifically how it sets Jews up to appear as delivering racist and classist subjugations, even when in a buffer role. The "freeze" comes not just from white fragility but from assimilated fragility. If we respond "like a person" we may respond as someone other than a middle agent, potentially causing a fracture in our structural role.

Still, "treating a person like a person" beckons. When I have the opportunity to respond in an authentic embodied manner, it disrupts the coded belief that I need my assigned structural role. It's been years now that with instruction and training and the support of numerous activists and friends, I am learning to witness other people's trauma without feeling that I should leave, escape. I learn to listen to Black parents at numerous marches and actions as they mourn their children. I learn to let it pour through me, to feel something of the grief, to let it fuel me to listen more deeply, to try to internalize something about the person, the life that was lost to police violence. I say "pour through" with the meaning of rushing water, how it can slam heavy objects over, how it can carve shapes in rock over time. Something must be altered and carved away in me. I have to be willing to be wrong and amended in the eyes of both others and myself, defamiliarized.

But this takes time, and it takes working against years of conditioning. I think of this slow creaky change over years when I watch Germans rigidly nod or when I walk up to a Holocaust memorial glittering in the center of town in the sun, tourists taking selfies. I toggle back into my own experience as a white person in Oakland to understand how people hold mass murder at the proverbial arm's length.

In his essay "Shoahtecture," Sam Holleran argues that many Holocaust memorials make an imposing statement but do not complete what he terms "the task of memorialization,"[3] by which he means the task of processing collective trauma. People today are still hurt by the history these monuments reference. Even as the last of the direct survivor generation passes away, their descendants are still affected by the fallout of mass murder, mass relocation, and the identification with new nation-states to which their families emigrated. Monuments may apologize, in their way, for a given event in time. But rarely do they touch on how these events tip forward into bodies living today, relationships, decisions.

I found Holleran's work in *Jewish Currents*, the Jewish leftist magazine that works often to connect state violence and repression globally with Jewish perspective. The magazine's analysis involves a nonexclusive relationship to Jewish suffering, which is one aspect of what I find so compelling in Holleran's piece. So much of Jewish writing about the Holocaust is solipsistic, but in Holleran's piece I feel I can breathe because the room is larger. Or, more accurately, the *building* is larger, or the neighborhood is larger—Holleran works to contrast showy museums and memorials (especially those designed by architect Daniel Libeskind) with artist- and citizen-led projects that inhabit and haunt how people interact with their cities now.

"It's easier to build monuments at a large scale. Fundraising for big, bold projects helps countries, cities, businesses, and philanthropists to feel that we have done something," Holleran writes. "Shoahtecture is showy, but, paradoxically, easily overlooked, meaning that big memorialization projects might be the first step towards forgetting. To truly disorient a viewer into greater empathy and contemplation, it may require a move away from the pharaonic scale of museums and mega-monuments and towards smaller, more direct intrusions on our space and our daily lives."

I love this word "intrusion" here, its physicality. The intrusion of my torso leaning forward over a beer stein and interrupting polite conversation, or of a German man's face leaning over mine, moving my hand up to brush his hair from in front of his eyes. Bodies revealing something that doesn't enclose but generates more and more. This intrusion does "disorient," as Holleran terms it. It turns my body in a new direction. And not just one direction. It keeps me spinning, swimming from one position to another. Victim, oppressor, Jew, woman, family member, friend. This swimming awakens the possibility of empathy because I'm awake now. Instead of being only an instrument of the Garden of Diaspora, I am allowed to anchor my boat on the bottom of a sea that shifts me back and forth, up and down as it swells and changes. I am safe now. Not to say that I couldn't be unsafe again, but in the United States, I am white right now. I am not cast in this whiteness or this Jewishness as one stone mold, but rather allow current experiences to also saturate the past. I can listen better, and more can cohere, make sense, make substance.

When I give my first reading in Berlin, in an elegant cafe near Mehringplatz, I feel a zing of panic as I look out at a room of straw-colored hair. Fine metal piping improbably holds up heavy slabs of wood for the tables and the chairs. Gigantic arched windows look out on dark water and night. People filter in and look at me expectantly, though it is not yet time to begin the event. I am perched by the front with the event organizer, and I set my mouth in an approximation of friendliness. I consciously relax the muscles around my eyes so that no one will feel I am already judging them or suspect that I am nervous. I lift my mouth slightly in the half smile I have been told makes my cheekbones bob forward.

"Do you need anything," the organizer asks. It's not really a question, because she has already brought me a glass of water in a beer glass, a beer in a canning jar, an extra stool where I am meant to set down my sheaf of papers while I read, and a brassy place to sit that looks more like a supermodel's hipbone than a chair. I shake my head. After ten minutes of sitting on this chair my butt is already painfully sore.

"I'm just going to run to the bathroom," I tell her. She nods once and gestures toward the corner. I walk quickly in that direction. I can sense heads turn toward me in the rows of chairs. I open a door in the wall, hopeful, and then can see that each bathroom stall is its own small room with its own sturdy wooden door. I open one and lock myself in. It's not easy to sit on a closed toilet. I lift the cover of the seat and pull my pants down to do what you're supposed to do here.

I do not need to pee. I pull out my phone and text my friend Allie: "At my reading. It's all ARYANS!!" Earlier today I had told her about the reading and that I planned to read the beginning of a story about my relationship with Michael, about my exploration of Nazi kink. Suddenly I am unsure if I can read this story to a German audience. Will they laugh? Walk out horrified?

But it is about to start, and I have not brought anything else to read. My friend texts back immediately though she is in a different time zone: "the ancestors say you are brave. The ancestors say you are doing the right thing." I can count on her to say things like this. Her words don't calm me, but they do make me feel that someone believes I can do this.

I leave the bathroom with my heart thumping and take my seat again on the gorgeous uncomfortable chair. The host introduces me briefly, but I do not hear the words. I stand up in front of the stool and the microphone and try to ham it up the whole reading. I read about Michael, *my Aryan*, daring them with the word. In this setting it doesn't sound that funny. (You might say: *wrong crowd.*) I can hear the audience breathe. The room goes very quiet except for my voice. I can't tell if they are listening closely, or just waiting for it to be over.

When I finish reading, several people raise their hands and comment on my courage, though they don't elaborate why they think I am daring. I smile sweetly and say "thank you." Then a tall man in a big raincoat stands up.

"Hi, sorry to yuck your yum," he says, "but do you think it's OK to trivialize Nazis, to make this all into your personal video game?"

He sits down, expecting, I think, that this will be a rhetorical question, that I will silently retreat. But I feel a flood of appreciation for the rift it seems we've made in the discreet civility of the room. I lift the microphone closer to my mouth so I can speak more softly but still be heard. I consciously release the gritting in my jaw.

"Thanks for that question," I say. "To me, this is not trivializing. To me, it is trivializing *not* to discuss these kinds of things." He begins to shake his head, but I continue. It's like I've always had these words stored up to say. "This is not a video game to me. Humor allows me to talk about dynamics that are very difficult to talk about otherwise." I can see that he is already seated and has turned his back to me, whispering to the person next to him. I call on the next person with their hand up, who has a genteel question about the research I am doing in the archives at the Jewish Museum.

After I am done at the microphone, they applaud, and I stand around while people come up to me to make the comments that they didn't get a chance to make in the larger group. A woman with curls very similar to my own comes close and tells me that my work resonated for her. I recognize the throaty vowels of her Israeli accent. She tells me she has been living in Berlin for years now but never brings "these things" up because, she says, "I just don't want to be that Jew, or deal with *that* asshole." She gestures toward the man with the raincoat, who's now got his arm around a woman over at the bar.

"You know what he'd hate even more?" she asks me and leans toward my ear to whisper: "stalag porn." It's not a secret, but it feels like one.

The term *stalag porn*, also known as *stalag fiction* or just *stalags*, refers to illustrated Nazi sexploitation books published in the State of Israel in the 1950s and 1960s. The conceit of these graphic novels typically involves an Allied soldier who is held in an SS prisoner-of-war camp (*Stammlager* in German or *Stalag* for short). The books often begin with female SS guards enacting sexual brutalization on the main character, a British or American male prisoner. The prisoner experiences a confusing attraction to his torturers. Most stalags end when the prisoner triumphs by overcoming the female guards and taking sexualized revenge against them.

Stalags were marketed as nonfiction, supposedly the chronicles of Allied POWs translated into Hebrew from the original in English. The books were published with fictionalized author pseudonyms like Mike Longshot and Ralph Butcher and included a fake translation note and fictional name of a translator. But stalags were all works of fiction written by Israeli writers, many of whom have since been identified as children of survivors of Nazi concentration camps.

According to the Jewish Film Institute, "for many in Israel, the stalags were both the only erotic literature available and their first source of information about the atrocities of Nazism."[4] Scholars have observed that stalags found their greatest audience in Israeli teenagers, many the children of traumatized camp survivors who got very little information about the war from their parents themselves. The popularity of stalags also rose parallel to the era of the trial of Adolf Eichmann.

"Appearing against the background of a transformative event in Holocaust memory in Israel, the stalags weaved fantasy and transgression into a cultural text that accompanied the trial," write scholars Amit Pinchevski and Roy Brand. "As such, they testify to the way initial revelations of the traumatic past were incorporated and imagined in the minds of young Israelis in the early 1960s."[5]

They respond "like a person." A faulty person in process of integrating nightmarish information.

Pinchevski and Brand trace stalags along the time line of Eichmann's trial in Jerusalem, which Hannah Arendt and others have termed the first national public reckoning with the horrors of the camps. Pinchevski and Brand invoke the attempt in Zionist ideology to construct a "New Jew" who was "deemed strong, courageous, and masculine, capable of defending his land and his people—the antithesis of the old Diaspora Jew, who was deemed weak, servile, cowardly and feminine." The weak Jew was particularly conspicuous during the time of Eichmann's trial, when Jews were described as trudging into gas chambers like sheep to the slaughter.

"A transformative process was set in motion whereby the definitions of what it means to be strong and what it means to be weak began to complexify," write Pinchevski and Brand, "The Stalags were an agent in negotiating this process." Stalags operated on the level of the visceral during a trial known for its massive scale: many have said that during the Eichmann trial, what was on trial was not just one person but all Nazis or, as Arendt indicates, the history of anti-Semitism itself. The very specificity of the stalags—down to their fake names and kinky, porny weirdness—counters the structured legal proceedings of the trial by emphasizing the human bodies involved.

These bodies are not boring or even bureaucratic. The messy mash-up of cartoonish stalag characters works against every way I've always been taught to think of the Holocaust. They invite you to play. Pinchevski and Brand describe how in the stalags, "evil is no longer banal—it is exciting. As such, these narratives constitute a counternarrative to the story of destruction—heroism, victory and sex as the ultimate triumph of libido over death." This libidinal energy triumphs through behaviors coded as beastly: "In the Stalag when it comes to sex, all are equally animals at base. Yet such animalization carries with it a kind of humanization: if all men and women, Aryan and non-Aryan, are essentially animals, this common animality is ultimately a basis of humanity." The revelation of physicality allows these characters—and, I wager, their readers—to move into more chosen relation with traumatic histories of the war.

Chosen, yes—but also chosen by the state, and serving political purposes. The stalags reinforced the aims of Zionist ideology and state formation by endorsing the use of force as necessary violence. They valorized a hot, strong, embodied protagonist who (while not Jewish) offered readers an opportunity to place themselves in a first-person experience of violent revenge against Nazis. Sex begins from what the body knows, and, here, sex conforms with what a political project wants it to know. If, as Pinchevski and Brand say, the stalags served to humanize by emphasizing their characters' shared beastliness, they did so in service of another dehumanizing project: keeping Israeli focus on the European front to eclipse the Palestinian and Arab refugees from the land on which they were building a new nation-state. The stalags show us which histories were being actively reinforced in the erotic imagination of their time.

Since that isn't my time, I guess it makes sense that stalags don't really turn me on. I feel only cynical reading about a busty blond woman slamming her boot into an American prisoner's knees so that he falls to the ground in front of her. I am cold as the early evening fog rolls in and rub my own hands together as she slaps him around. The zipper of her top slips down farther. I click the file closed, sleepy and, I now realize, bored. Stalags are extremely predictable; a fantasy reiterated to process the famously un-process-able realities of the concentration camp and keep the imagination held there.

I'm not their target audience. Stalags are the creative product and reflection of an Israeli audience at a different moment in history. I read with them, toward them, even if I do not relate, even as I purposefully redirect my own concerns to racial and political matters outside of the Middle East because I do not believe that Israel is the center of the Jewish universe, because we have so much cultural history and so much work to do elsewhere. I am reminded of Hirsch's "postmemory," in which a prior generation's trauma is processed by and through the next generation, "not by recall but through imaginative investment and creation."[6] Pinchevski and Brand draw on this, concluding that the less trauma survivors say, the more "creative liberties" a later generation may take. I'm extending this also to include the "less said" by the Zionism of my youth, by the early state-makers of Israel, whose silences, intentional and unintentional, lead me now to take new "creative liberties," to imagine outside of the New Jew, to imagine what liberation might mean where I am.

Liberation, liberties: to take liberties, in the negative sense, means not to be faithful to the original, to be disrespectfully intimate. I suppose that's what I must do in my postmemorial project. When I write of my own experiences, I try to stick with what I remember occurred, although I am reaching across time and place and cannot pretend it is all exact. I cannot speak for Jewish trauma on a large scale. I make so-called off-color jokes and connections for the sake of the audiences I hope will benefit from hearing them. I take liberties to expose a roughness that has been assimilated out of the identities I have known.

I want to reveal something that can't be solved, isn't clear, can't be shined away like Liebeskind's beautiful cement. I want to reveal that the story isn't over, that we haven't passed into whiteness in a perfect, solid way. It is less about whether I am a victim or oppressor, whether I am worthy or unworthy of speaking, whether I am hurt or healed. It is about the fact that we cannot trust state power to feel the same way about a given set of bodies forever, even if we feel relative safety in the United States now, in Germany before the war, in Israel if we ignore other inhabitants of the land and expect militarization, murder, anti-Arab racism, occupation and incarceration to keep Jews safe—which I personally do not expect, believe or find to be true in my lifetime. Hometown, motherland, site of cultural acclimatization: no matter the label, the state is not my safe house.

There is some hazard in refusing this house or home. I feel the hazard in the slow crawl I make across Berlin and Oakland and in between, trying to unravel subject matter deemed very officially impossible to understand. I am leaving a snail trail, something about me that everyone else can see. I will look back on this thinking having done something obviously wrong, obviously traumatized, a secret exposed, some toilet paper stuck to the sole of my shoe. It's not unlike telling a story around a dinner table and realizing halfway through that it's not going to be as funny as you thought. Still I keep telling it, hoping, more and more, that someone will explain to me where I went wrong. I'll have to blush, my hot cheeks the skin I can't hide, the skin that makes it clear that I am vulnerable, too. The more I unravel, the more the erotic potential of humiliation grows, and the more it eclipses the petrifying fear of being wrong, of falling outside the categories delimited by whiteness, intelligence, propriety.

Instead, I feel the draw of connectedness, of a possibly unlimited capacity to be included. The more stalag fiction I look at, the more yoked I feel to people I am not, the kitschy horrors surrounding me like long-lost relatives. I open the window again with my search for "stalag porn" and wonder what corporation is tracking these clicks on my browser. I never search for Nazi kink in incognito mode because I'd *love* to know what the algorithm thinks this search history means, what new ads it'll serve me for it. I feel the freaky power of nothing to hide.

Maybe it's the influence of the stalags, their blunt edge. Jews working out their trauma on their oppressors, cheaply, quickly, mass market. At first, I was ashamed of these children of Holocaust survivors for doing it so obviously, for leaving the world a glaring archive of their darkest fantasies. The voice in the back of my head: *It's bad for the Jews.* The desire to protect haunts me even as I poke. *How dare you tell a story that makes us look bad. Didn't you know better. Weren't you smarter.*

These lines have run through me the entire time I've been researching these worlds, even though I insist to myself and others that I am writing to humanize, that I don't believe that hiding serves us. I want to let it in, how silly the stalags are, how anxiously they make me giggle. I am able to release shame when I contact the eros of being exposed. I want to know what it feels like to let something genuinely affect me, to not prepare my guard before it arrives. Only rarely have I felt anything close to this, and those rare moments have come only in the context of skin-to-skin.

In *The Erotic Life of Racism*, Sharon P. Holland describes the possibility of fleshy erotic practices to enact and dislocate racialization. I first came across Holland's book in the days when I was googling "race and kink" to find out if I was alone in my explorations of kink that addresses identities. Many of what comes up in the first rounds of these searches is bad in the worst way—both racist and predictable—but Holland's book is not because she speaks of these topics in terms of how individual bodies move and shift inside the social orders they've been placed in.

"In racist ordering, relation is defined as those who shape time and those who stand outside it, as those who belong to your people, and those who do not," Holland writes, "Only grave trespass can produce another order altogether." This trespass is what I find myself longing toward, not the steely dissociation. I think of Jens, and how my own whiteness helps me understand why he freezes up. What if we act out freezing-up in a different direction: to freeze and make brittle or frangible the systems that hold us in the position of someone who "shapes time." To freeze with intent to crack. I wish to feel that frozen ice breaking around me.

This requires that hazard, risk in a form of disloyalty. Holland writes that those who shape time are those who decide what progress looks like, when and how a person will receive power based on their racial ordering. Holland's work centers Blackness, how personal desire is never inextricable from the Black/white binary. When Holland writes about time and trespass, she writes about a white world that determines who belongs in the categories of white and non-white. Holland's "grave trespass" destabilizes both time and belonging along said categories. The trespass mutates time and roles by naming them directly, letting them be funny, caricaturing them. It is "grave," this trespass, meaning dangerously consequential to all—not only those marked as racialized. It is grave because no one gets to stand neutrally outside of its effects: all bodies are demanded.

On the banks of the Landwehrkanal I guess Adam is Jewish before he tells me. Maybe it's something about how little he reacts when I tell him I am research-ing Nazi kink. He has told me already that he's kinky, and I recognize in him the reflexes of someone who has taught themselves not to be shocked. It is his slow, unflappable nodding, as if instead of protesting a strike his body simply makes room.

Adam tells me he's heard of Nazi kink before, in a lecture he saw once by queer artist and scholar Alexandros Papadopoulos. Papadopoulos suffered a homophobic attack that he chose to creatively re-perform through an eroticized exchange with a neo-Nazi over Facebook. Papadopoulos re-creates the scene of the crime with a different position of agency, a little like the stalags. Through this exchange, Papadopoulos attempts to understand how both he and his "gay neo-Nazi interlocutor" choose to perform their politics and experiences, center their own stories, and thus gain control over violent and precarious circumstances:

> There indeed seems to be a commonality, a type of "homo" that connected me to him—or, at least, his performance and my re-enactment of it. And the best phrase to describe this is "horny despair." I understand "horny despair." as the tendency to transform pain into horniness and horniness into despair when feeling defeated, whether professionally, erotically, or creatively. When I performed someone else's defeat and anger using my own body, these types of defeat felt interconnected.[7]

"Horny despair" enacts defeat and helplessness that was once externally imposed, but this time is done so electively. Many of us make this kind of move in a less kinky sense. When placed on the losing or passive side of a power dynamic, it can feel appealing to just give in, just collapse under the weight of assumptions or stereotypes, to trick our oppressor by doing what they imprint upon us. Papadopoulos reframes this move through its possibilities as pleasurable intervention:

> If some of us can turn sodomism into orgasm, then it might be also possible to transform pain—material, psychological, physical pain—into a form of pleasure. This is not a passive, over-positive, self-help acceptance of the world as it is, nor is it meant to suggest that if the world abuses you, you should relax and enjoy it. The point here is to fight back by inventing new languages of joy, new canons of beauty, and ultimately new ideals of professional, moral and social success.

Papadopoulos manages to dodge the problematics of self-help and the trivializing of kink by pointing to pain as foundational creative material. Not to say that misery equals art, but that misery can be radically acted with and on—by people insisting on their agency from a locus which was previously understood only as miserably unempowered.

The more I sit with "horny despair," the more I understand exactly how defeat—or, for that matter, mass murder—is not the end of the story. For it not to be the end, we need to continue to reveal ourselves, including our violent fantasies, including the backgrounds that may shame us, or those that layer power indirectly, confusing our understanding of victim-oppressor categories. The more I think about horny despair, the more inventive I feel.

I'm not on a search for a utopian wholeness, but for a continual opening that refuses to seal off. Theorists Lauren Berlant and Lee Edelman call this "living with negativity"[8] in their collaboratively written book *Sex, or the Unbearable*. Berlant and Edelman write seeking to maintain a rough surface, a "negativity" that refuses to transmute into blame, shame, and resolution. They write: "Ultimately for us, it isn't a choice between disturbance and transformational possibility. We are interested in the inseparability of the two, in what can never be predicted or controlled in any engagement with the world, with otherness, and thus with ourselves as well."[9] I glow when I read this. Disturbance and transformation are inseparable, ungovernably so. Could it be that I could be disturbed by history and still invested in engaging it in a new way? Could it be that considering it all this closely does not mean that I am necessarily disrespectful of others' trauma, nor necessarily pathologically stuck in an old world?

I think a lot about that comment at my reading, the one about the video game. At times I doubt myself—am I jabbing at the long resolved? Am I exaggerating an old scar? Are you bored yet? Maybe for the man who asked me that question at the reading the issue of Jewish genocide *is* resolved, and maybe he thinks I am making something like a video game because he thinks the story is complete. That man wanted me to accept the narrative as it has been completed, be done with it, *over it*, but I am not.

I read to understand why I'm so not over it, and what it might take for me to get somewhere new, somewhere closer to Berlant and Edelman's "transformational possibility." I flip through that Bessel van der Kolk tome *The Body Keeps the Score* that every therapist friend I have keeps on the bookshelf, though when you press them closely, they'll admit they've never read it the whole way through. "I know," I tell them, "Because so much of its already in our blood." There's something in our bodies that already understands how much we've been physically holding trauma and knows that our flesh must move to help us arrive, psychologically, in the present tense.

I read Jewish feminists like Melanie Kaye/Kantrowitz, who wrote in a moment prior to mine when activists were realizing how very white Jews were becoming and were trying to find the pause button for solidarity's sake. I read Resmaa Menakem's *My Grandmother's Hands* and Dr. Joy DeGruy's *Posttraumatic Slave Syndrome* to understand how other bodies have borne their trauma and genocide. I try not to make this experience mine, but I still read, believing I can learn from trauma with a different lineage than my own. I begin to notice how sparse my language gets when I'm writing about race. It's as if I can't be both clear and creative. In service of precision, I write shorter sentences. I repeat phrasing I have heard from others instead of inventing more lyric phrasing of my own. I begin to talk about this with other writer friends.

"Have you noticed your sentences changing when you try to write about race?"

Anne nods deeply in the Zoom window.

"Yup," she says, "my dissertation advisor handed my book back to me and said, *what if you tried just writing this as yourself.*" Anne is writing a novel that investigates her family's relationship to land in the American Southwest, though she expresses doubts about whether she should "take up space" with doing this at all. She'd asked me to talk about this together, specifically—how we are managing race in our work.

"I've been trying to write about my own whiteness in essays," Anne says, "but whenever I turn in an essay that references it, the editor asks me to take it out."

I unmute myself to ask, "why do you think they don't want it in there?"

Anne pauses for a moment and leans back against the blue couch behind her. "I don't think they're actively silencing a race discussion," she says. "The editor I'm thinking of is at a magazine that publishes a lot about race." She pulls up the email and scans it, her eyes darting back and forth across the screen. "Yeah, that's what I remembered," she says, "the editor said that my writing just wasn't as good—he wrote 'as *fluid*'—when I started to get into this stuff."

Understandably, magazines want good writing. But what if white writers can't write fluidly about whiteness yet, and that's part of the point? What if it's okay, even purposeful, that this writing comes out worse?

"Maybe it could be useful to show our bad attempts," I say. Anne waggles her head, half nod, half shake, and then smiles.

"Yeah, that might be true," she says, "because otherwise it's just getting cut out or covered over, even if we're thinking about it." I think back to the stalags and the messiness that they reveal: something that was published though regarded by many to be both foolish and morally wrong. I want sometimes to write like this, with a glimpse of skin allowed, a soft underbelly. The stalags are absurd. I try to be absurd about Aryans. If I know something is going to be ridiculous—even to be ridiculed—then I can push myself beyond what I think I am allowed to say.

Over years of thinking about race and trauma and porn, the internet begins to recommend books to me that are about killing, healing, or sex. One day my Amazon recommendations show me the philosopher Elizabeth V. Spelman's book *Repair: The Impulse to Restore in a Fragile World*, and I request it from the library without a second thought. It seems staid compared to many of the things I've been reading lately.

In this book, Spelman describes several ways that attempts at repair can cover or demand conclusion from something that is broken before all parties are prepared to move on. In her section on apology and reparation, she thinks through what one person seeks to erase in another when they apologize.

"When I offer an apology to you for my thoughtlessness, I am seeking to destroy the state of rupture between us," Spelman writes. "The consolation apology offers depends on its capacity to be destructive in this way."[10] Here, "destructive" is important because it implies loss. If someone wants to wipe the slate clean, the person who forgives them must erase something in their own feeling and experience for the forgiveness to feel valid. It sounds like Shoahtecture, how the monuments' magnitude communicates "we're done here." I am wondering what repair could look like that doesn't wipe away or erase, that allows us to build with or feel with rupture.

I think of the movement Adam made when I brought up kink, the way his chest caved in a tiny millimeter before he leaned back against the willow tree. It looked like a movement of integration, information soaked quickly into the body and the human reemerging, supple, to interact.

I remember Jens and Nas snapping at each other over the small table over the bar, how her body was so much more animated than his, her hands flying, his neck stiff. What I want for them both is agility, pliability. Where Adam and I sit, the branches of the willow form a curtain around us through which we can see. Usually, you can bend the end of a willow branch without it breaking. You can twist it together. I want Jens and Nas to be limber enough to braid with me and with each other. Not for one of them to fall away, disappear, become unconsciously servile so that the other can flower, turn to the sun—you get the idea. I keep at the plant metaphors because I can just barely picture what it means substantively for humans to do this. Entwined bodies: sex is the closest human thing I can imagine to what I am saying, and so I keep going back to twining limbs. It's the only culturally replicated image that lets us see bodies this twisted, this crip-like, this collective, and this close.

Adam's back against the willow tree is bowed but supple: a word very close to submissive but not quite it. Supple is filled with fluid, so it is not empty, but it can yield. It can yield when assessing what is inside, and what is outside. Yielding like water, how water moves in response to the space around it. Yielding, sloshing from side to side, multiple ends, multiple positions of power. I say multiple because I can relate to both the white man's compliance and making space for others, and to the dark-haired woman of color taking pride in her

96

inherited culture lest anyone try to wrest it from her or force its return to the traps of self-hatred. I can relate to the need to go mute, and I can relate to the need to be seen and heard and take control of the conversation when the city all around you insists on monuments but does not want to talk.

Supple: the body as the opposite of hard rock. Something supple takes one shape and then another in response but is never complete in its movement. I recall feeling swollen with possibility when I first began to look at kinky Nazi imagery, and how that sensation of physical swelling led me here, moving toward an interactive politics, moving toward Jens and Nas. It helps that Jens and Nas are a romantic couple because their togetherness implies a physical joining. Sex links bodies to make forms that neither body can fully predict or complete on their own. Holland's "trespass" does not let the forms lie still. We don't know what way the flesh will smush to one side, what exact folds will appear in the skin, how the leg will flex or twitch when it bends around another body or rises to point a toe up toward the ceiling. I fantasize toward this suppleness. It is just as sexy as the role-play itself, if not even more. It is the unknowable in another person that keeps me coming back to talk again, to read again, to play again.

Chaotic Neutral

I grew up with less body hatred than most. My parents didn't hide their bodies from me and my sister and didn't require we cover up the instant we got out of the shower. Maybe these behaviors are European remnants in the culture my parents' grandparents brought from the old country. To this day, members of my family will strip with ease, especially for help examining rashes, ailments, and skin conditions.

"You're old enough that you should be thinking about the family skin history," my mother says, rolling her pant leg back down. Maybe by exposing the marks where melanoma was removed, she can keep me from the same. My mother loves sun and heat more than most things, and when I think of her one of the images that comes most easily to mind is her closed eyes and reddening skin. Before showering, she'd turn the water all the way to the hot side and wait, one hand in the stream, until it was nearly boiling. As a child I'd sit anxiously on the toilet as steam billowed out from behind the shower curtain, worried that she'd faint in there. I'd call out to her just to make sure.

In the dark of winter in Berlin, I go to the sauna and think of my mother. She would hate this season here, the bundling and doggedness it requires. She would love the sauna, but she might have a difficult time on the way. In winter in Berlin it's hard to tell where you are going until you get there. You don't have the landmarks of cafés sprawling their tables onto the sidewalk and opening their doors. Light barely makes its way out from the windows onto the street, as if it too were preserving warmth for its interior.

I do not realize I have arrived at the sauna until I am inside of it. The exterior of Stadtbad Neukölln looks like many other buildings in the neighborhood, but once you open the front door the lobby is slick with marble and brass and I am impressed. I bumble my way through check-in with the attendant, who seems baffled that I do not already know how things work here. She hands me a small white towel and points me down a hall to the changing room, where I undress quickly and shove my things in a locker.

The first problem is the towel. It does not reach all the way around my torso, and though I am a small person I feel huge as I try to stretch it. I look around to see if anyone is noticing my struggle and feel like a teenager again, casting about for someone to tell me how to wear a tube top. I remember the one girl in the high school cafeteria who could pull off that kind of shirt, who had the perfect inch of skin exposed from belly button to low-rise jeans. I remember pinching my own armpits hard until they ached, trying to get the flesh to stay under my arms though it wanted to bulge at the edge of my new breasts. Even my parents' ease around nakedness couldn't protect me from what my body was not getting right, shirts made to remind you that the problem is you.

What's not a teenager about me now is I'll try anyway. I occasionally wear a button-down shirt though if they fit my shoulders right, they will never button without gapping at the chest. What remains teenager-like is my fear. I have always run hot and sweated easily, and in the locker room I can feel heat rising from my body already as I glance down the hallway, checking if anyone is pointing and laughing at my towel as a mini-dress. I look in one direction and then the other, and I realize I don't know how to get from here to the sauna.

"This is not what the towel is for," a woman behind me grins and just barely touches my hand where it grips the terrycloth. Her own towel is swung fully over her shoulder. "Put it under you," she says, and pats her own generous bottom. I don't know what she means, but she beckons, and I follow her from what I think is a respectful distance to walk behind a naked woman. We climb some stairs and the signs for the sauna begin to appear. The woman disappears behind a steamy door, but signs are all around me now indicating what the towel is for.

"*Kein Schweiß aufs Holz,*" signs first in German and then in English: "No sweat on the wood!" You are meant to sit on your towel, so you don't sweat on the porous wood surfaces shared with everyone else. In the dim light of a dry sauna, I spread my towel on a wooden bench. I crouch over the small white rectangle in a hopeless attempt to gather every surface of me on top of it. People near me whisper quietly to one another, and one man turns to me.

"Just relax," he says in English, his hand flat against his own towel as he leans toward me. As if it were that easy. It has never been easy, though my mother pressed down on my scrunched-up shoulder muscles or the gym teacher told me to *breathe before you explode.*

There's usually no explanation for why I'm tense. I'm quick to make a joke about ancestral trauma to explain why my heart pounds if I am two minutes late. Any presentation of rules makes me anxious that I'll fail. I breathe out slowly and remind myself this is supposed to be calming. The sauna's rules and goals are a system meant to help the heat steam away your tension along with your self-consciousness, enveloping you in its methods to arrive at tranquility.

I sit my butt over the towel and dangle my legs uncomfortably over the bench. I press down on my slick thighs spreading flattened across the wooden planks. Without looking I know where the one extraordinarily long dark hair grows from my outer thigh, nearly my hip. I pinch it between my fingers now and pull hard. It doesn't come out, but the predictable sting slows me down a bit.

"Relax," the man next to me murmurs again, and gestures an in-breath and out-breath, his hand conducting up and down his own chest. I wish it was the word itself that I didn't understand, because maybe then the physical demonstration would help. I nod, trying to reassure him that I've heard, that he has done the job of a convivial host.

That masculine impulse to tell my body to be chill. So familiar. It seems I am always tight when they want me to be loose, looking for instructions when they want me to already know them and obey. I remember crouching over Ben the first time we had sex, seventeen and a little drunk in his bedroom, listening closely for sounds of his parents. The sun had just set, and he hadn't turned on the lights. I could barely make out his face as he maneuvered around where he seemed hard and where I seemed soft. I remember settling my weight down onto his lap, our clothes still on, rubbing there and shifting my hips up and down like something I imagined from a porn. I remember his hands moving to my butt. I clenched and squeezed. A soft growl came up from below, and Ben's whisper, "relax." I didn't understand where he meant and squeezed harder. He grabbed my butt cheek then, hard.

"Tensing up isn't going to make this better," he said. As if he knew something about bodies that I didn't, when it was also his first time. Somehow, he got the rules when I couldn't.

"Be natural," he said, and I felt even more frantic. I knew I couldn't just lay my body down on top of his. That would be lazy or not enough. I needed to be told how to be natural so that I would do it right.

I try the steam rooms, because to enter those you leave your towel outside. I hang mine on a hook aside a massive ream of clear plastic wrap and watch for a little while as others tear off sections. The roll is the width of my arm span. An older person ahead of me rips off a long piece and holds it up in front of them, where it extends from their armpits to knees. It appears that you are supposed to get a piece of plastic to carry into the steam room where you array it on the opaque bench before lying on top. Impermeable now to the bacteria of previous steam bathers.

Or, if you are me, you enter the room with your chunk of warping wrap and can barely see. You creepily peer through the steam at other people's naked bodies until you find an empty patch to sit. I struggle to get the plastic wrap to lay flat on the soaking wet bench. My piece clumps and folds on itself. I frantically try to straighten it but eventually give up. I lie down on a clumped-up pile of plastic just long enough to accommodate about hips to mid-thighs. I choke meekly on the steam. Out of the corner of my eye, I watch other people who seem to maybe be sleeping. I stare down at my feet, and my scrunched-up toes that refuse to lie flat unless I push them down. I imagine belonging here, melting.

There's this scene I remember by the pool when I was young, probably ten or eleven, visiting my family in Mexico. We were sitting in the yard at our family friend's house, and I felt very mature reading my book next to my mother on pool chairs in the sun. I remember pointing out to my mother that she always made me put on sunscreen but rarely did it herself, and my father urging her: "let me do your back." My mother turning away from him as he sat behind her on the sagging pool chair, my father pulling down her strap in the back to apply it across her shoulders, and Arturo, the owner of the house, who looked over and requested teasingly in Spanish that my father pull the strap down even farther. I remember my mother's face scrunching up and my own body scrunching too, two pool chairs away, not totally knowing why but knowing Arturo was in charge, now. My mother turning to roll her eyes at my father as if asking him to do something, and my father shrugging, whispering, "he's just being himself."

Once the sunscreen was applied, my mother inhaled and straightened. I watched her. All of us at the pool watched her, my father, Arturo, even the younger kids in the pool conscious suddenly that something was going on. My mother did not look back at any of us but adjusted her towel along the slats of her chair, replaced her sunglasses on her face, lay elegantly back down, and closed her eyes. I remember the awareness that I was free to look at my mother's body, and how long her legs, how freckled her calves.

Only then did the static of the scene quiet, my mother's prone body in the sun. I learned something then about how female bodies move to resolve encounters, about what transpires to make tension clear. I think of that memory in the sauna as I try to lie prone on the plastic wrap and fail. I remember asking my father about it later that day, why Arturo had felt like he could make that joke.

"Oh, it's nothing," he said, "it's not rude. In our culture, bodies are more accepted." The "our culture" in contrast to American-ness because my father was born and raised in Mexico. My father brought me up speaking the Spanish of Mexico City and identifying with that place, but I grew up in the United States, and so tried to be okay with this way as well as with that.

By "our culture," he meant that Arturo had not been threatening or dangerous, that I should understand things were different by that pool. *Accept this*, he was communicating. *It's how the rules work here.* But it was an acceptance I couldn't quite duck under, because I'd been also in places where if a man leered at you, you were supposed to run. The more worlds I moved between, the more I doubted what I was supposed to do.

When I don't know how to fit into sauna culture, I read about it. As a child who moved through different cultures and messages about how the body was to be exposed, I was always reading text when I wasn't reading people, checking to make sure I had the right framework, the right tactic for that day.

I come home from the sauna and dive into the history of nudism. Nudists are always trying to explain why they are not sexual, or how they keep nude bodies free from sexualization. In one of my favorite examples, a man writes an open letter to the nudist magazine *Figaro*. It's 1917, and he's just returned from Siberia, where he served during World War I and the Russian civil war. In the letter, he describes going for a swim with a group of soldiers on the shore of the Sea of Japan. He mentions that they are "thunderously sexually charged," and warns "woe to the female creature, regardless of age, who fell into our hands." At the beach, the soldiers come upon a young Russian woman with her children.

"Without noticing [them], the young, beautiful woman disrobed first herself and then her children completely, and then took her children in her arms and entered the surf," the man writes. The group of men are so taken with this Madonna-like image that they lose all sexual urge. The writer concludes, "a naked woman who presents herself as innocent, free and natural is holy to every man."[1]

It's an ideal nudist situation because a body is presented to the eye without reservation. The *Figaro* letter concludes: "As they returned, they were so happily focused, and even the wildest and raunchiest among them were gripped by the deepest calm, sweetness, timorousness, and patience to everyone."[2] The soldiers achieve these higher states by watching people who hadn't exactly opted into being watched. The sunlit higher self requires that another self be translucent, less than human—that object that purity is enacted through. The mother on the beach makes herself fully naked before the gaze, and so the men can reach through her to their own betterment, her body the landscape on which their spiritual experience occurs.

The first time I meet Hanna, she tells me that she grew up in a commune, and initially it sounds dreamy. Hanna tells me that people were encouraged to accept their own naked bodies with all their imperfections. Kids were raised collectively, everyone pitched in to run the place, and all their learning was self-directed. Hanna is sharp in that autodidact way, with nothing to prove and everything to say. I tell her I have always fantasized about the commune life.

"Don't," she says, "it was very problematic." When someone whose native language is not English uses the word "problematic," you know they mean it extra.

I ask her what kind of problem, and she says only "the typical ones." She is done talking about this. All I can gather is that her father led the commune, and that she has never wanted a relationship with him since she left. I do not want to press her, so I go elsewhere. I use the distant route I can take around people when I have the internet.

The Friedrichshof Commune was the largest European commune to date. It was founded in 1972 in Austria with the stated intention of breaking taboos and established social habits. The commune was set up by the Austrian artist and founder of Viennese Actionism Otto Muehl, who opposed repressive bourgeois norms like the nuclear family and private property. Muehl is best known for transgressive and often violent Actionist art, for performances involving the smearing of feces and semen, all in service of destroying convention. I am first intrigued by how Muehl wanted people to try things they thought they couldn't do.

When Muehl started the commune, he described it as a work of art. He said his new creative canvas would be human community. To rupture what he considered artificial privacy and nuclear family norms, Muehl wanted everything to be shared. For this reason, children were raised by everyone and monogamy was shunned. Muehl developed "Aktionsanalyse," his own form of anarchic therapy in which people were asked to "break the armor" of all taboos in pursuit of higher consciousness. This involved a variety of performative practices like primal screams, acting out killing one's parents, and naked cuddling "nests." According to Aktionsanalyse, these practices could clear aside everything that stands in the way of true freedom.

Friedrichshof's intentions were, if we believe the best in them, good—to break norms that have caused suffering, loneliness, repression. Unfortunately, over time Friedrichshof became increasingly authoritarian, and the commune broke up after twenty-one years when Muehl was convicted of sexually abusing the commune's minors. As with many cults, the disavowal of taboos did not lead to safety. The "clearing away" of norms did not include certain entrenched repressive power dynamics around gender and sex. Muehl is said to have initiated children into their "free" sexualities by raping young girls and by sending young boys to be de-virginized by his "top wife." Muehl established a pecking order based on who had "released" the most taboos and obtained the highest consciousness, and meted out favors and power based on this hierarchy.

It's not a new story. One person imposed their creative vision on others without seeking feedback or inquisitive consent. Because cults build an immersive world around their members, it's hard for people to really consent, when they are inhabiting a nonnegotiable value system based on the leader's conventions. I have not been in a cult, but I have felt prey to conventions that feel mandatory. Growing up in a female body, I've been given to understand in countless situations that fitting in will mean safety, that rule-following will earn me shelter. If I can just have my nails the right length, marry a husband at the right time, my thighs the right circumference, my apology well-timed, my sexuality the right amount of pleasing. Friedrichshof offers me a bleak example of the illusion of this safety. The rules are always bent toward who wants to bend them.

As a teenager, I experimented little with taboos. That would come much later, but in the meantime, I got good grades, came home when I said I would, and argued little with my parents. In small ways I pushed the edges of proper—unbuttoned one more button once I left the house to show my burgeoning cleavage in a push-up bra, made a penis joke before I'd ever seen a single penis I wasn't related to. These experiments were quickly followed by the repercussions we've been taught to expect. A boy I didn't know well at a party pushed me onto the bedspread in an empty bedroom and, when I resisted, scoffed that he'd heard I was an unfair tease. "I mean, look at you," he gestured toward my neckline then turned, walked back to the party, and slammed the door shut behind him, leaving me in the dark to consider how much of this was my fault.

Or, "that dick," I said, to a group of us in the cafeteria, ranting about a guy who'd broken up with one of our friends out of the blue. I'd never used "dick" this way before, but I wanted to try it on. I wanted to be edgy and funny, one of those people who could say things about body parts and float above them, mocking. One of my male friends stood and leaned over the table. "You think he's a dick?" He jutted his hips at me, "I'll show you a real one," the baggy hips of his pants sagging over the table and almost into his lunch tray. Everyone laughed then, and he owned the laughter. He was the one with the dick. How dare I think I could use it to my own effect.

I took these incidents as data. As a cautious girl growing up in what we did not yet call rape culture, but I could feel around me as peril, I knew that some rules were there to protect me from the whims and crotches of boys, their anger that might flare up from nothing I thought I'd done, a curve of skin I'd let breathe in front of them. If I let my body out, it could belong to them.

Now that I look back—now that I have some space from a long, sticky cafeteria table—I can see how this fear is structured like other fears I have known. The fear of male violence compels me to believe that there is only one way to be safe: to stay within the functions and narrow set of manners laid out by patriarchy and its intersections with white supremacy. As a Jew, as a woman, as a partner, as a teller of stories, I should tell in a certain way, I should present in a certain way, or else. What's being offered in exchange for social control is a vague but coercing form of protection. If I step outside its rubrics, I'm on my own.

But I'm "on my own" more often now, in the sauna, in Berlin, literally because I travel alone and metaphorically because I reevaluate the coercions. Outside of my home context, I police myself a little less because I know less how to police. Don't know the etiquette, don't have the right black clothes or asymmetrical haircut, don't know which neighborhoods the white people say are okay to walk in at night. And I don't feel notably less safe, or any less safe than I do when I am playing the good daughter at a family holiday, when I dress not for comfort but for what I think someone else will deem appropriate. With some distance, I can imagine a different kind of protection, one not determined by how much I conform. I consider another version of safety constituted by how broadly, how generously I can pay attention.

Meine Keine Familie is a documentary film made by Paul-Julien Robert, who was also born into the Friedrichshof Commune, where his mother, Florence Desurmont, was an early member. I feel an easy jealousy at the beginning of the film as we watch children running naked and free through farmlands. But it swings quickly: most of the film is about Robert confronting his mother about the traumas he experienced growing up in the commune.

In one scene of *Meine Keine Familie*, Robert and another now-grown child of the commune sit in a kitchen with Desurmont. As they describe what Muehl inflicted on them, we cut to archival footage in which the whole commune gathers in a common room to watch people undergo Aktionsanalyse and other "happenings" facilitated by Muehl. In several of these happenings, children are forced into public competitions and embarrassing games for adult amusement. We see scenes of a young boy crying while Muehl screams at him to play the harmonica. We hear about another boy forced to have sex with Muehl's wife. We watch teens dancing and sweating with terrified looks on their faces. We cut back to a puddle of faces watching the children perform. They stare until some-one cues them to laugh, and they do, even while one child performer weeps.

The camera turns then to Robert's mother, who listens quietly as her son tells her how deeply these childhood experiences wounded him, how alone he felt without a stable parent figure. Desurmont is soft and passive in her responses. Her chin sinks toward her chest as if the only part of her body needed here is her ears.

I pity Muehl's mother. Her affect is so flat it's clear she too is disassociated, wounded. For years she was told that if she just relaxed more, she would be free. She followed meekly. Now, here is her son pointing at a set of human cruelties that are obvious in retrospect, but she looked past them at the time in order to conform with what she believed to be a liberatory project.

I watch the documentary several times, until even those early scenes of top-less farming feel tainted with backstory. Friedrichshof stripped the body down, but so little social programming was cut away along with the clothing. What's revealed in Friedrichshof nudity is more layers of what we already know.

I am most successful with the foot baths at Stadtbad Neukölln. I sit on a mar-ble bench and watch for a while without even attempting to do it myself. The woman next to me puts her feet in the ceramic basin, fills the basin with hot water, and then scrubs her soles with the pink scrub scattered in tins around us. She soaks her feet, then rinses. She looks up pointedly and stares at me before she stands to leave, but I shrug, less concerned. Watching feet instead of faces, I care less about being noticed.

I stay and watch the next person, and the next. I open the tap below me and fill the basin with hot water, then slowly lower my feet in to just above the ankles. I watch my skin pucker in the water, the scars from years of blisters, uncomfortable shoes and ingrown hairs from shaving across the top. I watch other people's feet emerge from the footbaths red and swollen looking, and then observe the fondness with which they dry their own feet in their hands. Eventually someone sets one of the tins of pink scrub down next to me, and I realize the tins are being passed down the line.

I pick up the tin, scoop some scrub, and rub it on the rough edges of the soles of my feet, the places where they crack and whiten. I scrub and watch, scrub and rinse. My feet tingle. I'll probably get it wrong no matter what I do, but it does feel like something is happening around the heels. When my basin grows cloudy, I pull the plug and splash water around it. Some clumps of pink cling to the sides of the basin, but traces of pink line other people's basins after they've finished, too. I stand, slip on my flip-flops, and walk off to put on my bathing suit, determined to do a few laps in the clear blue swimming pool downstairs before I leave. All out of order, to relax and *then* exercise, but I am relieved to do as I like.

In his book *Naked Germany: Health, Race, and the Nation*, Chad Ross traces how European nudism originally related to health. Historically, German nudist rhetoric held that by eliminating the barriers between inside and outside and allowing all of the body to be touched (by the sun, by the air, by the gaze of another), a person could remove individual impurities and, by extension, impurities in the culture around them. Ross explains that nudists believed that if their movement was fully integrated into society, there would be no disease.[3] The Danzig nudist Adolf Weide wrote a book titled *Verjüngung absolut* explaining this principle.[4]

I am reading about Germany speaking very little German, so I ask my friend Paulus to translate *Verjüngung absolut*. He stares over my shoulder for a minute, then says: "I think, *Absolute Rejuvenescence*."

"Rejuvenescence?" I repeat it back to him. He laughs and says it sounds wrong in English.

"It takes you too long to say that word." The sibilance twinkles between my lips and slows us down. That Latinate suffix -*escence* ("process or state of being"), meaning the state of being rejuvenated, the process by which one is rejuvenated.

Paulus is looking at his phone. "Maybe *Absolute Rejuvenation*?" It sounds correct with that more contemporary suffix: -*ation*, so that rejuven-ation means the *act* of rejuvenating, as if well-defined outcomes will ensue as we watch, means with ends. Paulus seems triumphant, but I am slightly saddened by this answer's neat product.

"No," I say, "say *Rejuvenescence* again."

"Why?"

"I love it," I say, "I love how it keeps going, -*enesensssss*." I let the sibilance go long, my tongue at the top of my palate while I smile at him. He watches my mouth.

"-*esensssss*," he repeats, his eyes on my lips, my eyes on his. As if we are learning a new language together. We haven't ever kissed, but he is looking so closely at my lips that I consider the possibility for the first time, the erotics of susurration.

"-*esssss*," I hiss it even harder, like a snake readying to strike, and he joins in. We both let a long hiss out until we break and laugh. Like any sound repeated for a while, the "sss" has become wild, alien.

"Do other words do that?" Paulus asks, "I mean that long -ssss." It is barely a question, more a moment for us to deliberate together.

"Association!" I say. "Asssssssssssss." I don't know how long Paulus will be entertained by all this, but I am excited. This is a game I always played growing up speaking multiple languages, and with one parent to whom English was something external, a dance made uniquely elegant by its own lurches into direct translation and rare vocabulary words. I can play this for hours, variations of the game where we say a word and listen for its strangeness, like my father used to lay out "beach" and "bitch," which in his mouth sounded the same and more like the latter of the two.

"Let's go to the bitch," my father would say on a summer day, and I would correct him even though he knew. "It's impossible," he would say, grinning, "they are so close." When something's not yours, it can seem that close, the blurred menu of foreign sounds. It is like this for me, still. I speak fluently, but I hear the slips. My language is always a little weird, a little cracked, a little off.

I don't usually correct other people's English because I don't inhabit its standards most of the time. I know that the way each of us speaks signals where we come from and who we have loved. "We cannot assume that repair is neutral," Elizabeth V. Spelman writes.[5] To repair language is to make it fit with a different person's set of places and relations. When people fix things, Spelman writes, they want the broken thing to be gone. Spelman details how repair can erase memory, whether we are thinking about a precious broken cup or a crime.

"If we wish to, as we say, pick up the threads of the past," writes Spelman, "that means we have to destroy the state of brokenness, a state that is as much a part of the history of the car or the friendship or the political relationship as any other state."[6] I wonder about a way to engage with the past that doesn't destroy what was broken and doesn't need it to be erased in order to make new information relevant.

I like the broken, but not because of some exotifying or aestheticized sense of ruins. I'm not interested in old, ruined things because it is sexy that they are run-down. When Paulus suggests I visit the "many excellent abandoned buildings" in Berlin, I feel jaded. I don't go up to the abandoned warehouse and compare its crumbling to my living, pulsing skin.

Ruins are part of me already. I want my father's split-apart language, the one that includes his slips into accents and borrowed words. It is a beautiful texture of language because it reminds me of a person I love, connected through the way we communicate, including immigrations and pains. If I tried to clean up the fragments, then I wouldn't be speaking as the person I understand myself to be.

My therapist friends might call this way of moving "trauma-informed." Trauma-informed care, as it's medically defined, assumes a past of harm, as opposed to assuming that harm has been erased or previously healed. I think with Spelman and I wonder about how not to assume away a state of brokenness.

For me, to feel safe means to make a net that allows the scary things in, too. I move in this direction because all the stories I hear about trying to be pure fail miserably. I fail miserably when I try to perform, and the communities I read about who say their rules are perfect—these fail miserably, too. A cult encouraging child rape and a sauna encouraging sweatless nudity are very different stakes, yes, but what I see by putting them together is how deficient rules are when they aspire to cleanse or sterilize us. The sauna I visit is astoundingly physically inaccessible, for example, and when I ask on my way out if there are any wheelchair-accessible rooms, the attendant frowns.

"This is a very old building," she says, "it wasn't built for that." No, it wasn't built for that. Systems of decontamination are built for their own reasons; around a population or person they seek to clean. I long for the clarity of cult-like rules but also resist them, knowing how gruesomely they manipulate. Their extremeness helps me see the more subtly gruesome on me. On the skin, in the room, across cities and states. My looking pans in and out, the micro, the macro, unconfined in scope. When my gaze keeps shifting, I'm less spellbound by control.

Pure Love

At the nudist resort in Los Gatos, the sun is still warm on my shoulders in November. I am in California now, trying to re-ground in where I live, what this place is, and what it means to be in winter when it isn't cold.

One way I know I am in California is there is a man standing close over me on the edge of the hot tub. He is not shy. "I'm Eric," he tells me. I think I'm not supposed to look at genitals at a nudist resort, but his remarkably large testicles are basically a foot from my face.

Eric won't stop talking. He tells me that he grew up in the Virgin Islands and finds it "traumatizing" to live anywhere else. "Everywhere else is outside paradise," he says. He claps me on the shoulder and announces that he and his wife are pregnant—a turn of phrase I've always disliked, the appropriation of someone else's reproductive labor into shared possession.

Eric tells me they are trying to settle down here, at Lupin Lodge, the oldest nudist resort in the western United States. I spare him a nod. I'm far past trying to get a word in edgewise with this guy. I stare resolutely away from him and hope against hope that he'll respond to social cues and leave me in peace.

"It's not the islands, but it's definitely a dream place to live," he says.

It's not the first time I've heard Lupin referred to in the same breath as paradise or dreamland. Its promotional materials use much of this language, referring to it as a "slice of heaven" minutes from the office parks of Silicon Valley. A fifteen-page history of Lupin and its part in the nudist (officially, naturist[1]) movement awaits me by the bed in the yurt and reads as a rocky road of hardships and triumphs. An innocent group of people fights off challenges and oppressions by those who just didn't understand their simple, pure way of life.

According to this narrative, Lupin was started in 1936 and played a key part in the forming of the naturist movement.[2] The booklet was written by former owner Glyn Stout and traces Lupin's participation in various historical moments of the twentieth century, including area fires and world wars, transitions of ownership and name, and attempts to keep the place financially afloat. In the 1950s, naturism hadn't really caught on in the United States, I learn, but with the social shifts of the 1960s and 1970s, the booklet tells us, "Lupin saw a resurgence of Lupin."[3] I read the sentence a few times to make sure that's what it says. The self-absorption of it seems too perfect.

Sinking in next to me in the hot tub, a woman with deep creases under her eyes and breasts tells me she's been a member since 1982, and that some of the original founders were from Oakland, where I've told her that I live. "They used to take the Oakland–Santa Cruz train line which stopped there—" she gestures past the children's play structure, and I picture the naturists heaving packages knotted with twine off a train platform.

Later, Eric brings his portable speaker to the pool, and out of the corner of my eye I watch him do some kind of aerobics. He swings his arms in loops, collapses his spine toward the ground, and tosses it up again. He smiles bigger than seems possible, the skin of his face strained across cheekbones and the sockets of his eyes. He looks over at his wife. Arms open again.

"We are going to change the human race, sweetheart!" Eric whoops and leaps into the pool, then surfaces and tosses blond hair from his face.

"You and me and that little baby, we are going to be pure love," he says.

It's very naturist to reinvigorate humanity. Many contemporary practitioners argue for the right to public nudity because, they say, it benefits not only their own well-being (for innumerable cited reasons, from fresh air to skin health and positive body image) "but also those of many non-nudists whose body image and, ultimately, life satisfaction, might be promoted by exposure to non-idealized naked bodies (i.e., bodies that fall short of prevailing aesthetic standards)."[4]

I am also told this at Lupin. "Doesn't it just feel so totally natural," a woman sighs as she lays out her towel on the slatted pool chair next to mine.

"I'm so glad my kid will be exposed to different kinds of human bodies," Eric says.

This aspiration toward acceptance sits strangely against the word "pure." When you're raised in a Jewish family of Eastern European descent, the word "purity" always comes with a sinister connotation of eugenics, especially when anywhere near "human race."

Turns out this connotation isn't baseless. Chad Ross has explored the origins of nineteenth-century nudism in Germany and found its roots in racial theory and utopia. "From its earliest appearance," Ross writes, "nudism established its goal as nothing less than the transformation of the German nation into a harmonious, strong, racially pure Volk by first transforming Germans into healthy and beautiful bearers of the racial seed."[5]

Well, when you put it that way.

Ross's analysis roots German nudism in the desire to recapture a sense of national belonging after the divisions formed by industrialization, rapid population growth, the swelling move to cities, and increased inequalities of wealth and power. He writes:

> In nudism, the declining German nation could only be repaired by first building better Germans, and Germans could only be regenerated by transforming their bodies. The body, of course, needed to be returned to its natural, naked state so that it could affect change upwards: first Germans, then the race and nation.[6]

We know this story about Germany, but it's also true that nudism was employed in service of utopian fantasy in several European nation-states. The move to recapture an original condition untarnished by current sociopolitical conditions is replicated elsewhere, and not just on the religious right.

When scholar Richard Clemison looks at such rhetoric in England and Spain, he notes how late nineteenth- and early twentieth-century European nudists on both the right and left justified nudism "as part of a search for the genuine against the artificial in modern life." He goes on:

> Both generally saw nudism as a means of freeing the human body from degradation and from the "lower" human drives such as sexuality, in order to attain a state of purity which was often equated with a particular interpretation of Greek forms and lifestyles. The right and left differed, however, over the imagery evoked to justify the elimination of "foreign substances" from the body.[7]

And then there's Maurice Parmelee, an early American promoter of nudism, who held that nudism would result in a "more beautiful mankind" because nudists would be motivated to "avoid deformations of the body," writes scholar Ellen E. Woodall. Parmelee saw nudism as part of a larger social revolution that would restore physical strength in humans and "free them from industrialization."[8]

Lupin, too, ascribes to purifying oneself through nudism, ridding oneself of the grit of social conditioning, cleansing oneself to reveal "higher" qualities and "drives." The resort has posted on its website "A Male Tribute to Lupin Women," a 1993 piece from the *California Naturist*. Also written by Glyn Stout, the text praises female members for the "extraordinary courage, trust and independence of thought" it takes to "overcome the body taboo," face "sexual abuse headlines," and "overcome complex social conditioning." Stout notes that "very few women accept, much less like, their bodies" and presents naturism as the answer to such difficulties: "Because it is so humanizing an experience, being nude with people also facilitates communications across gender, generational and genetic differences and makes us feel part of some great universal family."[9]

Whether it's anarchists talking about nudism as a way to dispose of entrenched Catholic values, or Stout gesturing toward a way for women to unlearn self-hatred and "differences," the message remains consistent: pure human goodness can be found by stripping away the trappings of the social world toward the (undefined) natural and (fabled) wild. Both positions echo the Christian idea of original sin, so thoroughly permeated in Western culture that it can go unseen.

When I reach out to Lupin for more information, I inquire about the community's associations with any religion or faith. I am directed to Brad Chibos, a Lupin Lodge member since 1981, who responds:

> Lupin Lodge has been a natural sanctuary for people of many different faiths. The club itself has always been run with respect for those faiths and nature itself. Lupin has never been associated with any organized religious or spiritual group. Many people do meditate, read spiritual material or practice yoga. Currently there are naked yoga classes. No religion or faith is ever required in connection with Lupin Lodge membership. We only require that people show each other and each other's beliefs respect.

This generalized sense that differences are dissolved in Lupin's sanctuary reflects a choice to ignore social context rather than acknowledge its role in the shaping of the community—a choice to look the other way, which has unfortunately plagued Lupin of late.

I ended up at Lupin because I was looking for somewhere affordable to get away last minute. Later, on Yelp, I learn that this happens to a lot of people. Lupin seems great to many from afar: cheap yurt, nice pool, sunny microclimate, beautiful hiking trails. And nudism, well, we live in the Bay Area—we've seen our share. "We can get down with that," my partner says when we pull up to the place.

It's not until I leave Lupin that I begin to learn the rest of the story. From an easy if slightly peculiar weekend, I get interested, curious, and pitch an essay exploring the aspirations of the Lodge. I feel a bit like I'm role-playing journalist here: the officialness of reaching out to Lupin for comment, comparing the language of different sources. This is not always the way I write, but the further I go into it, the more confusing and creepier the place begins to seem, and the more careful I want to be in examining different versions of the story.

Where Lupin's version is a series of misadventures, others see a pattern of worsening misbehaviors. Most media coverage of Lupin describes either the lawsuit against its owners for water theft[10] ("Lupin has historically and lawfully used upstream Hendry's Creek water that flows through Lupin's property," reads Lupin's official statement) or its rampant exploitation of workers. According to a 2015 article, Lupin recruited "people 'in transition'—transitions from prison, probation, broken relationships, or drug and alcohol addictions"—to work at Lupin in exchange for room and board.[11] Invited to "come live in paradise," individuals instead racked up debt to Lupin for "membership fees" and market-rate rents.[12]

In the amazingly titled investigative report "Bad News Bared," Jennifer Wadsworth writes:

> Though not certified as a sober-living environment, Lupin has also presented itself as a place to get back on one's feet. "They deliberately look for people who are in a desperate situation," said [Russ] Klein, who almost moved out several times because of what he calls rampant and passively accepted methamphetamine use on the grounds. "They have a twisted notion that they're some kind of a rehab."[13]

It's "twisted" because it's very difficult to heal in a place that won't acknowledge the structural power shoring it up. I think back to Glyn Stout's descriptions of Lupin as "so humanizing an experience."[14] Stout was co-owner of Lupin with Lori Kay during the time described in these lawsuits, purportedly running a resort that "humanized" people and helped them "connect with themselves." How is it possible that this discourse persists, even and despite its intersections with basic human suffering, and the harshly obvious facts of class in the Bay Area?

When I asked Lupin to comment on how the resort has been affected by the continued rising cost of living in the Bay Area, and how the tech boom has affected members of the community, Chibos responded that, "The increase in traffic on highway 17 has been a burden to some of our members when driving to the club," and, "Some people who have found housing to be far too expensive in the bay area have found a home at Lupin." I am struck by the continued rhetoric that encodes Lupin as an oasis—one need only reach Lupin and the brutal realities outside of it will somehow evaporate.

I felt an affection for Lupin on my visit there, an affection for the old-school Northern California feeling of ex-hippies who just want to be left alone to live in peace—but their peace exists only in a vacuum. I think of how Lupin described itself as place for "escaping the pressure-cooker of nearby Silicon Valley," while a former resident also described on his blog an increasingly disturbing difference between the clean, resort-oriented lodgings presented for members and guests of the resort and the "Maintenance Area" sign intended to discourage visitors from seeing the ramshackle trailers and tents where workers lived without septic systems or plumbing.[15]

One especially telling detail in Wadsworth's report on Lupin's wage theft is how the Stouts installed security cameras all over the property to keep an eye on workers, though resort guests are told that cameras are banned in keeping with naturist ethics.

"Nudism, while purporting to free its members from the ills of the capitalist, industrialized system, is a part of that system and, in fact, could not function without it," writes Woodall. In many ways, Lupin's travails form a very Bay Area story. Privacy becomes insubstantial when faced with the need to control information and labor. And then there's that desire to look past rather than reckon with what precedes or surrounds one's reality, whether "spiritual bypass" or "life-hacking."

When I ask Chibos how Lupin has addressed the lawsuits since their settlement and whether the resort has improved working and living conditions, he replies, "The arrangement that Lupin has had with the people who work and live here has proven beneficial for both sides since Lupin started in 1935. If Lupin Lodge was taking advantage of people it would not have lasted this long." This interior reality subsists only on its own logic without looking into the bare realities working on actual people.

"We are always working to improve Lupin so the membership and residents benefit from those efforts," Chibos continues. This work is missing any acknowledgment that true benefit would have to reconcile Lupin's utopian ideals with the economic and cultural conditions that surround it. The more that Lupin claims utopianism, the more I long for it to admit the ways it is nonideal, permeable, and full of need.

Lupin has shown itself willing to integrate some aspects of surrounding cultures when such integration benefits the resort. Wadsworth notes that by 2014 Lupin was hosting "all-night raves and fetish parties that they felt flouted the wholesome ideals of naturism." According to Lupin's own history keeping,[16] Lupin rented its space to these raves and parties to endure as a business in one particularly hard-up time, associating with Burning Man and other younger party scenes to host events that could bring in additional funding streams.

Journalist Nathan Heller has described the way that romantic and utopian ideals manage to persist in private life in the Bay Area,[17] even if not in public realities. But I think this story is larger than just this place. The paradoxes of Lupin show the porousness of utopian conceits when it comes to economics, the ways capitalism makes consistency impossible. To operate under utopian ideals with integrity means to acknowledge and participate in existing conditions, at least to the extent that this participation allows individual humans to survive, to reckon with the impossibility of paradise, and to laugh at the boundaries and paradoxes of human behavior. A nudism that claims total utopian purity is doomed to (at best) irrelevance and (at worst) injury of those who do not have a choice about participating in the wider economy. As much as it claims to "bare all," Lupin is as contaminated as the rest of us.

*   *   *

Our bed in the yurt is large and soft and has a king-size heating blanket tucked into the duvet. It is late at night, and my partner is dreaming, he will later tell me, that I bought a new car without telling him. Suddenly we're both awakened by a series of loud staccato shouts of "yes! yes! yes! yes! YES!" from out of the surrounding forest, followed by a few seconds of soft laughter. We grip each other in the dark.

"Sex?" I whisper, "was it sex?"

"Definitely not," he says, "it doesn't sound like an orgasm." I can just barely make out his smile. "I'd bet you a lot of money it's a win at online poker." This seems about right—while we were encouraged by Lupin staff to "detox" from the digital world while on the property, we spotted the Wi-Fi password (N8K3DW1F1) in a corner up at the lodge. I wouldn't be surprised if its signal stretches out here into the trees.

Name It to Tame It

In the cold, darkened hospital room, a sunset is illuminated on one panel of the ceiling. It is a screen of some kind, or maybe just an image placed over a fluorescent light. Either way, it is something for people to look at while the ultrasound moves inside them. As if this tropical sunset could take away the chill that sinks through my body as soon as I enter that room.

I have ultrasounds regularly to track the growth of my endometriosis, but I have not been in this room before. My medical insurance keeps changing and with it where I can afford to get the imagery done, so I get a new person each time, a new way of handling the gel and the wand.

I try to get this over with quickly. I have already laid down with my feet flexed and ready to spread when the tech enters the room and asks me to sit up. "I don't believe in stirrups, sweetie," she says, rearranging objects on the examination bed. She prefers to place a plastic-wrapped stack of sheets under my butt, she tells me, so my hips are elevated enough to insert the wand.

"I call this the bump!" She laughs. "I should patent it." I'm not used to people being nice in here, and I struggle to respond, my face still fixed in the silent grimace I assume for examinations.

"You know I've had these procedures done on myself," the tech pats her own stomach, "so I try to learn from what made me feel comfortable." I nod rigidly, the back of my neck sticky on the examination table. I am used to obeying and not talking to anyone.

It's been years now that ultrasounds scan for what is happening inside me: not a baby, but cysts and growths on my ovaries and in my abdominal cavity that continue to rupture and incapacitate me with pain. My doctor has said ultrasounds are the best way to keep an eye on me, to help her determine treatment. It says "elective ultrasound" on my insurance bill, though it never seemed like I had another choice. I sidle in to rooms like this one dressed in loose clothing, subdued. The kink of this occurs to me—it is dark, I assume the position, and I wait for the person who will manipulate my body. Under the conditions of someone else's power, I agree for someone to spread my legs and decide what happens next. But this time this tech is doing everything in her power to make me participate more.

"Go ahead into that bathroom and take off your pants and panties," she instructs me, "and don't come out until you've covered your bottom half with this sheet."

I shuffle to the bathroom, take off my clothes, and wrap a giant sheet of paper around me. It drags in a rustling white train as I walk the few steps from the bathroom back onto the bed. I raise my hips over the stack of sheets and the paper gathers loosely around my hips. The tech carefully pats the paper around me into place until no inch of me is visible from waist to knees. Only then does she sheath the wand in plastic and squirt gel onto it.

"Okay now, honey. Here comes the cold part," she says. I look at the sunset, and I barely feel it as the wand enters me.

Regularly I leave my body so that an explanation can occur. There's not a lot I can say about what happens in these rooms because I don't usually remember. I get little information from my body in the moments that I lie there. Someone else pulls evidence out of me and I attempt to get out of the way. I can't see much from this angle at all.

The only other time I attempt to get out of the way like this is when I give a reading of my own written work. I stand before a microphone or scan the eyes of a group in a circle and try to assess what is needed from me. I have plenty of practice giving readings, teaching classes, answering questions—but as I read I still calculate carefully how much longer to go on, how soon I can divert the attention. I read the words on a page that I have decided to read, and I rarely feel anything below my neck. The minute I start talking, I mostly disassociate inside the peril and demand of attention. It's hard to know when the attention will end, or what it might demand of me.

*   *   *

For many years, people never saw inside their own vaginas. The only people who looked up there were scientists. Moral scientific observation depends on this stance, in which a rational person stands detached from what they are observing. Even now, to be a good patient means to let them "have a look," to endure an ultrasound while someone stands over me who is not supposed to tell me any details about what they see.

In *Seizing the Means of Reproduction: Entanglements of Feminism, Health, and Technoscience*, researcher Michelle Murphy explains the "modest witness" who watches an event but does not get involved, and what it means to depart from this position. Murphy's work concentrates on small-group feminist self-help circles of the 1970s, and through them she proposes what she calls "an *im*modest witness" (emphasis mine)—a woman observing her own vagina with a pelvic self-exam. These women observed their own cervixes and vaginas with a mirror, and usually did so in groups so they could learn about the varied realities of vagina-hood. Murphy writes, "a naked woman observing herself was an *immodest* witness" who did not deny that she was watching. The fact that she had a visible body of her own was fundamental.

"I use the word *immodest* here to draw attention to the project of laying bare the importance of the subject in knowledge-making," writes Murphy, "and of challenging notions of chastity and modesty that prevented women from displaying, valuing or studying the female reproductive body." These women generated knowledge about their own bodies while recognizing the person making that knowledge.

Still, they missed many aspects of this subject-hood as they rejoiced in their own display. Murphy points out how these women declined to acknowledge the context of their work as intersectional, political, and racialized. White feminists offered norms about "the female body" that only applied to their white cis-female bodies as defined by conventional femininity. Looking through the self *at* the self means the doctor may be gone—but the human is still there, the human with blind spots and racisms and misinformation. The angle of the human eclipses the view.

Their gaze also blotted out many potential dangers in prioritizing exposure. Caught up as they were in the revelation of their own bodies, the immodest witnesses asserted that the more we could see the better. They merged with the growing discourse in American culture at the time that demanded exposure if the body required support.

It's dangerously easy to get people to comply when you require first that they strip away what they have known, what they have worn. I think of cults again, how they take the stripped-down person and remake them for their own purposes, often in the name of care. In today's medical context, that stripped-down figure becomes the quantified self, available then for targeted advertisements and compulsory treatment. When I want care, I must obey all requirements for photography and examination. In exchange for my privacy, I am offered the promise of results.

I imagine the speculum creaking open as a group of women gather round and peer in. I want to be on their team, but I fear its extremes and promises. The examination table groans beneath me as I lie back and wonder if it is steady enough to hold me.

In early 2018 I watched the writer Maggie Nelson interviewed at City Arts & Lectures in San Francisco.[1] Nelson was generous with her interviewer, turning rather erudite questions into answers for a general public, and deftly translating the interviewer's statements into actual questions that Nelson could answer. At one point, the interlocutor asked Nelson a question about queer femmes who are attracted to butch or masculine-of-center women, and what this means about the gender binary. The interviewer identified herself as a queer woman for whom this question was personally as well as intellectually important. Nelson took in a breath and drew herself up rather straight.

"You know," she said, "there are some things we don't discuss in mixed company." She looked out at the audience of over a thousand people, smiled politely, and flicked one hand forward, indicating that it was time to move on to the next question. Laughter flitted across the orchestra seating.

"Okay, but wait," blustered the interviewer, "I guess, I mean since you write about your partner and their gender . . . I'm curious to hear how this question relates to your work." Nelson's partner is the artist Harry Dodge, who identifies as gender queer and at the time was occasionally using "he" pronouns. Nelson turned back to the interviewer and shook her head once. Gently: "let's move on," she said.

Later I told a friend this was my favorite moment of the night. Much of Nelson's work gets categorized under the term "auto-theory" because it makes use of lived experience to develop new thinking, but with this comment she clarified that there are still boundaries to what she shares where and when. I love that she could gesture publicly that some conversations are only to be had with members of a particular group—in this case, queer people—because their topics are sensitive to incorrect analysis and harsh judgment from outsiders. Any one step she's taken toward revelation doesn't infinitely cede her agency.

I meet a new friend because several people I love have vouched for him. My guard is down, and I want to be friendly. I text him with enthusiastic exclamation marks that I've arrived back in Berlin for a few months and would be happy to meet whenever is good for him, but Sam does not exactly respond in turn. He texts that he is pretty busy but might have some time. He name-drops about other Berlin-based artists whose shows he is going to see if I'd like to come along.

"Sure" I type, then stop. I try to hold back this time and do not punctuate. Sam suggests we go see an exhibition at the DAAD Gallerie. He types the artist Lawrence Abu Hamdan's name incorrectly first (Hamdam), then blusters a lot over his correction. I draft a reassuring text but do not send it, and instead wait for him to tell me when he's free.

A few days later, I am already inside the gallery when he arrives. I am the only person in there, but I pretend I do not recognize him until he approaches me. Only then do I turn and smile.

"Hey," he whispers. He is tall and I am short, and I can barely hear him. I decide not to offer a hug.

"Should we look at the show first?" Sam does not make eye contact. I don't answer, just comply. It is a small gallery, and there is not far to go. We sit down on two of the stools in front of a large video projection, but a few stools apart.

A video plays in front of us. I try to concentrate on it, but the video is projected on a surface that I can see through, and behind the surface of the video a person sits at a computer in an office full of books. I can't tell if this is on purpose. It is sunny and late afternoon, and maybe the angle of light is wrong. Maybe soon they will pull down the shades behind me and everything will clarify. I squint to focus my eyes on the video instead of the light moving through it or the action behind.

In the video, Abu Hamdan stands in various rooms of an old KGB sound studio in Berlin and reads an essay he has written about walls and sound. As he reads the essay, various images enter the video that relate to the three sections of his essay. The first story I hear him read is one about a marijuana farmer in Oregon and the way police record sound to gain information about what is behind the walls around the farmer's property. They "see" through the walls using sonar and detect his illegal growing, but the farmer is eventually acquitted because this use of sonar is determined to be against privacy laws.

Abu Hamdan moves next to the trial of Paralympic champion Oscar Pistorius, in which a key witness offers testimony about what they heard through a wall. Abu Hamdan cites a speech by Ronald Reagan, and I struggle to grasp how these stories connect. I catch snippets of Abu Hamdan's arguments about how acoustics are mobilized to make everything visible, to penetrate privacy.

"Now, no wall on earth is impermeable. Today, we're all wall, and no wall at all," Hamdan reads. His facial expression is neutral, but he speaks diligently close to the radio mic, and I am not sure whether I need to be watching him. I tilt my eyes sideways toward Sam. I can just see the right angle of his shoulder in my peripheral vision while Hamdan explains the systems of torture and sound at Saydnaya, known as "the Mercedes-Benz of prisons in Syria." Prisoners describe the sound of beatings that vibrate the walls of their cells. The sound felt so close, Hamdan reports, that prisoners were always concerned that they were next in line for torture, even though beatings took place two stories above their cells through a security-grade thick concrete structure. Nothing was happening right next to them, but sound made it seem like it was. Abu Hamdan explains that Saydnaya is constructed around a central tower so that sounds from all corridors travel very far through and across the building. It sounds to prisoners like there are no walls and each person in each room is intimately exposed to all beatings. The most terrifying, restraining quality of the prison is the illusion that there is nowhere to hide.

At this point in the video, I become aware of an insistent pounding sound, warping as it grows louder and louder. "Torture rings through the porous and yet inescapably solid membranes of this structure." The pounding warps again and continues underneath the remainder of Hamdan's video, representing different sounds at different times, peeling away and back from the narrative until Hamdan finishes reading and leaves the room. The video lingers on someone in the next room drumming on a bass drum and I feel a calm settling in me as sound and image cohere. I have a moment then to notice what has coalesced in the video. I like that Hamdan has left the screen, hiding his own figure as the weight of the stories sinks in for the viewer. In contrast to the nonconsensual exposure of so many of his subjects, he backs away. He can move to a place where he isn't seen.

There's a seamless loop from the end of Hamdan's video back to the beginning, made even more enchanting by the continuity of the drumming sound. I haven't understood that the video is over, but Sam stands quickly and gestures toward the door. "Ready to go?" So I get up, too. Outside on the sidewalk I blink, bleary, and shiver in the thin sun.

"It was interesting how you could see through the screen," I say. Sam looks at me, maybe for the first time, and seems confused. He barely nods. "I think that was intentional," he says. I blush. All these years I've spent in galleries, and I never know the right way to talk about the art.

Eventually the two of us sit by the water. We drink coffee, and I try to hide how jittery it makes me. I tell Sam a little about my work, but not much about myself, really. It's easy to make artists feel you are opening up if you share about your creative process. Pleasantly, I can leave a lot out. Sam is reading about the Anthropocene, he tells me, and so we begin to talk about climate change and death, but all general, all in theory. We talk about bodies in the abstract, and we only get more specific when we move to talk about the friends we have in common. We have our first laugh when we realize we've each dated different members of a couple we both know.

"I guess now we're really connected," Sam says. I pick up a small clod of dirt and press it between my finger and thumb until it crumbles. "Something like that," I say.

I go back to see *Walled Unwalled* several times and watch it alone so that I can concentrate. When I go alone, I pick up the paper copy of the text of Abu Hamdan's essay and fold it away in my notebook. I reread the section in which the artist inventories the border walls constructed in the year 2000. Some I've heard about (Mexico–United States), some vaguely so (Israel/Area C), and some not at all (Brunei/Limbang). Abu Hamdan writes:

Today, physical barriers at sixty-three borders divide nations across four continents. And yet, all the time, millions and millions of invisible cosmic particles called muons are descending into the Earth's atmosphere and penetrating meters deep, even through layers of concrete, soil, and rock. Scientists have realized that these deep-penetrating particles can be harvested and have developed a technology to leverage their peculiar physical capacities to pass through surfaces impervious to X-rays.[2]

I google *muons* to check if they are real. (They are.) "Deep penetrating particles." I admire Abu Hamdan's assurance as he moves through these facts. This assurance does not have to justify the depth of its research or its associations. Though the subject matter is about penetration, his style does not seek to prove that it has seen through a totality. "Penetrated meters deep." The general plural of "meters" is expressly what Abu Hamdan seems to be going for: not exacting, but enough. Abu Hamdan does not offer or demand completion. He believes that some wall belongs.

I am back for another ultrasound, a few months later at the same hospital in Oakland, hopeful that returning to this same hospital means I'll meet the same kindness I did last time. As I check in, the person across the desk gestures to an iPad. "This is the consent form," she mutters. She scrolls past the entire document to the signature line at the bottom, assuming, I guess, that no one bothers to review the contents. I scroll up and attempt to understand the form, gathering essentially that doctors can use my images however they want.

Faced with these forms, I always wonder: what happens if you refuse to sign it? You can't get seen? But I am too tired to resist and have been in too much pain. I glaze over, scroll down, and sign. Maybe if I don't make a fuss someone will finally fix me. I think again of Michelle Murphy:

The subject-figure of the modest witness, with abilities for reasoned judgements, was supported by larger colonial, gendered, raced and classed figurations of what kinds of bodies were seen as having capacities to reason, and what kinds of labor were truth producing rather than merely instrumental.

Generations of feminism later, it's still too easy for me to slip into belief in the modest witness. I seek classification to understand how I am seen by others, to feel placed by them. My instrumental finger signs the document, my instrumental legs open and await that good old-fashioned medical truth.

As usual, I learn little from my ultrasounds. Month and after month, the blobs remain on my ovaries where they shouldn't be, and there is no new course of action, no answer produced from opening my legs. All I can say is that my insides exist and can be reached toward. I find a new coziness in this, my opaqueness, the way the doctor leaves me only partially visible, cloaked. It's another point of proof that the kind of surveillance I've been taught would protect me has its limits. When my body fails to be fixed, I learn I can survive as a body that doesn't make sense. When medicine fails, I learn I can survive as a cloaked figure, often even finding relief, comfort and understanding outside of the realm of solution. To be classified is not the only way to be held.

Just before she inserts it, the tech holds up the probe, now sheathed in its latex condom and dripping clear lube. She tells me to scoot closer to her side of the bed.

"I always have to ask," she pauses, "are you sexually active?"

"Uh, yes."

"Okay, because you're pretty young still—" I blink. I'm thirty-three. At many other times in history I would be considered past childbearing age, and pregnant women near my age are labeled with a "geriatric pregnancy."

"Well," her voice is soft, "if you aren't sexually active you know—I try to make sure people really need to get the vaginal ultrasound. Sometimes a teenager will come in here for an ultrasound and the parents says it's okay, but I still ask the patient. Because you know, they're like 13, 14 years old . . . I don't want to take that away from them." Though she doesn't say "virginity," I think that's what she means.

"I'm good," I say. "Go ahead." She gets a touch brusquer then, maybe so it doesn't feel like this insertion is related to any kind of relationship. There is no more eye contact as she inserts the probe. She is looking only at the ultrasound machine as she begins to twist the wand inside me. I breathe in sharply as she nudges my largest cyst.

"Breathe out, honey," she says, "I'll bet it is rough." A stab jolts at my hip and then streaks in all directions, down the muscles in my leg, up toward my ribs, twisting through my belly and souring my digestive system. I breathe and block out the tech and the probe as I try to visualize the pain traveling out of my body, a clear liquid that drips from my toes and fingertips and evaporates. I imagine that the pain will leave me.

The tech turns the probe and snaps the photos, looks up at the screen behind my head, that eerie moment when she knows something about my body I don't.

"Does it hurt when I press here," she asks, but I don't answer, because medical people usually ask what they already know. She doesn't repeat the question.

Once I had an editor who commissioned a piece from me about medical care and scientific touch. "Write about consent," she said. I drafted up a piece quickly, and emailed it out, only to receive a draft back two days later slashed with tracked changes and an email saying, "none of this really works." The editor had cut everything from my piece where I raged against the doctor's lack of empathy. She wrote that my argument did not hold if a doctor was doing something that needed to be done.

"It was an elective procedure," she noted in her comment bubble, "this makes no sense. They had your consent." Before I finish reading, my body is shaking. My hands are shaking. I have no idea what I am feeling at first, but after I sit and breathe for a few moments I realize I am more angry than I have been in years.

I call my friend Ayden, who also has ongoing medical concerns and interactions with doctors. Ayden gets it. She knows this anger I feel, and she knows that it just needs to be heard. Once I have slowed down a little bit, Ayden reminds me that "consent" comes from the Latin "consentire," to feel with, to feel together. It's exactly what I requested in my draft of that essay, and exactly what I didn't receive. Consent is not simply assent given so that a receiving body sprawls open. In the booming cultural understanding of consent as permission for physical touch, this aspect gets neglected: it's people agreeing to share an experience. And to share an experience means to know that it has its undetermined, shadowy parts.

*   *   *

It's hard to track when I started hearing "name it to tame it," but I'm pretty sure it first came from my friend Emily, who is a social worker. This makes sense: I think of the world of social work as one that believes verbalization has the power to heal. Dr. Daniel Siegel seems to take credit for the phrase, and for the process he implies by it. He argues that choosing words to describe one's emotional state invites the executive function of the brain and calms the limbic system and its production of stress hormones. Siegel encourages readers to verbalize to help calm themselves in stressful situations.[3]

But Emily uses this term a little differently—to describe dynamics she sees between two people who aren't acknowledging a conflict that sits between them. She uses it to talk about a tension between two lovers when one won't admit they are jealous of their partner's friendship with someone else, or to describe an unacknowledged power dynamic between two housemates, one of whom owns the house in which they both live. I love the word "tame" in this phrase because it's not "name it to *fix* it." To tame is to domesticate, but not necessarily by erasure—it is to bring something into one's own environment, knowing it carries its own wildness. Is there a way to tame without implying you can control?

When I show a friend an early draft of this writing, she tells me that she likes it, but she can't feel my body in it. WHERE ARE YOU, she writes in the margin. I am here but not here, my body flickering with absence. That's what it's like for me to be alive. Sometimes I can feel my body in great pain or pleasure or even a neutral state, and sometimes I can't feel my body at all. The longer I write, the more this seems reasonable. It's adaptive to have cloaks and walls as long as we are aware of them.

I try to tell my friend that this is the point, that my body isn't always there when I am writing, but I still feel I owe her something else. Even though the writing I want to do is one that keeps me partially cloaked. I want to write in a way that allows me to express and explore and play and move my body in space without then owing a reader everything, all identifying details or conclusions. I want to write in a way that models for a reader that we can see some, contemplate together, without owing anyone it all.

I think again of Maggie Nelson refusing the question. Is there a kind of writing that can allow a slow and careful process of consent? Can there be a kind of relating this way, too?

What if the practice of referencing, sourcing and crediting is always bursting with intellectual life and takes us outside ourselves? What if we read outside ourselves not *for* ourselves but to actively unknow ourselves, to unhinge, and thus come to know each other, intellectually, inside and outside the academy, as collaborators of collective and generous and capacious stories?

That's the academic and writer Katherine McKittrick, in her book *Dear Science and Other Stories*.[4] McKittrick writes as a Black theorist trying to track how she knows what she knows and to whom she can pay tribute who has not been given enough credit. While McKittrick does name many names, she notes that she has trouble tracing what she knows from where. She understands this as evidence that there are not sole owners of ideas. McKittrick tells us that she is "not focusing on reparation of the self, alone" but instead concerned with "unhinging," even "displacing the self."

I think too of the influence of money and class. I was raised to believe that owning things is protection, particularly owning property. If the apocalypse comes, you will at least have a place to hole up where you can assert your earned dominance. The more apocalyptic my world becomes, the more things my rich friends want to own: the best face masks to protect us from California's wildfire smoke, the stockpile of Paxlovid to mitigate the symptoms of COVID-19. And the more things they own, the lonelier they inevitably are, as this ownership distances them from a shared reality with the majority of working-class people who have to show up for their jobs even during the peak of the pandemic, who don't get to stay inside on the worst days of smoke pollution. They feel apart, because they *are*, because purchasing power keeps them that way.

While I don't own my own island or have a getaway stocked with canned goods that I plan to run to when my city burns or floods, I do have access to remote work and to panic-purchasing an expensive air purifier from across the country and overnighting it to myself. It's this privilege that makes me want to "unhinge." This access is part of what makes me so motivated to displace myself, to dwell in a more collectively generated, voluminous story, "capacious," as McKittrick so aptly terms it.

McKittrick encourages me toward the politics of a story intentionally unsorted, toward unlearning the closure I've been taught that I need to own, stockpile and be safe. "If white Jews remain complicit in white supremacy then like all white people they will be forever compelled to seek safety through separateness and self-interest," I read in that JFREJ report.[5] I extend this here to complicity in white supremacist capitalism, which also compels us to seek safety as separate. What if instead of singling out ourselves for safety or for threat, we cleave to a different kind of community, as collaborators in the positive sense, in McKittrick's sense, reaching for "capacious" stories, roomy and vast, in which the self is shifty, the narrative in flux?

While I want to affirm the effect of oppressions on individual bodies, separating out the individual is not the whole work. Here comes a bad joke about the Final Solution: I don't want to be finished off. But McKittrick affirms for me also that I'm not here to complete.

In the essay "Natural Processes," writer Ana Cecilia Alvarez describes an encounter with sea life on an ocean floor exposed during low tide on the Pacific Ocean. Her friends begin using the app iNaturalist to observe and classify the life that they see in the tidepools. Alvarez describes a moment in which she stares down at one single sea anemone and desires contact with it. After a few seconds, she tells us, she feels a hot zap in her brain that she interprets as the anemone telling her to go away, that it does not want to be known or categorized.

Alvarez writes that when we observe beings through taxonomy and classification, it "teaches us to see other life as proximate to us, rather than knowing ourselves as an extension of it."[6] When I read this, it's the first time I've heard someone describe so precisely what I feel in the ultrasound room. Only I am the anemone. I want to be an extension of life, as opposed to a foreign object for objective examination. To be an extension of the same life means someone else can't enclose me and say they understand it all. I am the anemone when I try to make others see and go away at the very same time. I do not want to own the narrative, even as I speak or write. I do not want to perform the ends to others' means. I want to be related.

Alvarez proposes that the zap she felt from the anemone might be read less as a rebuke and more as its gaze meeting her own. She thinks this zap was the anemone saying that it is not something to be seen through but something with which to be related. It sounds like consent, especially in a situation where different beings have different shapes of trauma and access to power. Defending ourselves is relational, adaptive. I zapped Michael, I think. We zap others so that they will remember we are alive, instead of being looked up or looked down on, knowing either of these positions to be a flat and deadly place.

How to Ride

I have this friend who always invites me to the Derby. It's not the Kentucky Derby, but the one in Oakland, California, a distant, campy imitation. This one friend loves to organize a group to go. She tells us to dress up "like you're going somewhere far away."

I never go but do get the email afterward congratulating us on such a great time. There are animated GIFs of ladies swooning and horses stomping. One friend replies-all: "The horses put us under their spell!"

In a GIF at the bottom of the email a lady leans clear over a railing with a tiny hat rigged sturdily to her head, tipping but secure. "That hat is everything <3" another friend replies.

"Wearing a hat is much like getting into costume, you might be pleasantly surprised to see what type of character you become. From the fantastic to the sublime, there are no rules or limits." I bring you this from the "what to wear" section of the real Kentucky Derby website, on which we are all encouraged to plan for the hat, with the option of a "fascinator," the official name for the tiny ones.[1] In a section titled "Hat or Fascinator," I find more description: "smaller than a traditional hat and just as stylish, this piece of headwear perches perfectly on your head and becomes more popular among Kentucky Derby attendees every time there is a royal wedding!"

In *Allure*, Aubrey Almanza tracks the rise of the miniature hats known as "fascinators" in western Europe, noting (as we might guess) that their name originates from the Latin "fascinatus," meaning "to bewitch, or cast a spell on."[2] Though hats had always been a part of British social life, the 1940s "saw the rise of 'doll hats,' feminine, miniature hats perched on the front of the forehead or nestled into an updo. In Europe, they were seen as a *pièce de résistance* in defiance of the austerity of the Nazi occupation." Though the most lavish fashion was frowned on in those severe conditions, Brits allowed themselves this controlled ornamentation.

According to Almanza, fascinator hats came to the United States from Europe through horse racing, which British settlers brought to the United States as a leisure-time activity. Along the colonial path, fashion travels too. When a race like the Kentucky Derby is billed as a high-class event, Americans look back to our colonizing culture. We look to Brits for instruction on what it means to be civil around competition.

I always hated competing, but I persisted on the swim team all through high school. I was just good enough to spend four years in the slow lane, where I would kick obediently along during our drills and mutely watch my own arm hairs float in front of me as I completed the glide at the end of the breaststroke. I preferred to elongate my glides before I broke the surface again because it was quiet under there. It was a slowed-down time just underneath the water punctuated by the scrape of the concrete walls against my feet as I made my flip turns off the sides of the pool, the shouts of my coaches and teammates only audible when my ears poked above the water. I had to pause eventually to look up at the piece of paper dampened against a kickboard at the end of my lane on which our coaches wrote the set of drills we were to complete. I tried to review the paper quickly and then memorize it so I could just keep going and not be noticed by the two men pacing the sides of the pool. Some days I completed my laps well enough and flew under the coaches' radar. But every few weeks I would have to be under their scrutiny. I would have to compete.

Every team member had to participate in our races, even those of us who lagged well behind the truly competitive swimmers. The day before the swim meet, we'd all gather around the posted list of who had been assigned to swim which race. I scanned the list from behind a few other girls, wondering who could see the small pockets of fat that pressed out of the racer-back of my swimsuit. Out of the water, there were fewer places to hide, so I liked to stand behind others. I scanned the list for my name, but mostly for the placement of my race in the order of the meet, hoping to be in events earliest in the day so that I could get it over with and cheer for my teammates from the side.

Our coaches would do their best to place me in slow heats, the phases of each event where I'd compete against slower members of the other teams. When my event finally came, I'd bend at the starting block praying not to mess up too badly. Or, if I was racing backstroke, I'd clench my calves against the pool wall, grip the handrail of the block and try not to push off before the whistle blew.

At one competition near the end of my junior year, I swam a 100-yard backstroke and for the first time noticed that there were swimmers behind me, their arms thrashing somewhere back behind my feet as I touched the wall to finish. I pulled up out of the water and looked up at the screen tracking us. I'd come in third place out of eight. Not last was a massive triumph for me, but I felt worn out by anxiety and not having timed my breathing correctly. I hoofed it to the girls' locker room before my coach could find me. In the haven of the locked handicapped bathroom, I stared into the warped mirror above the sink and noticed with horror not only the seared red marks around my eye sockets from goggles (a sure sign I hadn't placed them well). No, it was much worse than that. A few strands of hair had escaped my swim cap and were plastered in a rim of wooly curls to my forehead.

Oh, the drama! Yes, I was a teenager. My dismay at the errant hairs was both ridiculous and meaningful in context: Visible hair is the most obvious mark that a swimmer doesn't know what she's doing. If you place your cap well, it holds back everything so you can be a sleek animal slipping through water, and these were the rules that mattered to me at the time. If you place your cap correctly you usually have a headache for hours after practice from the pressure against your head. I wore these caps anyway, trying to look like what a swimmer should be. There were some caps made of Lycra or other soft mesh that were not as harsh on skin, but when my mother bought me one of those, my coach forbade me using it. The only worthwhile caps are severe. The taut latex or silicone flattens everything. You should leave the locker room showing nothing.

Even this, the one time that I'd swum faster than usual, I'd failed—failed, I tell you!—at being a swimmer, because I hadn't been able to keep my hair back.

I'd always known I was only weakly attempting to be on this team. This scene was meant for bodies who could perform sleek and reserved.

The buzzer rang for halftime, and I knew I'd be noticed if I lingered any longer in the locker room. I ripped my cap from my head, shook out my hair, pressed my fingers hard once against my eye sockets in an attempt to get the blood flowing, and slipped out the door to the pool. I opened it cautiously so as not to scrape anyone's bathing suit bottom and mingled into a clump of my team members gathered by the diving board, where our two captains stood to lead a halftime chant. I moved my hands along with the motions everyone else was doing, my voice blending with the other girl-voices rebounding off the tile.

> Who da who do who da
> Who do you think you are
> Oh, you think you're sexy
> Oh, you think you're cool
> Uh, we're coming up
> Uh, to show our STUFF!

Here is where we all knew to explode, leaping from a faux-humble crouch up into a flying jumping jack. Or, some of us just stood up and spread our limbs wide, not trusting that we wouldn't slip on the wet poolside. But our captain, Whitney, sprung into a perfect fly jack, as always, everything about her body tight and toned except for the slight vibration of her flip-flops as she lifted into the air, smiled, and landed, poised. She bowed.

We cheered and high-fived, uplifted by Whitney's glowing skin. No one cared what my body was doing then. I enjoyed swim team when I got to follow. I could fit in enough. I could admire and support others more than display the power or performance of my own body. We moved as a group to sit on the edge of the pool and watch our team's two divers compete, their midair spins and twirls something I'd never be expected to do. My knees bumped casually against those of my teammates, ease flooding my body as the adrenaline retreated. I didn't want to compete, not even for third. I didn't want my body to be measured and held up to ambitious standards. I wanted to witness, not to be the star. The tips of my hair tickled my back, and I pulled it to one side over my shoulder to match the long, wet locks of several girls next to me. It dripped across my collarbone. You know a swimmer is done for the day when their hair is down. It's the moment when the physical standards release.

My mother asks why I am still getting sunstroke at my age. "Sweetie, I think you're old enough to do better." I do know, but I am very committed to not wearing hats. I trip often when I'm hiking because I'm dizzy and haven't covered my head sufficiently from the sun. The old handkerchief I've draped over my head floats away down the trail over the Berkeley Hills. I chase after it and accidentally stomp it deeper into the dust. I pick it up, look up at the friend I'm hiking with, and shrug. She laughs.

"You're never going to wear a hat, are you?" I shake my head.

"Hats are for straight hair," I say. My type of curls crush easily, and even a few minutes under a hat means a wadded mat on my head for the rest of the day, flat along the top, betraying the shape of my skull.

At high school dances, my swim teammates and I would make a different kind of formation, usually a circle that was porous enough to accommodate the approach of boys. They would always approach from behind, so you had to know the signs. I have a clear memory of once dancing to Ginuwine's classic R&B song "Pony," feeling especially fluid in my hips. I was smiling across the circle to a friend when she gave a quick thrust of her chin to alert me to someone behind me, and without further notice a Boston Red Sox cap was slapped backward on my head. A few seconds later a lap ground up against my butt from behind. With the voice in my ear of a boy I knew I knew but couldn't quite identify by his slurry whisper: "Wow, your hair is just like my poodle's."

If you're horny, let's do it
Ride it, my pony

My friend Avery tweets: "If I were to give a high school commencement address, I would advise them to be VERY careful what music you listen to for the next four years because it will affect you your whole goddamn life."

My saddle's waiting

Come and jump on it

The song didn't just show up at dances. It was one of my team's favorite
"pump-up songs," and we demanded "Pony" from the bus driver on the way
to every swim meet. Our coaches somehow endured sitting straight-backed
in the front seats of the bus with forty teenage girls behind them screaming
this chorus aloud. I can't say I understood what the hell I was screaming, but it
meant something, to try very hard to yell words that held almost no meaning
to me. The lyrics about sexuality bled into sports and competition. I pounded
the metallic walls of the orange school bus to the rhythm and bounced in my
plastic seat.

It only mattered that the song was loud, shared, and dramatic. In *Notes on
"Camp,"* Susan Sontag defines camp as, "the sensibility of failed seriousness, of
the theatricality of experience. Camp refuses both the harmonies of traditional
seriousness, and the risks of fully identifying with extreme states of feeling."[3] To
be able to inhabit the song without it being mine, knowing it meant something
to someone.

Now, looking back, I aim for camp in this story. I'm no longer the hormonal
teenager frantic to fit in, or at least fly under the radar. Looking back, I tell a
campy version of her story that serves my purposes now. I'm intentionally using
her to play to my own ends. She can consent to this because she is me.

I wasn't competitive at swim team, but I was a high achiever in academics and
stressed plenty about coming out in the top ten on honor roll and doing well
on standardized tests. Swimming was one environment in which achievement
mattered only to *other* people. My parents had encouraged me to swim "just to
get exercise," and they regularly rolled their eyes at the swim-team parents who
urged their children to shave a few more milliseconds off their times. I floated
and kicked. I moved my arms enough to participate and for my skin to grow
dry with the daily exposure to chlorine. The competitions were high stakes for
other people, and that was fine for them. I sang along relieved when it was over.

My experience of swim team set me up well to do the writing that I want to
do here. When I play in sexuality, in hair, in fascination, I am joining the team

to learn how it's performed, to push the roles so far that I can understand what they are hiding.

Fascinator hats are tiny for reasons both practical and symbolic. Some designers say fascinators became popular as fancy British people began to spend more time in crowds, without a wide berth of personal space. In *Vanity Fair* London-based milliner Stephen Jones explains that his clients used to wear hats only in the carefully choreographed and amply spaced seats at fashion shows or church pews.[4] But in the 1980s, these same clients started going to nightclubs and crowded spaces. They weren't willing to let go of hats entirely but needed something that wouldn't be knocked off their heads or hit fellow clubbers in the face. People needed to notice that the wearer was wearing a hat without the hat getting in the way.

"They're supposed to look like a caprice. Something that means nothing," says Jones. "And things which are supposed to mean nothing—they actually mean everything." Decades of queer theorists raise their hands. Fascinators tip away from meaning whenever necessary. They are fragile, diminutive, and dodge the fact of their own faculty.

I identify with the comfort of this dodge. "Top me," I joke with a friend as we struggle to decide where to eat. "You be in charge," I tell my partner so that he will choose the movie for tonight. The terms invoke sexual domination but are not restricted to that realm.

"It strikes me that bottoming is heavily coded as absenting oneself of responsibility for or complicity with social power," writes Kay Gabriel.[5] Here Gabriel is in discussion with Billy-Ray Belcourt and George Dust about a purported "top shortage" in queer circles. Belcourt, Dust, and Gabriel conclude that this shortage corresponds to a widespread shirking of responsibility and power.

"I'll suggest that top/bottom mirrors the animal/human distinction, that it's a gradient of dehumanization. The top isn't afforded innocence or subjectivity. The top is the brute," writes Dust. A mighty brute can be held responsible, where a humble pet—as we know from Berger and from the alt-furries—can enjoy (even benefit from) power without having to worry what it means.

"It's not a top shortage, it's a brute shortage. This is the dynamic people are crying out for," Dust writes. "And maybe that helps explain why this supposed shortage seems to be a completely white phenomenon. Anyone who gets inter-pellated into this interaction as a top is going to be more critical of it."

I think of swim team again, and its setting in my predominantly white sub-urban high school, how much early coding it gave me in power and race. I was on a bottom rung as a slow member of the team, but I also placed myself there by the way I understood my body: too curvy, too freckly, too many hairs sprouting from crevices and planes. Too far from the illusive tall thin light body to aspire toward it. The other girls competed for beauty on a level I wouldn't have thought to attempt.

Through casual jokes and social cautions, my family had subtly commu-nicated that I was different from the Protestant and Mormon majorities of my school. I didn't yet understand my interpellation into whiteness, didn't yet understand the way assimilation made my skin color more alike to theirs than different. What I knew was that they fit in better. For them, successful confor-mity was a few trips to Walgreens away. I remember watching, enthralled, as my teammates plucked individual hairs from the joints of their ankles and hogged the hair dryers to blow out their "do" after every practice.

"I'm disgusting," Whitney would tell her blurry reflection above the locker-room sink. There was pride in it. What disgusted her were qualities that she believed she could remove on her way to first place. I never aspired to win.

I think of my teammates under the hair dryers and I am reminded of Stella Goldschlag shaking out her hair. It's a weird comparison—the stakes of com-peting for a swim meet are awfully different from the stakes of competing for one's life. Indulge me for a moment while we look at them together for the sake of camp, for the sake of highlighting (and, hopefully, interrogating) one body playing at white. Because assimilation and its associated fears are also, I see now, what obscured the distinctions between these stakes—and what persuaded me to believe that every compliance was a mortal necessity.

Stella lived for a time as a white phenomenon, a top. A savage role she wanted to benefit from but never wanted to admit. Stella testified during her trials that she was coerced into the job of catcher by her husband Rolf. She clung to this, but others disputed this claim. One witness in Stella's 1967 trial reported of Stella and Rolf that "she led him to water." Who is the horse here, and who the rider? If Stella led Rolf to water, that means that she led his innocent animal force with her cunning, decisive control. The instinctual need for water puts innocence in the all-powerful molding hands of evil. If Stella leads Rolf, she manipulates this purity of his need to put his brawn behind her aims.

At the end of the war, Stella attempted to lead power in another direction. In his memoir, Peter Wyden describes how Stella attempted to maneuver herself onto the side of the Allies after the war. "The Germans had an evocative word for what [Stella] needed to think about doing: *umsatteln*, resaddle, switch to another horse, but quietly, very, very quietly," he writes. Here the horse propels Stella forward alive. If she falls off, she might be trampled. Or, maybe worse, she might be left bare to display the force in her own body.

I never wanted to display force. I never wanted to be tested on my own strength, always wanted to hide it behind the systems and cadres of others. It is also a gendered story that I've learned from watching women hide their power so as not to be intimidating. I watched my most muscled teammates pretend they couldn't even lift a six pack so that a boy at a party would not feel threatened and would do it for them. I watched my grandmother prepare a lavish six-course meal and then wave off any compliments, claiming it was just good ingredients or hungry mouths. There is gendered conditioning here, generations of socialized belief that attractive women do not display their power. There is also fear behind this story, fear of taking credit. What will people think of us if they notice that we are strong?

If we are strong, they may critique us, attempt to take us down. I drive into the face of it here, with an outlandish link between a Jew-catcher during the Holocaust and me hiding out between swim team heats, a possible belly flop of a comparison. I must fully flop in order to stop denying I have power.

Throughout her trials, Stella claimed that she was helpless over any power that others ascribed to her. "Sounding almost like Hitler when he held Jews responsible for Germany's problems, Stella blamed her good looks for her troubles," writes Peter Wyden. Stella told her judges that her beauty was "a thorn in the side of the Jewish Community." Here Stella concedes that she is a fascinatrix, but the source of that fascination is out of her hands. It's not her fault that she's beautiful or that other people hate her for it. It's not her fault that she rounded up others: during her trials, Stella insisted that she only became a catcher because Nazis tortured her, manipulated her, and forced her to do their will. Wyden writes:

They turned Stella into a witch and really she was just a girl. People today have no idea that when you were in the claws of the Gestapo, you had to be prepared to have your teeth filed down, one by one. Stella had wonderful teeth . . .[6]

The witch, the claws, the teeth. More than enough ingredients for a decent Dom/sub scene. I wonder if Stella were alive today, if she'd be earning the big bucks as a dominatrix.

It's easy for me to transfer Stella's image into a different era because she appears so malleable, hollow. The more I read about her, she seems less a person and more a stand-in for whatever someone wants her to be. "Thus, the camp sensibility is one that is alive to a double sense in which some things can be taken," Sontag writes. "Some things," or some people who can double-time, double down on either side. "It is the difference," Sontag goes on, "between the thing as meaning some-thing, anything, and the thing as pure artifice."[7] Stella entertains for her survival but leaves little that seems true at her core.

It is easy to make fun of artifice because it purposefully leaves space open for meaning. Fascinator hats, too, leave room for us to step in and decide what they are. Do they mean something or nothing? Whose side are they on? They do not tell us this clearly, so we must decide. It's a paradoxical bearing in which we as viewers hold all the power to determine meaning, but the hats and their wearers hold all the power to duck away. When Irish hat designer Philip Treacy describes how one of his favorite clients wore her fascinator, he says, "It was as if she was not wearing them—like they happened to be there to entertain herself and whoever came in contact with her."[8] Her performance of the fascinator is successful because it merges with the scene.

Treacy is famed for fascinators he's designed for Sarah Jessica Parker and Madonna—and, maybe most notably, for Princess Beatrice of York to wear to the 2011 wedding of Prince William and Kate Middleton. Beatrice's fascinator was a blush-pink "gravity-defying" contraption that projected upward from her forehead in an eruption halfway between an octopus and a ribbon tied in a bow. Grandiose and outrageous, it made quite a show at the wedding, and on the internet, where it spawned a world of GIFs and memes, many of which depicted a different object (toilet bowl, vagina, the princess's own face) erupting from the center of the octopus sculpture above her head.

Princess Beatrice did not enjoy this treatment. She notes in an interview with *British Vogue* that it was tough on her to receive such an intense and mocking level of media interest, but she knows that she and her sister, Princess Eugenie, are responsible for staying positive because they are public figures: "there's no point being angry with anyone for beating us up—we just need to shine light and love in the world."[9]

To call what happened to Princess Beatrice a "beating" exaggerates it so that she can appear as an innocent victim. Sontag again: "Camp rests on innocence. That means Camp discloses innocence but also, when it can, coopts it." Beatrice invokes the simplicity of "light and love," the innocent stance of someone who only receives the gaze and does not direct it.

Beatrice continues: "We are the first: we are young women trying to build careers and have personal lives, and we're also princesses, and doing all of this in the public eye. . . . We want to show people who we are as working, young, royal women, but also not to be afraid of putting ourselves out there . . . it's important that it's real. We're real."

I watch the sisters back away from their power. Though they are people with tremendous privilege and many staff members working to curate their personas, they want to come off as simple and authentic. It pays to abdicate power, because with this abdication the blame can fall on someone else.

The fascinator ducks away from the hit. The fascinator leads without incurring blame. Let's not forget the translation of the prefix *fascinat-*, "to cast a spell on," or "to hex." If someone is fascinated, they are under someone else's influence—not their own. Here's Virgil in his Eclogue 3, 103: "*Nescio quis teneros oculus mihi fascinat agnos.*"[10] "I do not know what eye hexes my tender lambs." Some scholars say that the tender lambs refer to children, to the belief that young people are easier to cast spells on because "their pores are more open, their juices less formed and the fibers of their bodies more delicate and sensitive."[11] Others say someone's literal livestock was cursed, but in either case it all happens in the passive voice. The actor doesn't appear. It's hard to trace the hex when everyone is looking down at tender skin, fleecy tufts of wool.

I spent so much time yelling the chorus of Ginuwine's "Pony" that I never learned the rest of the song beyond its bouncy groove and weird, burp-like hook. But now I go back, and I see it.

I'm just a bachelor
I'm looking for a partner
Someone who knows how to ride
Without even falling off

I guess it made some sense for a competitive swim team to chant this song, with its implication of endurance. It was a very strong team. Several of my teammates went on to qualify for the Olympics. We always won our longer races, and our coaches were proud of our zero-disqualification record. We entered every single race, even if entering meant entering someone like me, someone who occasionally would flail and choke and finish a full two minutes after everyone else.

This happened more than once, and I can still feel the shame of looking around on my last lap and realizing everyone else in the race was already out of the pool while I swiped my way through the water alone. Even then, my teammates would high-five me when I finished and congratulate me on completing. We were well-mannered and weren't ever mean when we won. A real top doesn't need to show off.

Stella made her fatal mistake by gloating too much over her successes. She was a *griefer*, a catcher of Jews, and seems to have noted this with honor. During one of her trials, a witness reported overhearing Stella boast that she'd "made a wonderful catch today. . . . I dug out an entire nest of illegals."

I read this and imagine Stella's face loom large over a hole in the ground as a litter of kittens stare up at her with giant terrified eyes. Her maniacally smiling face fills the sky above them.

Stella denied this comment, but the imagery of it stuck. No performance is flawless: eventually some hair slips frizzy from the swim cap, or a comment comes back to bite you. It's believed that the "nest" comment was crucial in the deliberation of the jury that sentenced Stella to detention and later to imprisonment.

Wyden describes how the Jewish newspaper *Allgemeine* railed against Stella during her 1967 trail: "She can't be excused by pointing to the system that 'turned humans into beasts.' What we are is within ourselves." The newspaper argued that to call Stella a beast was to fail to inscribe her with enough responsibility. Her beauty was not the gentle softness of the dumb hexed lamb. It was cultivated prettiness, calculated theater.

Stella was trained for this job, and not just self-taught. Wyden finds details of "Stella's elite contingent, carried in Berlin Gestapo files under the never-published name of Jewish Scouting Service (*Jüdischer Fahndungsdienst*)." It's estimated that about twenty to sixty young men and women worked in this capacity for the Nazis, who Wyden says were referred to as "stool pigeons" or *Spitzel*. He writes: "These renegades bore some resemblance to at least certain of the often pitifully beleaguered Jewish Council of Elders that had to help run the fenced-in ghettos into which starving Jews would shortly be herded in every Eastern community." The resemblance is that these groups deflected blame from the Nazis and, later, took the fall.

These Jewish Councils of Elders are those mentioned famously in the Eichmann trial and in Hannah Arendt's coverage of said trial, in which Eichmann testified that the cooperation of Jews was "the very cornerstone" of the Final Solution. As has been well traced, Arendt was publicly condemned for pointing this out. Her coverage of the trial noted that the Holocaust would not have been possible without the Jews who were placed in charge of organizing their own communities for ghettoization and deportation.

Everyone hates this part. No one likes to admit that they were bundled into the *fascio* of brute force, and so became the force themselves. I struggle to admit any desire for my own power, because I have seen too many examples in which the person who competes the hardest is the one who must run the most difficult races. You race in one direction, but the system in power isn't static. Why aspire to be a top when there's no assurance in it? I prefer to be the sloppy slow one, the innocent rider flung about, not the horse tromping sludgy through the mud.

What makes life different from camp or role-play is when you're some of both. No, let me rephrase that. What life can learn from role-play is how very "both" you can be.

When I listen to the song again, what I hear in "Pony" is how it diminishes itself. *I'm just a bachelor.* The comfort of *just* ripples through the song: it's undulating. It's easy, flirty, awaiting.

Gotta be compatible
Takes me to my limits
Girl when I break you off
I promise that you won't want to get off

Ginuwine offers something he's convinced we want and won't be able to stop doing once we begin. The animal. Who could blame us for leaping astride?

A good ten years after I was on swim team this song had a revival when it was featured in *Magic Mike*, the movie about male strippers that so many women I know love because of the permission it gives them to consume, to indulge in a kind of sexual attraction that is lightweight, silly, does not sully their reputations. When Channing Tatum strips to "Pony," the cheering never stops. Everyone wants this scene to go on forever.

In the trailer for the sequel, *Magic Mike XXL*, Tatum's character has retired from stripping but still cannot help dancing to "Pony" when it comes over the radio. The song reveals some inner undeniable truth about him, even as he shakes his head and tries to resist.

If we're gonna get nasty, baby
First we'll show and tell
Till I reach your ponytail
Lurk all over and through you baby
Until we reach the stream
You'll be on my jockey team

Ginuwine himself gets to be a bottom in "Pony," a team member, *just a bachelor*. The rhyme between "stream" and "team" is muted and soft.

"While 'Pony' may ride the equestrian sexual metaphor a little hard, it's still better than your average bump and grind," *Entertainment Weekly* concluded in 1996.[12] Not good, not evil, just better than average. The song is on a team that defines why it's good.

In the most popular press photo for the musical version of *Stella*, the actor playing her wears a black hat, one she's seductively flipped off one of the male cast member's heads. It sits lightly, jauntily on her, yet stays attached as she twirls. I'll chalk this one up to professional hair stylists and touch-ups during scenes—there's no other way a hat like that would stay still on curly hair without ruining it. One more testament to Stella's campiness: a hat that leaves no trace.

There is only one photograph I can find of the historical Stella in which she wears a hat. It appears to be black and white, though in some versions the photograph has been tinted so that Stella's jacket is green, her lips ruby-red, her hair straw-yellow, and her hat a reddish brown. She looks proper, well-dressed, and stares calmly into the camera. Some kind of fur hangs in front of her pockets, maybe mittens. I stare back. She seems both the opposite of me (neat, collected) and the same (cautious, dodging).

"The work of postmemory, in fact, is to uncover the pits again," writes Marianne Hirsch, "to unearth the layers of forgetting, to go beneath the screen surfaces that disguise the crimes and try to see what these images . . . both expose and foreclose." I'm writing into Stella for this reason, to contest what I can understand about myself or the way I've been organized. Of course it's important to let the horrors of genocide warn us against fascism and repetition, but what I'm aiming for here is to confess the ways that I too have tried to cozy up to power and follow the rules in order not to expose myself to danger.

Until we reach the stream
You'll be on my jockey team

Stella rode well for a while. She ducked under the theater of other people's commands. In this photograph of her, I see a person protected by what she sits inside: a jacket, a hat, "something that means nothing." Some hair that rebounds. A person who fits in well, a human who joined the team.

Identifying with aspects of Stella is muddled and absurd, but it's an absurdity that helps me do some delicate work. It helps me realize that Stella might be less an aberration, and more normal than any of us would like to imagine. I find this especially useful in the moment when I am writing this, as fascism and extreme forms of nationalism continue to rise in the United States and globally, including in Germany. If I am going to play and make light in the realm of fascism, I need to stay attentive to how it is happening now. I can't duck out of that one. I gesture toward "Pony" because it brings in the flamboyant, the pop-ish—it makes role-play stagey and clear. It's so clear it makes me look at myself, the part I'm playing now and how she is different from though influenced by who she was then, and who she was near then. I must be very careful—and very specific—about what power *does* inhabit my body, even when it flickers, even when it changes from place to place. I am liable, too.

I am relieved to find a German writer who might orient toward liability, too. The German Jewish writer Max Czollek challenges the idea that Germany has moved past its Nazi history—or, for that matter, that any of us have. He attempts to replace the action of moving past with a continuous scrutiny of how the past moves in the present.

The complex compound words of the German language serve Czollek well to bring multiple spheres together. He describes a mainstream German consciousness as a belief in "overcoming the past *Vergangenheitsbewältigung*." As a counterpoint to this, Czollek suggests "*Gegenwartsbewältigung* [overcoming the present],"[13] which, he writes,

> proceeds from an awareness that we are living in a post-National Socialist society. This inverts the familiar modes of interpretation for the surge of rightwing thought because from the perspective of *Gegenwartsbewältigung*, it would be surprising if those outdated ideologies did not continue to manifest themselves in the present.

I notice my spine straightening against the back of my chair, lined up perpendicular to gravity. It's as if Czollek is looking at the landscape in front of him and saying *of course*. It feels so basic. *Of course* the past is moving in us today. It would be naive and also dangerous to assume it is over and sealed off.

Looking closely at right now requires additional work in cataloging long-gone evils. Czollek continues, "*Gegenwartsbewältigung* means an attempt to shape our present in a way that the violence of the German past will be impossible to repeat."

If we could admit that the past laps through us still, what kind of new thinking could we do? What kind of alertness could we bring to our relationships, to our politics, to the way we navigate the menaces we see in our communities and governments? I imagine that we would more easily admit our own complicity. I imagine that we would zoom in, spend less time on sorting who is correct and more time on our interactions. This is also a form of postmemory: "uncovering the pits" not to lie down in them, but to look at the bodies alive now. The possibility of healing is more likely for me when I don't have to block anything out.

I try out forms of this, in this writing here, and my attempts to connect it with the racialized trauma I witness today. When I return to Oakland in 2016, I return to a group of white-identified friends my partner has gathered to talk about how to show up more considerably for the Black Lives Matter movement around us, not just going to the big protests, but considering where in our friendships and our neighborhoods and our work environments we could do more. When he opens the first meeting, he acknowledges, "I know many of us identify in other ways in addition to white, but I'm going to ask us to focus on that for now. Not trying to make us feel bad with it, just trying to acknowledge how much power we have," he says, "Or, at least, I have," he stops again, clears his throat, "I guess I shouldn't assume everyone has the experience of this, I know—" he looks down.

"It's fine, Josh," Jake says from across the room, "we all don't know, but we're trying to see what we can do." Jake shifts on a maroon pillow on our wooden floor, and various things creak beneath him.

"Yeah, thanks," Josh says. And that's how we begin. Nothing gets fixed by this group, and there are plenty of moments in which someone backs up and says they don't like how we're generalizing. We stop at those points and reconsider. We keep having to stop and reconsider. That's most of what this group does.

"*Gegenwartsbewältigung* therefore does not aspire for normality or catharsis," Czollek writes, "but rather, for the awareness that both we, ourselves, and our society require ongoing attention and care."

Czollek lets go of catharsis. He lets go of the process of purifying the past. In its place, he says, we must look at what seeps into how and who we are.

I write to track this seeping. I write to ask: If it's true that Stella existed, what can I watch for more closely in myself? I write to ask: Who are we, now, knowing all this, holding it all together?

The fact that Stella existed changes and alerts something in me, even though we were not alive at the same time. Stella believed that assimilating toward the dominant power was stationary and could protect her. From my moment in history, I can see this didn't work, that time went on from Stella's and we integrated more information. I need to keep writing to keep learning. In Czollek's ongoing-ness, there's no hat that can keep our status defined, no delicacy nor severity that can keep me white enough, my hair controlled enough to be invisible. There's no Ginuwine "stream" that we'll reach where we'll be beyond the jockey team and all the hurt will be over.

I don't mean to say that we should act as if in constant danger or that we should always be on the run. During the Trump presidency I had plenty of conversations with Jewish friends about packing our go-bags, panicking in a way that felt ancestral, recognizing that the powers running government institutions might turn against us in the way they have before. But this panic isn't what I'm advocating for, nor what I see in Czollek, nor what I see in the lessons of Stella or fascinators perched on the heads of people denying their own force.

I'm advocating for finding integrity in being switchy, instead of using it to dodge. I want to notice that I am on a team that adapts, and currently holds the privilege to adapt.

"Privilege is not the same as power," writes activist-organizer Scot Nakawaga in the JFREJ report.[14] I'd never seen someone articulate this so clearly before I read it there, and it's become extremely important to how I understand integrity. Being adaptive, to me, means holding both the material privilege I have now *and* the knowledge that it is fleeting. It's hard to do! But only when I hold these together can I participate in an opportunity for liberatory action beyond a Jewish story. Nakawaga continues: "privilege is not a bulwark against white nationalism and other fascistic movements for those who are targeted, because privilege is conditional and hinges on [who] is in power. It is important to address antisemitism as a lever of white supremacy and anti-democratic power arrangements and movements."[15] I teeter on the lever. I am switchy and slippery in time, and so can make contact with a larger, much more powerful potential solidarity with the masses of humans whom white supremacy and patriarchy seek to control.

I read Czollek and lean back in my chair, a chair at an artist residency in Santa Fe, New Mexico, where I am editing this book. I have terrible hair days in Santa Fe. The dry air both wilts and snarls my curls. But I go out anyway, without fixing it, with the peculiar bravery of feeling like no one knows me or will notice me much. This place isn't my home, nor is it either of the two places that form the poles of this book. Even so, I remind myself again, I am not homeless. I am not teamless. I have relationships to place and home, and they are constantly adapting as I meet new people, take new jobs, occupy new spaces and times.

I put my feet up on the chair across from me in this quiet room swept clean so that people can make things in here that matter most to them. The Ginuwine song's still in my head, even after all of this reading. It sticks. It stays attached to me.

Lurk all over and through you baby

I love the word "lurk" in the song. He's prowling, he's waiting around. He won't leave.

I won't leave. Finally willing, meeting fear of failure with desire. Close reading a song that won't hold all I'm putting on it, I lurk in the failed space.

Lurk all over. The role of assimilator or collaborator will always be coming for us, asking us to twist a certain way. If I recognize that this darkness lurks in me, I can turn and look right at it. If I can see the motivations or needs that make me desire assimilation, maybe I can escape habitual actions, and meet those needs more explicitly instead.

Testing Testing

When I first met my partner, he had just injured his cremaster, a muscle most people don't know about unless you are really obsessed with penises. The cremaster carries the testicles up and down, further from or closer to the body. People only tend to learn about it if they have a problem—the muscle usually afflicts men who jog without sufficient support for their testicles, straining the cremaster as it tries valiantly to hold the testicles steady.

The cremaster moves the testicles to regulate the temperature of the scrotum. Sperm stay alive at the ideal temperature of sixty-eight degrees Fahrenheit, and the cremaster works hard to preserve this temperature: it links up to a system of muscles and fascia from the oblique muscles to the pelvis, a delicate loop that controls how much surface area is exposed and thus how quickly body heat moves away from the testicles. This arrangement is why testicles hang low when it's hot out, and high when it's cold. Like many delicate systems in the body, we only notice this one when it stops functioning.

Two months into our relationship, my partner asked me if I wanted to take a bath with him. He brought in candles and tried to make it a romantic night, but the true motive was that he had injured his cremaster, and his doctor had said that heat would help the sore muscle heal. In the warm soapy water, he snuck in care for his own injury while folding his large body around mine from behind. As our relationship deepened, I looked back on that night and realized it was a test. Could we take care of something weakened and still feel sexy together? Could we allow for him to be soft?

* * *

Ten years later I was at an art museum in Berlin. I had been sad and solitary while struggling to finish a project. Back home in Oakland two of my closest friends had new babies, and I was missing the baby showers, missing the births. I was sad about missing out, but sadder still about the yawning contrast in our lives: as they settled into the well-worn grooves of family life I was out here, alone in Berlin, trying to finish a thought. What was my life compared to theirs? If I wasn't growing up the way they were, what was I doing?

I moved my body around the city but felt often like a shadow, recollecting myself. I made some new friends, and listened warily before I spoke, assessing what parts of my life back in California felt relevant enough to share with these people, mostly artists, mostly collectivized in their activism and collaborative performance work. They had each other, and this legitimized their lives; they mirrored for one another the normalcy of living from gig to gig, growing from performance to performance, living their politics in their shows. Dropped in amid them, I could measure myself not by human births and nuclear families. What parts of me were important here? I could feel the enjoyable edges of potential reinvention, but I hovered there, unsure.

Often alone with my books—or, more accurately, my pdfs—I thought about being a person, and attempted also to *feel* about it. In one of my loneliest moments, I read Harry Dodge. In *The River of the Mother of God: Notes on Indeterminacy*, Dodge reads Hannah Arendt in search of what it means to be ethically social. Dodge describes how "one can be more readily social if one allows oneself some time and space to think (simultaneously alone and together with others)."[1] It is public space of contemplation that allows one to think something through—not entirely alone but given space around one's body and mind. Being given space makes me a bit more able to hang out in the sensations of my own body, more trusting that my body too could have information for me.

And so I took the very long walk to Hamburger Bahnhof, a quiet, airy contemporary art museum where I knew I could stand next to others a few feet apart, alone but amid. I come to museums when I am lonely because they are legitimized spaces for staring and thinking in public. I can think my thoughts but also spy on how other people are reacting to the art or situation. I watch for how their reactions interfere with my own.

Upon entering the museum, I went first into the exhibition titled *Der Elefant im Raum*.[2] The title excited me because so much of my experience in Germany involved that historical elephant in the room of National Socialism. But, in a twist, the Elefant in this exhibition referred not to politics or genocide, but to sculpture itself, the Elefant being the form of a physical art object and how it takes up space.

The German artist Joseph Beuys featured heavily in the exhibition, especially several of his pieces made of felt. I walked around them on the shiny wooden floor, remembering the 2018 film *Werk ohne Autor* in which a character based on Beuys slams piles of lard against walls and fervidly repeats "dur *felt* and Der *filz*." In this film, the Beuys character says that he works with felt and fat because these are the materials to which he has the most immediate emotional connection. He instructs the main character in the film—a young art student under his charge—to discover for himself the materials with which he feels this kind of immediacy. The Beuys character recounts the story of how he was nursed back to health by nomadic Tatars after his plane crashed in Crimea during World War II. All of this is based on Beuys's own personal mythology, though records show that Beuys was in fact recovered by Germans and there is no evidence of Tatar involvement. It's largely agreed that Beuys at least partially invented this story to develop his creative persona.

In *Der Elefant im Raum*, Beuys's supple materials felt extra theatrical, placed as they were against the planked floor and the white wall, under the high rounded glass ceilings of this museum designed inside the dramatic arches of an old train station. Pacing around them, I found myself impatient with the sculptures, recalling the movie and Beuys's tidy explanation, how it constrained what I was supposed to see in the felt. I wanted to speculate more widely.

I rounded a corner to get away from the Beuys and tried not to step on squares of felt arranged in the middle of the space. I noticed a smaller room to the side of the main exhibition and headed in that direction, looking for something legitimately cozy instead of something soft that I couldn't touch.

The smaller room was a rectangle with only a few objects in it. As I stood in the doorway, I saw first that the room was dedicated to the work of American artist and director Matthew Barney, particularly his series of films, *Cremaster Cycle*. On opposing walls of the room hung framed stills from various films in the *Cycle*. At one end a bench faced a large screen showing *Cremaster 1 (Choreography of Goodyear + MS Goodyear)* (1995). The room was glossy white, its walls glistening against the glass display case set up just underneath the monitor screening the video projection. In the case were a few props used in the filming of *Cremaster 1*, most notably a clear plastic high-heeled pump.

I moved toward the glass to inspect the props, but someone cleared their throat, and I realized that standing to look at the pump meant blocking the view of anyone watching the film. I hovered nervously to the side of the case, then moved to the bench, where I sat compliantly. The clear shoe glinted at me from across the room, flashing reflected colors from the screen above.

Cremaster 1 has been sometimes referred to as the most "feminine" of Barney's *Cycle*, which is, after all, named after this muscle around the testicles, and deals, among many themes, with masculinity and its discontents. The *Cycle* is maybe best known for being difficult to get through, and according to critics, requires great concentration and dedication, a kind of strapping feat.[3] From the bench I watched one film, not the whole *Cycle*. Still, sitting there I felt inside of the project—encased in this smaller room and inside of Barney's aesthetic, his carefully curated world.

I was somewhere in the middle of the film. The camera moved between groups of women, each in high femme makeup and costumes that indicate their delineated roles. The bulk of the film transitions between two tracks: in one, dancers form grand formations across a football field, over which two blimps fly. In the other track, we see inside these blimps, where bored flight attendants smoke and eat grapes from giant tables, underneath which a woman dressed all in white satin appears to be trapped. She moves ever so slowly, steals grapes from the table above her through a vulva-like rip she tears in the tablecloth with her long nails. She silently and painstakingly waves her legs around in those clear plastic high heels. She seems to be controlling the dancers down below on the field, as the patterns she creates with falling grapes predict and echo the movements of the dancers.

The best-known scenes of *Cremaster 1* are referred to as "fallopian imagery," including scenes in which those falling grapes trace the outline of Fallopian tubes and uterus, and glamorous dancers do high-kicks in old-Hollywood style. To me, though, the grapes seemed less like a human ovum and more like sperm. They fall from great heights and dance in a circumscribed direction. They are solo travelers, alone together in the same film, not finding one another because they are each so dedicated to their own targets.

*   *   *

A few days later I'm meeting Lukas, a German friend I don't see very often. We hug over his bicycle, and I feel acutely how solo I have been. My body caves toward his, eager to be absorbed in our interaction and forget my own projects and concerns. I pull myself back physically, hoping he will not feel my need. We stand apart and I wonder what next. I suggest that we find a place to settle on the grass and talk.

Lukas nods, and we walk to the Landwehrkanal. He asks good questions, and peppers me with many, earnestly trying to catch up. *How are you? How is your work? How do you feel being here?* I speak slowly, feeling careful before his friendliness, wanting to check if it is genuine. Lukas spreads a blanket that of course he happens to have in his backpack. We sit down a few feet apart from each other, though in the past we've touched with ease. We've been lovers, but mostly friends for years now, and it's never been confusing—there's always been a clarity to our communication, a trust that we want to know each other but do not want to bother or intrude. We live far apart and don't try to maintain something that's difficult over distance. When we go a long while without seeing each other, these boundaries can feel high, like I can barely see Lukas over his politeness. Gradually we work our way back to the intimacy of the past. Our talk today feels formal, obligatory somehow, and I notice I am breathing shallowly, waiting for the time it takes to grow comfortable again, for when that toggle will turn on to closeness, the way I remember us laughing easily together over plum-flavored ice cream last summer. Every time Lukas asks me a question, I ask it of him in turn. I watch his face as he answers me and I have a hard time concentrating on his actual words, more taken with the variations of color in his facial hair, his eye creases, and the minutiae of his gestures that I hadn't remembered in the years since we saw each other last.

Lukas begins updating me about on his mother's health, and then something stings me very sharply on my little toe. I notice it but make no sign or sound. I take in the prick of it and continue listening. Only a few minutes later, when I slip away to the bathroom, do I investigate the area. It is red and hardened, but not swollen. It's not a bite or sting I've seen before.

I take a while in the bathroom with my toe pulled up over my knee, inspecting. Someone knocks on the door and jiggles the handle.

"Uh, yeah!" I exclaim, never knowing how to respond from that position. *Wrong*, I think. Wrong language for this country, wrong thing to say, wrong activity to even be doing in the bathroom. I slip my foot back into my sandal, open the door, and return to the blanket on the grass, where Lukas has a patient look on his face and is staring out at the geese on the water. I ask him what one is meant to say from inside the bathroom when someone knocks.

He doesn't understand, at first.

"I mean in German," I say, "what do you say when someone is checking if you are still in there?" He laughs.

"You say: *go away, I'm shitting?*"

"No, really," I press. I want him to give me something sincere, a useful phrase for polite exchange. I am weary, now and already, of this conversation, the surface we can't seem to break. He senses my impatience and shifts his posture, turns away from me and stretches his legs toward the water. "Okay, the correct word would be *besetzt*," he says. Meaning, *occupied*.

"It's the same as squatting in a building," Lukas says, "or Occupy Wall Street." I can tell he's proud of the reference he's made, and he leans toward me. "Or you could be *besetzt* with your work?"

I sigh, and he looks back in my direction. "This means something to you," he says. At last, things are loosening between us. It's *besetzt* that does it. I remember Harry Dodge and Arendt, Arendt's insistence that free thought primarily takes place in dialogue with another, and how Lukas is reaching for this, for co-thinking. *Besetzt.* I feel the spongy sense of where this word could go. I tell Lukas how many hours I've been spending at the computer feeling blocked, how it seems impossible to continue, that it's all been pointless and this book impossible to write.

"But this is how all artists feel." His chin tilts down toward me, his hand now very light on my calf, consoling. His finger slips across the tendon, down to my foot and encounters the red bump at my toe. He looks up with concern.

"Something stung me a few minutes ago," I say, pulling away from his hands.

"A few minutes ago? You kept it to yourself while we talked?" He seems disappointed, left out.

I straighten. "I'm upholding my masculinity by not showing pain." I mean it as a joke, but also feel a showy pride.

As always happens when you learn a new word, I begin seeing *besetzt* everywhere, first on posters about an upcoming protest in which activists will occupy a building slated for demolition. And then I spend a day waiting for Diana to get back to me about our plans for tonight, *besetzt* with the ongoing annoyance of anticipation. I've been waiting on her and cannot tend to anything else. It *eats up the day.* Jeff texts a group to say we should come to the park tomorrow for his birthday, but "no big deal" if we are not already *besetzt*.

I show up at the park and drink warm beer on another blanket, this time surrounded by gay men who are engaging in a conversation about penis shape and size. I nod and pretend to care, fake total enthrallment in this topic about which I already know far more than enough. I let myself be overtaken by the conversation in the soupy heat of the night. It's relaxing in its way; I'm sucked in without having to participate. Tonight, I'll be a "chill" person because that's who these people bring out in me.

It was my uncle who first taught me how not to be tickled. It started because he'd tickle me as a young kid and then I'd try to get him back, but he'd sit motionless and relaxed against the couch. I would stare into his face as I scratched harder and harder into his armpits and his waist, but nothing. His jaw would barely move. I was frustrated by this imbalance between us, but also awed. My uncle explained to me that if you concentrate hard enough while someone is tickling you, you can relax your muscles and control the sensation, or dull your reaction to it. We made it a game and practiced together until I could feel the input of a tickle but control the response, soften my body around the stimulus. It took my full concentration, to the exclusion of all else. If he started talking to me, I would lose control and be ticklish again. I had to seal myself off totally to play.

The longer I sat in the white room watching *Cremaster 1*, the more I felt welcome to space out. It wasn't the loop, the forty minutes after which everything begins again. No, it was the feeling of watching images that were familiar but exaggerated, the campiest version of normative gender roles. As beautiful as the images were, I closed my eyes and didn't feel that I was going to miss much.

"Rather than reading Cremaster, we are encouraged to consume it as high-end eye candy, whose symbolic system is available to us but hardly necessary to our pleasure,"[4] write critics Alexandra Keller and Frazer Ward, "meaning, that is, is no longer a necessary component to art production or reception." The film presents a set of symbols and images that meet whatever the viewer wants them to be, or whatever the viewer associates with them. A kind of junk-food manna. We are not nourished by it but can notice in the film's content the symbols we're already carrying around. I think of BDSM, the symbols of rope or paddles or chains, the rooms in which I watch a person lead another person by a chain locked at their throat. In BDSM play, the play absorbs the outside world, including histories of slavery and imprisonment. These histories are taken up by a "symbolic system," as Keller and Ward write.

I sink into the bright lips and outlined eyes. I sink into the bench at the art gallery. I sink into the symbols. Keller and Ward continue: "Left to its own devices—and it is all devices—Cremaster places us in a framework of mutually assured consumption, consuming us as we consume it." I watched the woman in white tear open the tablecloth and sneak a grape through, and I watched her calves move weakly across the planes of her confinement. These devices are ones that I already know, and already know how to use, so I eat them up as I go along, snack on well-known modes of patriarchy, not disrupted. Placid.

It was nearly silent in the gallery as people moved in and out of the room, catching a few moments of the film and drifting on. I felt powerful with my eyes closed, having staked out my place on the bench and stayed icily still. My affect was flat, and I felt vigorously immune, mountainous in that Zen-sense. Was this power, to let it all wash around me, and stay? Like when I conquered the tickles: instead of resisting the touches of gender, I accepted their omnipresence in my space, but stopped reacting. Could I live among them without being engulfed?

I do not understand how a joke has not been made about the "seminal nature" of Barney's *Cremaster Cycle*. The *Cycle* has been referred to as "seminal" on occasion, but I haven't seen it couched ironically. Seminal: Groundbreaking, strongly influencing of what comes after, creative in the sense of birth. What comes after is linked to the original thing whether the latter thing chooses or not, like a petulant child standing in their parents' shadow pouting, *I didn't choose to be born to you.* The *Cremaster Cycle* occupies a room and something oozes from it. Something wraps around us that owns the place.

I left Hamburger Bahnhof and took myself out to lunch, something my friend Allie had suggested I do for "self-care." I usually roll my eyes at this overused term and how it mostly applies to purchasing and intake, but I accepted it this time because I so craved instruction. "Order yourself something special," Allie texted. I try not to engage in this kind of consumption, but I was very tired, so I got an iced coffee with some kind of homemade nondairy milk made from an exotic nut the waiter only knew the name of in German. It sounded right, and the coffee came in a fancy fluted glass, but as soon as the glass hit my table, a wasp arrived and began circling. I tightened.

A few years before, I would have screeched and run away immediately. I was notorious as a child for my skin's intense reaction to bee and wasp stings, but over time I'd learned the adult behavior of waiting it out. I stared at the insect as it moved from my elbow to my plate. When my salad arrived, the wasp was interested in that, too. I lifted my fork and took tiny bites to my mouth, closing my lips carefully and setting the fork down as far as possible from the insect.

I breathed in and out, making no sudden movements, no jerks. I clenched my inner thighs and feet in case I would need to jump up, but I kept my surface soft. Like the tickle, I could hold this out only to the exclusion of all else. I didn't think any good thoughts about the art I had just seen, and I didn't allow my mind to wander. I didn't eat much lunch, losing my appetite as the fear sloshed in my belly.

The difference from a kinky submission: I wasn't relaxed. I wasn't performing this acquiescence to feel a part of something or connected to other people. I was presenting a silky facade in defense, feeling some (even small, insect-sized) sense of danger. Not distilled, I was frazzled.

I pulled out my book and then notebook and pen. I tried to read and write but failed. The wasp whizzed by my ear. I couldn't concentrate, my skin itching with tension, and then, suddenly, as the wasp moved to the back of my hand, I stood before even considering whether I wanted to leave. I gathered my things in a clump and marched away from the table, hot, itching. I was fast now, away from the wasp, opening and closing a door to the restaurant so it couldn't come through. I paid for my lunch at the counter and shut myself in the bathroom for a moment of peace, finally caring little about whether anyone had noticed I was fleeing an insect. I stood in front of the toilet and ran my hands across my arms and legs, squeezed my own bicep. The skin across my arms was red and prickling, my body suddenly rippling with an outsized anger.

Sarah Ahmed uses the term "feminist snap" to describe the moment the feminized body dramatically refuses something it's been tolerating for a long time. Even if one event precipitates the snap, it is caused by a sequence of events to which the subject has not been reacting. "Senses can be magnified, sometimes after the event, in a way that one may not just touch lightly upon the issue, but cling on the detailed recollection of components 'too overwhelming to process,'" Ahmed writes.

I live among and tolerate for so long that when I snap, I don't fully understand why. Though I recognize this as snapping, it does not necessarily come at a sensical moment, here with the wasp or otherwise. I don't have a clear "detailed recollection" of why rage rushed me when it did, just as I cannot tell you for sure when I first got sick, or even when for sure I understood myself as kinky. Ahmed's "components" ring through me like Barney's "devices," the tendencies and traditions that I tolerate. There are moments here and there, months when I go along, unable to sense what is wearing on me. Until abruptly my senses magnify, having held taut, having been unable to focus on much but my tolerance: for the wasp, for the film I watched for longer than I meant to, for the fat and the felt and *Der Elefant im Raum*. An exhibition with a name that gestures toward an awareness of secret undercurrents, of powerful forces at work, but then neatens everything around it, doesn't spill an ounce.

I don't trust myself around an exhibition like that one. It's campy enough to make me feel like we're playing, that's only a tickle, all in good fun. But to stay calm in its presence, I have to numb out. The price of rising above it all is too high. Under my surface something readies itself for the sting, protective, preoccupied. The stillness that comes over my body in the *Cremaster* room is my body trying to blend and camouflage so I will not be a target.

These moments are so subtle that they seem fine until I break. In the break is an opportunity to reassess. In a country that isn't my own, surrounded by people who haven't known me for very long, I can protest my own moments of meekness. A snap, a pause to reorganize how I relate to my physical body and to my womanness. The nuclear families back home in Oakland, the aspirations of couple-hood and home ownership and stable career. The liberal assumptions about what political positions I will take. Which forms of living do I want to take as my own, and which do I want to leave behind, seeing newly where they agitate me?

It's not a binary between these two options, to be sure, and there's no one correct course. I can't expect to slide through white rooms without colliding with danger. I can't expect to sit on a blanket over the grass and have no creature touch me. I can't expect Lukas to open up to me without exposing something of myself, too. It's all different, but it melds in the imperfect politics I'm building around myself.

I came to the museum in the first place because I was lonely. Harry Dodge describes loneliness through how much is permeable or shared. Dodge writes: "I am interested in the thinking of solitude as vibrantly contaminated by companionship and loneliness as a kind of stark, depilated situation of non-collision."[5] I might still be receiving information during periods of noncollision, but what I do receive fills my space not as companion but as current, alluvial. I am lonely when I do not get to interact with what comes through, those "depilated" limbs continuously slipping past me, far too smooth to grab.

In the opening scene of *Cremaster 1* the dancers stand in their heels in careful rows. The women in the front row hold up their giant orange hoop skirts to reveal most of the length of their legs. Their toes tap very slowly in front of them, a tiny movement that feels incongruously intimate for a group to make, like a coordinated nervous tic, an unconscious mind-meld, or body-meld. They look like objects more than people because they act so robotically together. They move perfectly in sync and do not stop to question what a body does. They are controlled, contained, conforming. These depilated lady legs rock me nearly to sleep. So sleepy that I crave a jolt. I must keep testing, test something else out.

I was disappointed to find that there is no etymological connection between "test" and "testicle." There is good stuff in its origins, still—testicle comes from the Latin *testis*, a witness. It's the softness that sees. Many *Cremaster* scenes transition from one to another via one image that expands to become an entire separate landscape. We pan out from the tapping toes to a football field and two blimps that fly above it. The blimps surveil what occurs below them but also are caught up in their own worlds, the heels and grapes inside.

Inside of every world is yet another. Worlds I know and worlds I don't. I think of my friends in Oakland who are newly parents, inside of a new kind of family world about which I understand little, but I can text them and see what they are willing to share with me. Maybe they will offer stories that I find alienating or boring, and maybe they will explain aspects of their experience that will let me in. A *testis*, I can potentially witness. *Testis*, I learn, originally meant a witness to virility, to that which can generate life, novel starts. The testicle suggests an observer of patterns as they form the world. The testicle is delicate *because* it observes, a receptive action in which it makes itself available to the possibility of new harm. The testis and the testicle both need to be cared for. As I do, also always enclosed and suspended in a system with its own agreements.

Yes, I just compared myself to a testicle. I'm jealous of them, sometimes. Once my partner understood his cremaster injury, it became something he could talk about with other men. I encourage him to bring it up, because I think it's a funny story, but also because I like what happens when he talks about it. Often, another man's eyes will widen, and he'll realize he once had this injury too, but never knew exactly what it was. "I thought it was just unknown crotch pain," they say, as the cremaster becomes shared terrain between them.

A warmth unites these men, though soon they move on to "cream" jokes. Yes, the cloak of dude behavior moves in quickly to cover over the reminder of fragility. But just before that happens, they acknowledge that they share a delicate something, something that usually moves in and out of sight in its soft sacs, the cremaster carefully tucked between layers of spermatic fascia. Listening, I find myself coveting this moment of exposure. I am aiming for something like this. Exposure with just enough protection to talk about it. An admission that our bodies are *besetzt*, occupied, with activities we cannot fully control.

I listen to these men laugh together. They laugh about the alien-like blobs that move toward and away from their bodies though they are not cognizant of telling their testicles what to do. What's funny is this strange combination of conscious and unconscious, what they choose and what they can't. The balls will keep jiggling as they've been trained to do, and they might get torn as they dance.

On Fascia

When my grandfather was alive, he would not allow German products in the house. He had been a pilot in World War II, but I knew nothing about what he saw during his military service or where his hatred rooted. It filtered down slightly in the next generation. When I was twelve and taped a magazine ad of a Volkswagen Bug to my wall next to the picture of Freddie Prinze Jr. in *She's All That*, my father looked at the ad and smiled.

"Our family used to hate Volkswagen," he said, but it was nostalgic.

"Why?" I knew but wanted the verbal explanation.

"Better not to give the Germans any of our money." He shrugged. I came away with the impression that my father had never set foot in the country, and years later I am nervous to tell him I am going back yet again to Berlin. Over the phone, I explain it as a work trip, as if someone is forcing me to go there though I've labored hours over a travel grant to do research and planned for it for months.

My father sighs, but then, quickly, "I bet you will love it," he says. It is only then that I learn that in his early twenties my father traveled through Germany with three Jewish friends, that they intended not to stay long but spent one night in Berlin and felt straightaway that they had to stay longer.

"Why?" This time I am asking for real detail, but I get little. "The people, the city, the architecture—" My father stops. I can tell there is a closed door behind his response, maybe sexuality, a transgression, or something else he does not think it necessary to explain, at least not to me. It's okay, that pause, because it means my father gets to choose discretion, too. He too can let some doors stay closed that mean something to him, and I don't necessarily need to know why.

"Berlin is the most permissive place," my father says. Something expands behind him that will stay a glimmer, only communicated in the way he will smile in the video when I call and tell him about the friends I am making, about the art, about the coffee he would love, about my long walks discovering corners of the city that both spook and charm me. Something will give way enough that we talk for a good half hour before mentioning "The War." Long before it comes up, I will tell him my feet hurt from my wanders, and he will recommend a German brand of insoles.

My father has had plantar fasciitis for years now and has warned me to start wearing better shoes. "You can't avoid it," he warns, "it'll come for you." I ignore him until the day my heels begin to throb.

A fascia (/ˈfæʃ(i)ə/; plural fasciae /ˈfæʃii/; adjective fascial; from Latin: "band") is a band or sheet of connective tissue, primarily collagen, beneath the skin that attaches, stabilizes, encloses, and separates muscles and other internal organs.[1]

I stand in this country and feel my substance twist in its presence. I mean the very fascia, the connective tissue that sits under the skin. It angles a different way, walking on different textures, feeling I am watched in a different way, wanted in a different way.

Nora and I become friends first because we share this experience of gaze. We are both American with parents born elsewhere, but we meet in Berlin. At the cafe in Neukölln our folding chairs seem creakier than everyone else's, our voices louder too. People passing by glance at our faces and then our bare legs. We agree that people stare at us in Germany much more than we are used to.

"I'm magically hot here," Nora jokes. We laugh and people turn to scrutinize our brashness. We try to let our voices fly for each other.

"Are you 3G?" Nora asks me. She means "Third Generation," a shorthand used to identify the generation of people whose grandparents were Holocaust survivors.

"No," I say, "just regular old Jewish trauma." She smiles. We are allowed to think this is funny together.

"That's why they think we're beautiful," Nora says. Her gaze sweeps the street. "It's what we have that they don't." I feel the void of this, the way the sidewalk swamped with light-skinned Germans floats our rickety café table on a riptide toward them in the still, hot air.

Attraction here is an equation, less about my own qualities and more about the abyss in another. I have always felt my own attractiveness to be tenuous and dependent on conditions. I wasn't hot in high school, round and awkward, still learning how to hold my body up. The experience of playing shadow to bodies who mattered more formed me so consequentially that it surprises me still when others find my body worthy of gaze. I sense my skin pull toward where it is wanted.

Like ligaments, aponeuroses, and tendons, fascia is made up of fibrous connective tissue containing closely packed bundles of collagen fibers oriented in a wavy pattern parallel to the direction of pull.[2]

As I've aged, I've grown into my body with more gentleness and even pride, but I still feel a double experience. When I dress in the way I think suits me best, I receive compliments and eyes catch on my shape, but when my hair is up in exercise clothes I can easily disappear again. People will tell me they didn't recognize me when they saw me out running. There is something I like about this sleuth-spy feeling, my costume obvious, the performance of attractiveness carefully chosen and easily taken down. It's a superpower that I can move in and out of being appealing.

Ideally, your fascia is healthy and therefore malleable enough to slide, glide, twist, and bend, pain-free.[3]

When fascia works well it is orienting. It helps you stand in place, like I stand on an uneven street and shift slightly to see Nora coming around the corner to meet me for the second time. I move back to sniff the smell of baking bread behind me. Nora comes closer. We hug, and the fascia in my ankle help adjust my weight so I will not topple over or tear something.

Fascia turns the body with ease. It glides along the surface of the muscles so that they can do less work. I coil my speech like fascia, with fascia. Like language, fascia moves where it is needed. I followed the root of *fasci* to "band" or "bundle" in Latin, a vocabulary from yet another location. Now the words haul me here, along Berlin's streets. *Fasci* maneuvers to allow me to keep moving with people. I slink around Germany and then slide myself down along its length.

No one asked me to track my family's pain, my people's history. No one asked me to tell this story on their behalf, to memorialize the place my body held. What I have to say is my own urge to bring things together.

I did not come to Germany and say, "my family came from here." Because my family moved through. They came from Poland and Lithuania and Ukraine as far as I know. Some died in territories under German occupation during the 1930s and 1940s, but not the ones I know the most about. It is different to experience the phantom of World War II in our stories and fears when the family I know best fled before it, in the 1920s, to the United States and Mexico. The line breaks. In its place are stories that do not conclude, or stories whose only conclusion lacks detail.

It's true my great-grandmothers left the old country. They left behind their siblings, parents, and cousins, and they never heard from most of them again. My *abuelita* tried to find her aunts, wrote letters, and called offices, but no one returned the letters or had anything to say in response. In the blank space is the inference of murder without the affirmation of its particulars.

In Germany I tried to avoid the invocation of murder, first because I did not want to, and later because it felt too vague, too inconclusive compared to other people's careful survivor tracking, their lists of names. The branches of my family extend and strangle when I look up into the tree. I look up the long scroll my *abuelita* has curated on Ancestry.com and wish I could say the names correctly. This standing and looking and not knowing them is one of the family roles I take.

"We make ourselves in relation, of course," writes Harry Dodge, "and our senses keep us from wrapping ourselves around things so hard we wrench meat from bone. Another way of saying it is that pain produces things: proximity, velocity, and establishes a rhythm for relating."[4] The secrets of my family bond them to me and me to them. The gaps in the family stories keep me coming back, keep the tension held between us. Even when lacking content, they hold us "in relation." I cycle through the same stories again and again, each time faster, more impatiently, each time trying to find a way to build a conversation, one that can never be full because it's only me writing here. Anyone else's version would be written differently.

"You need to give up and just say what you think," my friend Eleni says. She reaches across the table to refill the water glass I've drained. I've told her I'm scared of speaking on behalf of my family, let alone on behalf of the Jews.

"You'll definitely be wrong sometimes," she says, "but I know you," she winks, "you'll be willing to back down." Eleni wears a leather harness over her business-like cotton button-down shirt, and a collar around her neck with a metal ring in it, the kind of ring a Dom uses to attach a leash. When I point this out, she shrugs, "it's in fashion," which, she's right, it is. But we both know she means something by it, something that has taught us both how to be brave.

I have no last names to look up in Germany, no apartment where my ancestors lived. There is that cliché of the crumpled yellow paper from a great-grandmother's hands, the apartment number she hid in a dusty jewelry box for years and handed her grandchild just before she passed. No, I do not have that.

What I have instead is words and where they break. The words interrupt themselves—my *abuelita* says her father was conscripted into the czar's army and he took the first possible ship to escape. My mother breaks in to remind me that her grandmother also took the ship alone. It was a different ship to a different port, but the competition now is for the separation, for how many siblings each of them they left behind or how young they were when they departed. My mother describes how her grandmother tried to bring the rest of her family over to the United States, but they never believed it would get that bad in Poland. "And then they were gone," my mother says.

"*Fallecieron*," my abuelita concludes, *they perished*. They are speaking about two different family lines in two different nation-states, but the story twines together as two languages attempt the end. The words that I use to explain family compound and blur together. The cadence of my sentences is drawn from my father's native Spanish, my mother's English, my abuela's Yiddish, Russian, Polish, Hebrew.

I am a native English speaker, but I have always spoken with a roving syntax that other people experience as poetic or playful, and that I experience as automatic. I incorporate the accents and phrases I've heard. I stare into the face of English where I was born, English where I meet the word *fascism* and try to use it as best as I can. But because "native" next to "language" floats, insecure, I glide between them. Whenever I encounter a word, I try to hear beyond it. Here comes the lure, to follow *fasci* in and through.

No, I do not have an address to search for in Germany. I do not have people to search for with different spellings of my last names. What I have instead of origin is a search in sound, in the generous creep of the verbal, the oral.

Yet again in Berlin I am on an unstable chair, gripping my laptop on a café table as if it will hold me steady. The chairs seem to always be tippy. Maybe they assume a person is strong enough to stabilize on their own. I sit in the patio of a cafe and the sun is bright enough to make it difficult to type, and bright enough to warm my feet under the table. The woman across from me smiles and says something to me in German. I shrug apologetically.

"Oh," she points down and switches over. "English. You have beautiful feet." I have never seen my feet as beautiful. They spread broad and flat. My high arches fall easily and the top of my foot strains and bulges with bursitis where it's unsupported by the thin soles of my shoes. Maybe it's that my feet are exposed today in this sun, and their visibility makes them notable. I look over at the woman's own feet, which are encased practically in the kind of thick-soled black platform boots that make so many Berliners look equally ready to dance, climb a mountain path, or stand and salute. When I brought home a pair of these that I'd bought at a sidewalk sale, my Berlin roommate said I'd gotten my very own "Berghain boots," invoking the name of Berlin's best-known nightclub. I haven't worn the boots yet because I'm sure they will feel foreign. I look at them in the closet and tell my roommate I am working up to it. Berghain boots are the opposite of most of my shoes, the floppy kind I wear today that make a person seem like she might melt into the very sidewalk.

"They look through me and see whatever they want to see," Nora says. We are listing the funniest comments people have made about our bodies in Germany.
Can I touch your hair?
What a mournful smile.

In Elaine Scarry's classic text on aesthetics, *On Beauty and Being Just*, she writes, "No matter how long beautiful things endure, they cannot out-endure our longing for them."[5]

Your people are so sensual.

These comments are so obviously stereotypes that when people say them to me, I feel they are reaching past my body toward something out of time. The comments are funny because I'm not even there. Someone looks at me, hungry to place an object, and I happen to be that object. I do not exactly feel that my own body is being looked on as beautiful, but rather that someone is trying to sort and catalog for their own purposes. Placing me as an object makes less work for them.

> Fasciae were traditionally thought of as passive structures that transmit mechan-
> ical tension generated by muscular activities or external forces throughout the
> body. An important function of muscle fasciae is to reduce friction of muscular
> force. In doing so, fasciae provide a supportive and movable wrapping for nerves
> and blood vessels as they pass through and between muscles.[6]

Information passes among fasciae, reducing friction by connecting the body to itself. Instead of two forces rubbing up against each other in contradiction, fasciae smooth out difference, keep the subtle movement for itself.

I am supposed to just accept these comments. I am supposed to nod and smile and take a compliment. But if I do, I maintain whatever norms the other is projecting. When I question the comments, when I write about them or list them with my friend, we interrupt. We point out that something is being invented, more than factually described.

Because I understand this sort of attention as transient and contingent, when I am on the receiving end, I can't help but think too about the moments when I am in the gazing body, the one guessing about and categorizing other people, wanting to know what they are like, though naturally they too are being continually invented. From multiple angles I feel this pull.

> Fascia is consequently flexible and able to resist great unidirectional tension forces
> until the wavy pattern of fibers has been straightened out by the pulling force.

When I entered my thirties, my friends also began to warn me about plantar fasciitis. Women I know have begun changing over to comfort shoes in droves, and I ask them if they miss delicate footwear. Liat shrugs.

"It's one-hundred-percent worth it," she says. I see she walks with ease, trusting the ground in her sneakers. I don't have this bearing yet, still clinging as I do to the light, flat sandals of my youth.

"Eventually it won't be a choice," Nora smiles as she picks up my sandal from the floor next to her couch. She bends it in half with one hand. "Eventually your feet will give out."

When inflammatory fasciitis or trauma causes fibrosis and adhesions, fascial tissue fails to differentiate the adjacent structures effectively.[7]

When fascia fails, muscle and bone rub up against one another, their difference obvious.

"Trust me, you'll know when something stops working," Allie says.

The Wikipedia page on Fascia begins:

For other uses, see Fascia (disambiguation).
   This article is about the human body. For the ideology, see Fascism.[8]

The word ambiguates, and ambiguates again. Both are about the human body. The strain comes when I try to keep them apart for too long.

You're all so intelligent.

That wisdom in your eyes.

Your people are so expressive with your hands.

I'm jealous. Jewish women are so liberated in bed.

The flow of generalizations moves about me, and I feel that same riptide of being here not exclusively as myself. So many other bodies swimming with me, living and dead.

"To bring us back to the body is a risky move indeed, but my attempt here is not only to make that move but also to understand it as a move toward the relational, rather than the singular," writes Sharon P. Holland. "Therefore, the 'body' . . . is simultaneously forever absent and always already present,"

Holland continues. Yes, my body is here in Berlin receiving the comments, but at the same time is looked over in service of a cultural story. Yes, a stereotype erases my individuality, but if I can see this while it is happening, I can catch it in my hand and curve it on itself, bend the shoe. Holding their assumptions in my gaze, I might challenge both of our positions in the dynamic.

I feel this option when the woman in the café looks at my feet and labels: beautiful. My knobby toes with the hair curling up from the knuckles. Instead of accepting beauty, I poke at it, point at it. What does it say about the person speaking, about me, about the two of us in space? Her beauty label challenges the victim story, the dirty Jew story, the endless suffering that lives on when the stories end with *fallecieron*. It challenges the haunting by making it clear how much can shift.

Elaine Scarry argues that beauty is valuable because it liberates us beyond our individual egos. "At the moment we see something beautiful, we undergo a radical decentering," Scarry writes.[9] This is not beauty as in admiration, but beauty as in reorientation. Looking down at the feet, looking up at the sky. I am somewhere in the present.

Scarry cites Simone Weil, who writes that beauty requires the beholder "give up our imagined position as the center. A transformation then takes place at the very roots of our sensibility in our immediate reception of sense impressions and psychological impressions."[10] We are impressed upon, moved aside for the sake of superior structures.

Something we consider beautiful presses on the body, and the fascia move to allow. A system of tissues shifts. I laugh at a stereotype. I poke at what we've been carrying, something unbearably heavy. I play with the standards that make beauty. It allows me to put something down.

No one asked me to tell this story, but I felt the charge in my body, the desire to stop carrying a bundle on my back, a rigid set of pain points. I am stretching, trying to see where we can be made more flexible. I follow *fasci* into Germany and the word contorts again, into my feet, between ideologies, into my mouth as I giggle with Nora about how awful I am at saying German words.

"It's totally excusable," she tells me, "Jews don't want their kids to do German." She learned to speak it anyway, and she helps me to try to say the name of the German city "Mainz," where it's possible that maybe some of my family is originally from.

"Where else . . . ?" Nora doesn't need to finish the question. I can see she really wants to hear, her glass of shimmery green tea set down. I know that she also has a long list of answers to this question, that her parents were born in South Africa, a country Nora does not think of as home. Because home is unstable for her too, she is ready to listen carefully and not presuppose. She is here for the names of small towns across an array of nation-states and even for the inconsistencies and chasms.

"From so many places," I start. I tell her the long version of my family story, the various fragments that do not cinch. Someone is caught on a train and escapes and ends up on a horse, a boat, another mode of transportation. Someone hears that they have a cousin in Mexico, and so they take the boat to Veracruz, then somehow find their cousin in the morass of Mexico City before cell phones or email. The name of the street where my great-grandfather landed in Mexico City is exact, but little else. Little is known about the town where he was born or what his family was doing there prior to the events that made them leave. It's an origin story of passage and flow instead of source.

Over the years of considering Jewish memory, I've talked with many leaders of Jewish organizations and scholars of Jewish life and culture. Many of them are intrigued by my pursuits, by how they've brought me so much closer to Jewish identity than I'd ever been before. "But what is Jewish about all of this," one scholar asked me, "if you're not engaging closely with the exact history, or with religious or Biblical texts?" He put into words a fear that I have long imagined lies behind Jewish institutional brittleness: What will Jewish identity become if it continues to evolve away from tradition and toward reinvention? What will be left to pass on? Is it being watered down?

I can understand that this fear is real, especially for people who are closer in proximity to the trauma of genocide than I am, but also for anyone deeply committed to a version of Jewishness as they personally understand it. But strictly circumscribing what it means to be Jewish has driven so many of us away already. To reproduce culture necessarily means to reinvent it.[11] Because I've been given freedom, here, to really stretch the boundaries, I am more engaged with Jewishness and Jewish history than I ever thought I would be. I am fascinated. I have given up my power to refuse what presents itself.

"Berdichev," I say to Nora, "Mlawa." I feel my mouth move around the names of towns and cities. I've never been to those places, and I don't speak the language of their inhabitants. It helps me, though, that Nora is listening, and she does not appear to judge me for not knowing more. I remember Fred Moten, that "terrible trouble" that having been diasporic does not mean that an uncontaminated origin story awaits you. Nora does not seem to mind when the story drifts into uncertainty, because she knows more layers on top of it now, more happening in this very moment as we stare at the cloudy water of the *kanal*, when I ask her to help me speak a few words of a language that I'll never fully get the hang of. Speech does not stop where it stands, but thrusts itself from the body speaking, moves again and again.

"Confronting antisemitism is a necessary precondition for collective liberation,"[12] concludes the JFREJ "Understanding Antisemitism" report. When I look at the report again, now, I see movement all over it—movement in the sense of collectivization and social movements for justice, but also movement in the way it speaks to shifts, to Jews trying to get out from under the anti-Semitic tropes designed for us.

"The goal is not to crush, it's to have us available for crushing."[13] That's Aurora Levins Morales again. If I can move, if I am mobile, then I am less available for crushing. I am less available to be crushed by anti-Semitic scapegoating, less liable to crush others without understanding that I am doing so, less available to be crushed by the bulk of inherited trauma.

I have been reading Tirtzah Firestone's book *Wounds into Wisdom*, in which she studies Jewish ancestral trauma, the way it is carried through epigenetics, and how descendants of historical oppression might learn to release it. "Two elements are key," Firestone writes, "a safe witness and the ripeness of time."[14]

Time mellows our process. The time is ripe now because I grew up secure enough not to fear for my life. I do not blame my grandfather for his hatred of Volkswagen, or my father for his initial caution around touring Berlin. Their time was a different time from mine. I am living when I can do this, a time in which I am safe enough to turn *fasci* over in my hands and see it for what it is: a functional bundling, a term flexing the muscles of context. And I feel secure that I have found witnesses, people who can lean with me into what is funny and playful about *fasciae*, the eerie way *fasci* pulls differently on different audiences, gleams in one moment and terrifies in the next. Nora laughs with me, Michael listens and cocks his head, RA invites me over to their sickbed, Berivan points at genocide over time. They witness, and something rests.

Nothing is fixed, but some things are released. "Repair is conservative,"[15] Elizabeth V. Spelman writes, meaning that it tries to restore and preserve a past before trauma or destruction. The action of repair, as Spelman thinks through it, wants the past to be able to stay as it was.

But what if I don't? What if I want to know the past but the way I carry it forward is not still? I walk over very old streets in heavy clogs, and my ankle waggles from side to side. There is no perfect statis for my muscle. What if there is no return? What if we let go of the idea of continuity with what was?

Inevitably, my feet begin to ache, orbs of pain form in very center of my heels, and I cannot walk effortlessly. I wince, I limp, I pick my way from cobblestone to stone. I am surprised to notice that even then I feel elegant, attractive, because I've redefined what that means to me. My walk bears the consequences of unwise shoe choices, and hopefully it will soon bear the consequences of something else.

I keep moving, though I begin to consider wearing Acrosoles or Birkenstocks. I stop in front of a German shoe store that displays the styles of sandals that I used to think were very ugly, but I now consider. I examine the arch inside of one shoe bed and the very wide toe box. *Maybe I'll change soon*, I think.

"It's extremely Jewish to start over," my friend Mónica says. Change may in fact be more faithful to my origin story itself, the one involving continual movement. "Jews always reconstruct," she says. Mónica is both a poet and a rabbi, a rare combination of someone equally committed to spiritual and artistic practice. She reminds me that one common way to narrate Jewishness is through a story of tectonic shifts, periodic transformations, and rebirths.

"I have the rabbi's approval!" I text Nora. On paper, with her rabbinical credential, Mónica is the best source to tell me I'm a good enough Jew. In lived experience, she is also a great source—brimming with soul and humor together. But it is the "on paper" that matters here, because it plays with hierarchies, with the authorities from whom we're supposed to seek approval.

"I've been liberated by the rabbi," I text, "She says my weird sex story is Jewish." It's the nontraditional tradition: a socially normalized "kink" in the system.

Sorry. Puns, too, have been passed down.

*   *   *

"Don't stop there," Nora says. I've paused at the turn in the story when my mother's mother arrives in the United States and finds some work in a dry goods store run by Jews in Pennsylvania.

"That's the predictable end," she says. One thing that draws Nora and me to each other is we are both writers, both averse to clichés in language and forms. She won't let me get stuck here.

If we let our bodies keep talking, something scary might happen. It's scary because we don't already know it. I speak of words that learn from the past and of the potential of language to transform in place. She might use words to describe me, and their meaning might adjust in her mouth, or in mine. I do not expect us to finish, to be finished. My diction continues to develop.

None of this can be standardized enough to apply to everyone in the same way. You can't tell every Jew how to describe themselves, how to pray, or how to heal from what ails them. In her book, Spelman spends a full chapter speaking to the pros and cons of the methodology known as restorative justice, particularly in contrast to the criminal justice system. In practices of restorative justice, the victim and perpetrator of a crime meet along with community members to discuss the harm done and to determine what kind of action will reconcile the two parties and allow them both to reenter social interaction.

"Proponents of restorative justice celebrate how parties to a conflict need to be creative, flexible and practical, while critics see these features as invitations to improvisation and arbitrariness," Spelman writes. I'm struck by how applicable this feels here. When I choose to work on a relational level—with witnesses, between people, in present time—the solution is specific. What restores me personally—what makes me feel I can laugh, speak, move—is likely not right for others. But it works for me. I'm ready to transmute what *was* into what *is* moving. This requires improvisation, participation in what follows from here.

"What happens after?" Nora asks again. I open my mouth and notice that my lips are very dry.

"I think things were up and down for them for a while," I say. I clear my throat and reach for lip balm in my bag. I'm not sure what I'll say now. Will I wonder about why my grandfather studied oral surgery when his father and grandfather had been rabbis? Will I talk about my *abuelo* and his brothers selling trinkets on the beach in Veracruz, though no one has explained to me how they saved up enough from that to start a construction business? Will I say something about class, and how it began to shift for them once they owned their first home? There are many directions to go, many people with varied experiences of being Jewish in their new country, of working, of parenting, of going to school and learning who they were or should be. I'm not sure which story I'll say next. I want to leave it open, so that there remains so much to say.

Formula One

"You Americans don't know a fascist when you see one," Emil tells me. As if it was a simple thing to spot. I am visiting Emil in Copenhagen on the way home from Berlin, and when I explain to him that I'm tracking *fasci*, he gives me a long, hard look.

"It's just a story to you." As he shakes his head, the soft lighting of the lamp next to us reflects on his balding scalp, closely shaven how men do to make it less obvious when their hair is going or gone. The shine against stubble and skin makes me feel gently toward Emil, and I indulge him. I stretch my legs out on his couch and prepare for the Eurocentric lecture, for whatever it is he wants to prove to me.

"Around here," he says, "a fascist is not a theory. You want to see a real fascist?" He asks. He drags his laptop toward him and googles for the story of Max Mosley, former CEO of the auto-racing organization Formula One. It comes up quickly: In 2008 the tabloid *News of the World* leaked a sex video featuring Mosley, which the tabloid declared a "Nazi-style orgy." Emil reads that phrase aloud.

"What the hell is a *Nazi-style orgy*?" I ask. I laugh, though Emil's face is serious, determined to teach me. This happens in our friendship's dynamic. I let him play the authority. It's an act.

"I don't know, but he does," Emil shuts the computer before I can scroll past the few fuzzy images. Later, while he is napping, I pull the story up again and read the transcripts of the video, in which Mosley is first "punished" by five sex workers, and then later fakes a German accent (though he is British) and administers corporal punishment to a "prisoner" in a striped uniform.[1]

178

I scan through a lot of legal and media back-and-forth documenting Mosley's attempts to get the video banned. The tabloid that released the video defended its right to provide the public with "the truth" of Mosley's kinks. The legal manager of the tabloid released a statement demanding:

Why are German military uniforms worn?

Why does he issue orders and threats in German to women who cannot speak German?

Why does he deliver and count out beatings in German to women who cannot understand German?

Why does he put on a German accent when speaking English?

Why are the victims of these beatings in German made to put on sinister striped uniforms?

Why the head lice inspections, the forced shaving of body hair and the sinister references to inmates being housed in "facilities"?[2]

These are obviously leading questions, but when you dig into it, it's not so clear to me that this is exactly about Nazis. The tropes used in Mosley's kink scenes are also evocative of prisons or other torture scenes—very little specifically conjures "concentration camp," as the tabloid's coverage would have us believe.

I listen to Emil snoring in the next room and look out at the window washers cleaning the all-glass building across the street. Emil wanted me to be offended by the sex tape, but I'm long past abiding with other people's standards for offense. What kind of failure is this one? It's a productive one if it takes me somewhere I want to wonder about. I wonder not the same "whys" that the tabloid asks, but, instead, why people care so much about this video. What purpose is it serving to sensationalize it? Why the need to make Mosley out to be so bad?

First, there's an easy answer: What made this whole scandal significantly worse for Mosley was the fact that his parents were famously into Nazis. His father, Oswald Mosley, led the British Union of Fascists beginning in 1932 and was married to Max's mother, Diana, in Joseph Goebbels's sitting room, with Adolf Hitler as an honored guest. The revelation of the sex tape was an opportunity for belated revenge against Mosley's parents, and also a chance for British media to take a public stand against anything fascist. There wasn't room for play when Mosley's powerful family was already so implicated.

When Mosley pleaded before London's High Court asking that the video be banned, the judge denied Mosley's injunction, saying, "Although this material is intrusive and demeaning . . . the granting of an order against this respondent at the present juncture would merely be a futile gesture,"[3] given how far the footage had already spread. It does seem pointless, Mosley's attempt to stop search engines from linking to the video, but this unrealistic request in its way supported Mosley's broader attempt to make himself out to be a victim. He came off as "futile," weakened, nonthreatening. He successfully turned the story away from the details of his actual sex life (or, as the tabloids put it, "racial shame") toward one about ineluctable forces conspiring against him.

I want to better understand the history here. I want more of a sense of what the British public sees in Mosley, what haunts them when they watch these rather campy videos. I find the particulars in a YouTube video of a 1977 interview with Lady Diana, Mosley's mother.

"Mrs. Mosley, your family has been described as a 'savage tribe,'" the interviewer begins, "now do you concede that title?" Diana Mosley smiles charitably. She is a striking woman with incredibly high cheekbones, posh British accent, and well-coiffed waves. She dodges the question, but as the interviewer circles closer and closer to the specifics of the Mosleys' association with fascist figures, Lady Diana Mosley draws herself up and puts on an amused, matronly expression.

"I've always loved clever people, even when I was very young. And I made a beeline for anyone I thought clever or amusing," she says. I can imagine her smiling at Hitler and Mussolini from across the room, admiring their uniforms, their clipped speech.

The interviewer asks Lady Diana to describe the first time she met Hitler. "What was he like?" She delivers the question nonchalantly, as if out of innocent curiosity.

"He was a very interesting and fascinating man," Mosley replies. Her eyes open with a long blink, invoking how very much she wanted to see.

"How did he strike you? I mean what did you like—why did you like him?"

"He was a fascinating man." Mosley seems to be humoring the interviewer. "Well, he was charming, but it wasn't only that he was charming," she explains, "He was completely different from anyone we'd ever met before." This is what haunts this family, and why the label *fascist* keeps sticking to them. Fascist is the phantom of being duped, overcome. Fascist is the specter that threatens to suck a family—a world—of innocents in with that charm.

When Emil wakes up from his nap, he's forgotten already about Mosley and I don't choose to remind him. I don't need him to know about the YouTube videos I've watched, or that I've already scrolled through pages and pages of British fascist history. But I want to know more and more, a lust for research, following filaments and themes that hold no assurance of wholesome resolution, and only make sense to me. I can feel the draw of the browser window that I left open on my laptop, and I'll keep reading tonight on my red-eye home to California. My eyes ache wanting to get back to it all.

Having grown up in the 1980s and '90s, when I think of being "sucked in" by something one of the first images that comes to mind is from the film *Who Framed Roger Rabbit*. Maybe it's a strange association, but most of us remember the first time we watched something sexy that we knew we weren't supposed to see. For me that was this movie. It was Jessica Rabbit, the fictional cartoon wife of Roger Rabbit in the film. I remember the movie was on television on a late afternoon at some after-school program I attended, and I remember rough carpet against my forearms and calves as I lay in front of it. I remember the tingling I felt across the back of my neck as Jessica entered, and the look of rapture that came over the male characters' faces, how they stared as her breasts bounced against all laws of gravity.

Who Framed Roger Rabbit was also my introduction to eyes popping out of someone's head. In cartoons, this move usually happens when a (male) character sees a sexy woman and his eyes swell out of their sockets, sometimes traveling clear across the room or falling to the floor, retained only slightly by a thin ligament. This is sometimes accompanied by "an ahooga horn,"[4] the two-toned exclamation of pure lust most recognizable from Wile E. Coyote and Bugs Bunny.[5]

Who Framed Roger Rabbit is one of the few movies in which characters who are *not* cartoons experience the metamorphosis of this eye pop. Upon its release in 1988, critics lauded the film's combination of live-action and animated characters. This combination allows cartoon behaviors to cross into human bodies at crucial moments in the film. The ultimate reveal in the movie occurs—in a scene described by *Rolling Stone* to be one of the "top scariest in a children's movie"—the character of Judge Doom turns out to be a "toon" after masquerading for most of the movie as a person. This transformation is what makes it so terrifying, and it's signified by a change in his eyes. After Doom is run over by a steamroller, he peels himself up off the floor and blows himself back into shape with an injection of helium. As the helium enters him, his eyeballs pop out to the floor and are replaced by cartoon daggers. The eyes popping out clue us in to the fact that Judge Doom isn't human anymore and is not operating under the rules of other people.

As I watch this scene over again, the eye pop strikes me as less exclusively about sexual seduction and more broadly about disorientation from norms. The eyes bug out when a source of power *fascinates*, disorients people so fully that they can even become not-people. Here they become cartoons, exaggerated, larger than life. I enjoy living fleetingly in this world, where power is only play and eyes can reshape themselves when they want to see.

I missed the lesson on how to use the word "fascist" that everyone else in Oakland seems to have gotten. The police are fascist, the newspapers fascist, the mayor too. I wish I could just go along with it, but I'm disturbed by the way the word skims across the city. The street cleaning is fascist when it gets my friend Ariel's car towed.

"Fuck those fascists," Ariel whips the slip of paper through the air, the paper that says she's left her car in a street cleaning zone five times now without paying the ticket. Five times a charm, five times means your car has a yellow clamp immobilizing one back tire. We are sweating and stressed and not in the mood to wait. It's hot out already at ten in the morning and whipping dry wind in the late fall I've come home to. It's fire season. In weather this apocalyptic, it's hard to take on any responsibility. You want to make it all someone else's fault.

"It's completely unfair." Ariel turns away from me, and I can see that the skin of her neck has reddened, her pale skin that blushes at everything, the short-buzzed hair that reveals her nape and shoulders. It's not the time to question her, though I do wonder if the boot is unfair, exactly. I know that the system of citations and fines falls unfairly on those who can afford it least,[6] but Ariel has gotten so many tickets, and it hasn't been a major inconvenience for her or drain on her financial resources. She can afford the fee. I've overheard her at a Friday night shabbat potluck groan that she knows she needs to move her car before she goes to bed, but she just doesn't *feel* like it. Instead we sing another Jewish song, this time "B'rich Rachamana," an after-meal blessing. It's the short and simple version, the bare minimum for gratitude after your meal, a one-liner in Aramaic: *brich rachamana malka d'alma ma'arey d'hai pita* ("blessed is the merciful one, ruler of the world, creator of this bread").

Aramaic was the secular language in biblical times, the one spoken daily when Hebrew was reserved for prayer. And so this blessing is already in some ways casual, quotidian. The version I was taught feels even more assimilated, re-assimilated to American contexts, because it is sung to the tune of a Shaker hymn titled "Sanctuary."[7] We follow the Hebrew words with the English words of that hymn: "Oh lord prepare me / to be a sanctuary / pure and holy, tried and true / and with thanksgiving I'll be a living / sanctuary for you."

After all my time spent contemplating purity, those lyrics strike me as strange, at the very least. Creepy, even. Ariel leans over the edge of the couch and puts one arm around me, and we are definitely mocking the song as we belt it, "pure and holy, tried and true." Ariel has a beautiful voice, and she lingers operatically on that "true." The song's language is very Christian, and that's precisely why it sounds funny to us. I'm enjoying how foreign purity feels, how silly.

"I hate them so much," Ariel says the next morning, standing in front of her car staring at the ticket under the windshield wiper. There is no one in sight. It is a weekday just after morning commute time in Berkeley, and Ariel slept on my couch because she didn't feel like driving home last night. She pulls up the ticket and hands it to me. To get the boot removed, $140, plus the outstanding ticket fees. I nod, trying not to agree fully but also not to contradict her.

"I hear you," I say. I fold the ticket in half, hand it back, and offer to drive her to work. I don't want to upset her, though I miss the playfulness of last night. I'm not sure why her reaction is so big, why this is having such an impact on her. For years I've sat in popular education and antioppression trainings in which we set ground rules at the beginning on a white board or large clipboard. Always near the top of the list is some version of "see intent versus impact," that rule that asks us to remember that if someone hurts us, they might not have meant it that way.

Increasingly, though, this rule is frowned on in these same rooms, and in some of them it's getting crossed off the list—"I don't need to try to understand when someone hurts me," one participant will say, or "it's not my job to do that labor." Ariel is in this camp. She is not someone to see the nuance in things, and though I've sometimes admired her for this—the way she stands uncompromisingly for refugee rights at her job, the unapologetic stridency with which she explains to people why they are wrong—I never want to be the one arguing with her. She will rise from her metal folding chair and face the room to explain how oppressive a rule is, staring us down as if we were her enemy. Ariel is the kind of person who will plow you over to explain how she's right, without necessarily factoring in interpersonal warmth. I am aware of how bravely this goes against gendered training that keeps women conciliatory, apologizing, prioritizing niceness above all else. But when I say the wrong thing in front of Ariel, I sometimes feel scared. Not afraid for my physical safety but concerned that it doesn't matter to her that we are friends. It matters more to her to pick a side.

Once, I was talking to Ariel about what news we read and how every source of media is tainted these days. We were ranting, tired of parsing the perspective of everything before we read. We sat in a park to rest under the redwood trees and watch some children grab fistfuls of sand and throw them into the air. Ariel began listing journalists, which of them we can trust, how one in particular is a *fascist*. I looked out at the children in the sandbox and did not respond. The journalist Ariel mentioned was my friend, Lara. Maybe used to be my friend—we haven't been in close touch for a while, and we disagree on some things, but I don't usually let go of people that easily.

Lara would never use the word *fascist* to describe anything, in part because she is Jewish and rigid about a spade being only a spade. I thought this over for a second: If Lara was herself a fascist, she might bring along with her the capacity to *fascinate*—this capacity to obfuscate, to make herself irresistible, the deception of her friendly smile. And so how would I know? Maybe I'd been duped.

"I've known her for a long time," I said to Ariel eventually, "I don't agree with her on everything, but I think she has a good heart." I forced myself to keep looking at the playground, feeling the sweat at my lower back, the pressure in my chest knowing I wasn't siding with the team. "Lara was really kind to me when I was at my worst," I said. I remembered Lara holding me close on a ratty couch as I sobbed about my first major breakup. I remembered her making sure I made it to the therapist's office, texting me after to check in, assuring me it was OK to take Lexapro for a few months until I could regularly get out of bed on my own. I remembered her taking me dancing once I could and how fully we celebrated then, in our early twenties, that I felt alive again.

"She was a loyal friend," I said to Ariel. "That's important to me." I spoke slowly, as if I were blindfolded and guessing at what had been placed in my hands. I turned to look at Ariel as her face scrunched and the rest of her body pulled away from me. I wanted very much to backtrack, to give her what she wanted. But I couldn't do it anymore, that plunge between good and evil. I couldn't follow it when I knew the person involved.

Ariel stared at me, shaking her head. "She advocates for everything we know to be wrong," Ariel said.

"I don't know," I said, "there are some things I think it's okay to question."

"You should think through that one a little more." Ariel zipped up her backpack. "We do not like her." She spoke for a "we" she did not identify, and I wasn't sure if I was in now or out.

"I cannot muster the 'we' except by finding the way in which I am tied to 'you,'" writes Judith Butler, in "Violence, Mourning, Politics," their essay in which they argue that relational ties are undermined by politics. Butler describes how we demonstrate which lives are and are not worthy of compassion by how much we are allowed to mourn them publicly. Butler writes of the semantic experience of trying to relate to someone outside our immediate relationship, saying that we can enter this "we," "by trying to translate but finding that my own language must break up and yield if I am to know you. You are what I gain through this disorientation and loss."[8]

When I didn't know the right thing to say to Ariel, I felt this loss but also a potential. I couldn't step into the "we" she was describing without a murky field opening before me, one that included both Ariel and Lara threaded through me, a "we" adjacent to the one Ariel meant but not the same. I am in a disoriented "we," as Butler says, one in which language does not pin as easily on its targets. If we were in actual physical or psychological danger I wouldn't allow this disorientation—if someone was truly pinning targets on Ariel and me, I would run from that person, and do everything I could to divide us. But we are safe, right now. Lara is not armed or threatening the rights of people I love. I am safe enough to stay in the disoriented "we."

Is there a way to pay attention without aiming to mark the subject as bad or good? Throwing around "fascist" reminds me too much of Lupin or

185

Friedrichshof, commanding we must strip ourselves of evil only to layer on additional coercions. I am not immune from mistake or reactivity. I don't believe anyone is immune in this way, and I don't expect to be made all the way decent.

It is always easier to decide that someone is bad. It is easier than holding on for the dizziness of reaching toward them, speaking toward something uncertain and not pinned down. But, as Butler writes, if we allow some of this disorientation, we allow relationship. Butler continues: "This is how the human comes into being, again and again, as that which we have yet to know."[9] Reading Butler I think of the "switch" in BDSM terms, the person who does not always occupy the role of top or bottom, Dom or sub. I think of how I only feel I'm really getting to know someone when I get to see them play multiple roles, or how turned on I feel when my usually mild-mannered partner makes strict demands of me in order to change up our usual dynamic. "The human comes into being, again and again."

"Maybe you'd like slapping me?" My partner asks one night, when we are tired, and our sex is a little rote. "You can try, if you want," he says, picking up my limp hand, "call it research if you have to."

I flush, too known, too nerdy. I am willing to try it tonight. I want to be something else from what he knows me to be. I make my right hand firm and flat, all the fingers lined up, the muscles so engaged they begin to shake. I look at his cheek but not his eyes and slap him resolutely and fast. I pull my hand back a few inches from his face. Only then do I look at him.

"What do you think?" I ask. I'm guessing he's not into it, but I want to let him tell me.

"No, what do *you* think?" He touches his jaw as if checking for results.

"I don't know yet," I say. I bring my own fingers to his jaw, to the indentation between the bones. Together we check out what the skin feels like there, and it's the most intimate we've been all night. We are not sure but feeling. It's what I can do now that I don't think I could before. Before Michael, before Nazi kink.

This touch is also why I can't bring myself to throw around *fascist* and close it off. I don't want to toss that word in the direction of Lara and assume her known, tagged, inhuman. Sitting at the playground with Ariel, I watched as she swung her backpack over her shoulders, and I restrained myself from apologizing.

"I have to get going." Ariel stood up from the park bench. She took a few steps, turned back to wave once, and walked away behind the trees. I stayed for a minute, jamming the toe of my sneaker into a crack in the concrete.

Later I'd call Ariel and we'd talk about something else until we forgot this moment. We'd talk about whether the person Ariel was dating wanted to move in too quickly and where we wanted to go camping next weekend, and I wouldn't hold our earlier interaction against her. I remember how tired she is, how much she's read, how eagerly she wants to support antioppressive politics. This is inside of my "we," too—that Ariel feels the need to defend herself and others in ways that I don't. I understand that the use of "fascist" is one exhausted way of turning the page, of using old information to explain new. It's just not one I can tolerate now.

One thing to know about Lara is that she can make anyone feel welcome. People tell her their secrets and their best anecdotes because she listens very carefully and notices immediately when something is important to you. She follows up with questions that show she remembers what you care about, and she suggests relationships and other stories you might enjoy. Lara knows I have been looking at Nazi history, and she tells me about a German friend of hers. He usually refrains from telling her much about his family, she tells me, but one day he mentioned casually that he found a knife with a Nazi insignia in his grandparents' attic. He told her then that his grandfather was in what the family referred to as "the German Marines."

"But he wouldn't say Nazi," Lara says. "I asked him if it was a swastika on the knife and he wouldn't say."

"How could he miss a swastika?" I ask her. It seems impossible to us both, a symbol you can't unsee.

During the first half of the 20th century both the fasces and the swastika (each symbol having its own unique ancient religious and mythological associations) became heavily identified with the authoritarian/fascist political movements of Adolf Hitler and Benito Mussolini. During this period the swastika became deeply stigmatized, but the fasces did not undergo a similar process.[10]

While both the swastika and the fasces had histories and usage prior to the way the Nazis used them, the swastika constricts after World War II, and the fasces widens to hold more. I imagine that this is why "fascist," too, stays open. The visual symbol of the swastika cannot be as easily translated into a different form, cannot evolve as quickly as language. But words shapeshift and travel with usage. With this malleability, derivations of *fasces* are both suspect and usable, up for grabs.

I'm not the first to notice how we use "fascist," but I am cautious in listening to others on this topic, knowing how quickly it inflames. In *The Temptation of Innocence*, the French philosopher Pascal Bruckner questions the contemporary use of "fascism," saying the word "means anything that opposes or challenges an individual's inclination, anything that restricts his whims. So then, who is not affected, who does not suffer and have a right to complain?"[11] Bruckner's book opposes the stance of the victim, which he argues is used widely today to justify carelessness and oppression.

I want to give a disclaimer here, because Bruckner also makes some wildly irresponsible arguments about gender and privilege. Many people I know would place Bruckner on the "bad" side of intellectual discourse given these issues, similar to how they do with Sarah Schulman. But that's what happens when I research in the way that I want to—I want to include Bruckner in my thinking, to include the deliberations of someone who has considered this victim stance, even if not all his ideas are sound. Without completely trusting Bruckner's reasoning, I also do not wish to throw him out. Again, I find myself loyal to speech that sometimes gets it wrong. I don't justify all of Bruckner's arguments. But I never expect an immaculate mind.

FASCIST. The word blares in white spray paint along the highway median, then echoes on my retina and spreads across the buckled concrete on my way home. I co-own a house in East Oakland, an area of the city that is gentrifying more slowly than other parts, or where the forces of gentrification have not fully peaked. Black Oakland has not been as gentrified here, and the storefronts advocating Black Power scatter across Foothill Boulevard with its Black churches, street taco stands, and carts selling cones of *frutas*.

My partner is driving us home when sirens blare and OPD cars pull across to block the street, and both of us take out our phones to record what might be happening, because we are white people trained to keep an eye out for police violence against our Black neighbors. In meetings we have been told this is one way that we can support the struggle against racist policing. If we are going to live here—and, with our presence, bring up prices, potentially threatening the integrity of the community that already exists in this place—we might at least intercept this form of repression.

I zoom in on my phone camera and try to catch what's happening behind one officer's back. From this angle I capture only officers speaking to one another, and almost nothing of the people they are in the process of arresting. Once the police cars clear and we are ushered forward, my partner slows the car by the clutch of people on the side of the road and stretches across me to get a better look out the window.

"It's not our business," I hiss at him, my hand tight on his thigh. But we are both already seeing something we have seen too many times: two Black men with their hands up and chests against the police car. I look away because I don't want to spectate. The victims of state oppression in this neighborhood do not usually look like me, and so if I stare at them, I am an onlooker, not a part. I am not from here or from this. The story is not mine to take or take shelter inside. This time, from our car, it feels like my looking is too much about my own education, and I don't want my own education to take place on the backs of someone else's trauma.

"Let them be," I say to my partner. He turns the wheel and his head together, to the left, away from me and away from the sidewalk. Our car jerks suddenly down and up again, but neither of us react. We are used to the streets here being uneven, to the city lagging always in fixing potholes and fissures. It is not easy to drive in East Oakland. It is even more difficult to bike, the way we used to get around when we lived in Berkeley, which has far-better paved streets. It's not easy because there is no way to get from the 580 to High Street without falling into a deep jagged hole in the pavement or swerving entirely into the oncoming lane. Even on the highway. Just before the exit for Fruitvale Avenue the concrete dips and you are plummeted momentarily into a crater. I know the hole is there, but it seems to pull me toward it. I never see it coming soon enough to turn, and I curse it every time I fall in.

The Latin "fascinare" has three meanings: 1. Deceive, to hallucinate, obfuscate. / 2. Attract irresistibly / 3. Make evil eye.[12]

As I loop through *fascist*, I keep looping back through *fascinare*, through the way this root explains the workings of the evil eye. I look for where I can find it in my own ancestral tradition, and for this I need to look to Yiddish, where many mystical Eastern European folk wisdoms are stored. I don't understand much Yiddish but can grasp the meaning of some phrases through gestures and context. Until recently, one of these phrases was "*keinahora*," a Yiddish derivate of the Hebrew "*kein ayin ha'rah*," meaning: "may there be no evil eye." I heard my grandfather mutter this under his breath during a family conversation about what to do in the case of my parents' death. He murmured it, like clearing his throat, and no one seemed to react. It was the familiar unknown, like oxygen we knew theoretically was there but didn't need to investigate.

Until I do. Reading further I learn that "*kein ayin ha'rah*" derives from rabbinical discussions of how someone can bewitch or harm someone else by looking at them. If an eye looks hard at someone, it can take what is theirs. We say "*keinahora*" when something desirable or good is happening to us, so as to deflect potential eyes from it. In Ashkenazi tradition we are supposed to say, "what an ugly baby," when looking at a newborn, because a compliment might bring on a jealous gaze that wishes to curse. It's a nervous tendency, one that deflects admission of power, a related move to what we do when we call someone else a fascist. We duck, as if eternally on the verge of being hit.

Butler again: "Loss has made a tenuous 'we' of us all."[13] When we paint ourselves as victims, we are held together by loose threads and superstitions. If the evil eye or the source of power is always elsewhere, "we" are held together only by the shunning of strength, the insistence that we have none. "Compassion is an admirable inclination, but it weaves between mankind a sense of solidarity only in pain," writes Pascal Bruckner.[14] This gives us little room to move beyond the frail ties of pity.

At a neighborhood meeting to organize against police violence, the person next to me keeps muttering "fucking fascists," but when called on to comment will say nothing else.

I know the word *fascist* is often intended to create solidarity, to wrap together experiences of violence so that we can understand them as interdependent and intersectional. I am careful with the word not because I am looking to claim fascism for my own, or to say that the graves of my people are more important than those of another. I do not want to compete for pain. Instead, I am looking for how fascist orients us: how people in bodies like mine recycle stale roles in oppression when we obtain the right combination of fear and access to power. I call the roles "stale" because they are very old and because they are not actually any good to eat, digest, no good for us in the end. When I get a whiff of their staleness, I make contact with some other options for how to behave.

"Oppression does not make people better: oppression makes people oppressed," writes Joan Ringelheim. Ringelheim writes in the 1990s and is considered the founder of women's Holocaust studies, notably for her refusal to believe that genocide gives Jews an exclusive moral stance.

"There is no sense in fighting or even understanding oppression if we maintain that the values and practices of the oppressed are not only better than those of the oppressor but, in some objective sense, 'a model for humanity and the new society,'"[15] writes Ringelheim. Instead of glorifying my neighbors because they are more targeted by the police than I am, I want to tackle the present together, to learn more about the present time of one another's lives, to celebrate a birthday on the block or to make a plan for resource distribution during the next earthquake. Environmental disaster is one (convenient!) common enemy; a way we can turn our fears away from one another and toward a significant shared threat.

It's taken me time and work and thought to get here—the course of the writing you see here now, years of living in Oakland and Berlin and elsewhere, years of conversations with people in which I repeated old stories and only gradually began to break them down. Years of slowly realizing that I am secure enough to participate. Some of this learning had to happen with Jews, by reflecting on my own Jewishness. For a little while Ariel and I were both in a loosely organized group of white Jewish women and nonbinary people called "Burning Bush Collective," in which we met to process where race was coming up in our lives, read and educate ourselves with texts by Black leaders, and organize to offer our support for Black-led movements.

"Burning Bush" was yet another disoriented "we"—we shared some cultural history, though each of us experienced our Jewishness differently. We called it "Burning Bush" to play on the biblical story in which God appears to Moses as a burning bush, and as a light vagina joke on "bush." We spent hours processing how far to lean into this—we liked the joke for interfering in an otherwise extremely sincere environment, and everyone present that day did identify as possessing a "bush"—but how far did we want to lean into this sexed identification with gender? It wasn't unflawed for our politics, but we ended up letting it stay in the name of not being perfect, and in the name of not spending our whole meeting deliberating on our name when our intent was to support others.

It's funny and also cringey now when I look back at the over-processing navel-gazing meeting of a bunch of white Jews. But it's important to me in retelling this story to include the parts in which we caught ourselves over-mired in our own identities, realized we wouldn't ever get this right, and then moved on to the more important things: who was locking their bodies to the doors of the Oakland Police Department next weekend, and how much bail money we could raise. I want to show how self-involved we could be before and between, spinning our wheels, stuck in the mud.

I do not want to get stuck in "woman" or in "Jewish," even as I need a place to process that history, as I do here. Even as I process here, I do not want to lionize my own history to excuse my own implication in the forces that threaten people who have lived in Oakland much longer than I have. The oppression that my ancestors experienced elsewhere does not qualify me to escape anything, to treat anyone poorly, or to overlook where my body sits now, what it enacts as it walks or drives here in Oakland.

"No, I was born in Boston," I say, when Rick from two doors down asks if I grew up around here. He flips the hot dog on the grill with tongs and nods. "An East-coaster, huh?"

"Sort of," I say, "though my family hasn't been there for long." I want to say something about the alienation of gray New England shutters and assumed soft pastel Easters, about my family painting their house in bright orange and bringing smelly fishy food to public places. I want to say something about what it means to me to live in California, but I am not sure how, yet. I nod, and let my answer be partial. I think of Fred Moten, one of the minds I admire the most, and how often when Moten speaks he leaves open possibility. "What I want to believe—" he begins, before offering a theory, "it might not be true . . ." Or, "I'm asking questions as if I were making a statement," he says, when aware of potential contradictions.[16]

I want to believe, and it might not be true. A state in question. I come home from Europe to Oakland, and I sit down. I sit in my car or on the park bench or on my front porch, and I grow faint in the heat, with the sense that the connotation of my body keeps changing and I must speak precisely if I want to keep up. I have not escaped the phantom of my own people's genocide, and yet I know the peril of words that describe something as more static than I believe it to be. I try to clarify my relative safety and not assume that other people experience the same. There are places where it makes sense to touch into the immense grief of the murder of my ancestors, places like Burning Bush and potlucks full of white Jews talking over one another, trying to guide each other gradually toward a more precise politics. And there are also places and moments when it makes sense to only listen and await instruction.

I come home from Europe to Oakland and I interrogate "fascist" because it reminds me of how persistently I need to pay attention. I need to pay attention because where I am situated is always changing, and with it how to hold my own story. What is changing in it, live? I try to write in a way that belies some of its liveness, some sense of continuous replacing. I remember Édouard Glissant, the Caribbean critic and thinker who wrote against linear origin stories because he believed these to be always regulated by structures of power, advocating instead for identity constructed in relation—and not only constructed in this way, but potentially more resistant to structural control when understood relationally as such.[17]

I remember Glissant and I think of "fascist" as a word with Latinate origins, yes, but origins that change over time. What Latin means and how we understand its cultural origins shift as time continues and historical analyses continue to unfold. When I study "fascist," I see it fumble from one situation to the next like someone thrown by uneven ground, stumbling and then picking themselves up, looking one way and then other, patting themselves and checking that they are intact. Today, this word might be useful or even necessary for someone else's mouth to use, but in my white Jewish mouth, "fascist" flattens. It is a ghost that scares away the possibility of change.

"To ask for recognition, or to offer it, is precisely not to ask for recognition for what one already is. It is to solicit a becoming, to instigate a transformation, to petition the future always in relation to the Other,"[18] Butler writes. I bring up the history of my people to ask for a future. This is less solid than name-calling, more ghostly, because it allows for echoes without pinning us to a certain grave. We have the tendency to claim that power dynamics are static because we don't want to notice that which is more frightening. It is more frightening to have to do something, to have to figure out how to respond, newly, based on present-time information. It would be much easier on my brain to get to apply past patterns to present reality. But a different response is required of me now.

The response required is so intricate, it is impossible to deliver it immaculately. To aim for immaculate is precisely beside the point. I am implicated, I am always sick, my mind is never going to be clean. I recall Alexandros Papadopoulos, the artist who reenacted his homophobic neo-Nazi attack. "The point here is to fight back by inventing new languages of joy, new canons of beauty, and ultimately new ideals of professional, moral and social success."

As I return to Oakland, I try to replace the need for immaculate with the fight for a new language, a grimy, encrusted tongue. There are not easy words for this language. It is a mixture of thinking and listening and feeling and acting, a speech in the process of making itself. A place where the canon has not been set up. You see me now: I stop, start again. I am not sure how to word it. I am a person who finds my homes in language, and the language shifts under me now. I try to let my words reflect this.

From the comfort of my own living room, I write to Emil. It's been a few months since I saw him, and I am ready to bring up again something I think he's probably forgotten.

"I read more about the Mosley sex tape," I text him. I add a shrugging emoji. "Not convinced."

"Of what?" He texts right back, though it is late at night in Denmark.

"I don't think that's what makes a fascist."

"Oh, whatever," he texts, "you probably liked it."

"Liked what?"

"His role-play. You love submission."

I wonder if he's right to pin me there. If that's why I am so quick to forgive, to mold myself around what Mosley thinks is OK. Sub where I started; lowering myself and wanting to be treated as beneath. But it doesn't satisfy all parts of me, especially now that I see how many more options there could be.

"I don't think I'm just a sub," I text back, "I'm switchy." The chameleon whose desires depend on the scene in which she finds herself or the partner with whom she is paired.

"You have to try more before you know," Emil texts. He has told me how he's begun to, probing the edges of being a Dom and beyond, trying restraints on himself as well as others, exploring the limits of his pain tolerance. He has sent me links to play parties and dungeons I could check out in Oakland. I sit at my desk and twist both of my ankles behind the legs of my stool. It's a move I've been doing for a while now, pinning my own body to a chair. Do I want to go somewhere where someone else does it first?

Oh My Love

Mostly I seek the promiscuous feeling of being alive.
—Lisa Robertson[1]

I watch an older white man flog a younger Black woman, and I try not to get in the way. We are at a party intended for this purpose, in a room intended for this purpose, the walls lined with tools I don't understand and won't approach unless someone wants to explain them to me.

The woman is taller than the man, and more muscular. Before they began their scene, I watched her duck her head to meet the dungeon master's eyes and tell him it would be her first time under a flogger. He asked her several questions, none of which I could hear from a few feet away, but she answered softly, already docile, and he seemed satisfied.

Now he arranges her along the wall where she spreads her legs and reaches up to grip the large metal handles. She stretches her limbs against the wooden planks, turns one cheek to the wall and nods at him to begin.

The *whap* sound of the flogger on her back is rhythmic, lulling. The gentle whir through the air and then the landing of leather on flesh, the marks appearing quickly in even maroon stripes. Later I'll tell a friend, "The guy clearly knew what he was doing," an assessment I make mostly based on his pace and his tranquility, almost blankness, his arms and torso sturdy and certain with a deep concentration on the task at hand. The woman breaths out faintly.

I am at the club to experiment, to find what additional kinks linger in me. Thus far I know I like to watch, though I check first for the rules, whether it is okay to sit on one side of the bondage room, whether it is okay with these two people that I watch. I asked before I sat, and they both nodded dismissively, as if my presence were just another apparatus in the room among the whips and irons. My exact wording is not important for this part as long as I get their consent. A new way I'm relating to speech.

I sit and mold myself into a corner bench built into the wall. I am covert but still here. I watch, and my body begins to relax with the cadence of the flogger. My back rests against the wood, my bare thighs sticking to the leather upholstery where my underwear ends. This underwear isn't kinky enough—no straps or metal buckles, just the bright blue lacy pair I keep for special occasions because I like how it fits—and probably signals me as an amateur here. But what I want is to look, and my underwear won't determine how well I pull that off.

The woman against the wall closes her eyes and straightens. The flogging seems to go on forever, his patience and her receptivity not tied to any achievement but her willingness to stand. Even though I know that she has consented, a busybody in me begins to worry for her, a concern that was not requested of me and is categorically not my business. It is the movies surfacing in my head, the descriptions of slave punishment I read in Toni Morrison and Zora Neale Hurston, the scenes of a woman enslaved being beaten by her master. Before I can catch myself, I am fixating on her brown skin and his paleness.

I try to talk myself away from dwelling on the racialized dynamics. It's interference. It is not up to me to decide how the scene feels to those who are a part of it. I've engaged with partners in ways that other people deemed dangerous or abusive, and I've known they weren't dangerous for me. I think it's OK for me to wonder what it means to this woman to be beaten in this way, but it's not for me to determine. The two of them are immersed, and it is not my scene to disturb.

"Sorry," I whisper under my breath, for no one to hear. The word gyrates through the overapologizing gendered dynamics I know, the white lady freezing I know, trying to find its way back to this room. When can an apology be a kink, too? I think of my most recent apologies, one to my old friend Michael. We were out of touch for years until I saw a thin man on the street in Oakland with gray-blond hair pushed back high over his forehead and was reminded of Michael when the wind pushed his hair into his face at the *kanal*.

I considered for a while before I pulled out my phone and texted Michael an apology. I guessed that was probably what would hook him, and I decided I wanted to use that route in.

"Hi Michael, so sorry I've been out of touch," it began, "it's been a busy time." I pulled power over into my court, pretending he had been trying to get in contact but unable to reach me.

"How are you? I know politics have been bad over there this year. Sorry!" That second apology I didn't intend, and only noticed it after I sent. I restrained myself from writing more to explain it. I put down the phone.

"Do not worry!" He responded the next day. Always not soon enough, but I excused him the nine-hour time difference. I read the text over again and waited while the app indicated that he was typing. "We are doing well." My chest went tight. I waited.

Quickly a picture arrived of him with his arm around a woman in the snow. In the picture, she held a Christmas wreath regally in front of her abdomen. "My girlfriend. We hope to have a baby soon," he texted. ":)" The old-school smiley face seemed exactly right for the traditional happy ending he was conveying.

It wasn't what I'd hoped for, but what had I hoped for, exactly? I had wanted that zing I felt when Michael was absorbed in looking at me. His gaze and his interest disturbed my interior enough to arise and show itself. He brought something out in me that wouldn't have come out on its own, without the magnet of someone else's desire. What I wanted from him wasn't boundaries or polite deflection. But I hadn't been in touch with him sufficiently to know anything about his life, or what shaped our communication from his end. Time moved on from the moment in which I met him, and all we were left with was the inherently unwieldy continuing future.

"Oh, sorry to bother you. You must be busy!" I scrambled to text. "Wishing you all the best." I set the phone face down on my dining room table and tucked my fingers into fists to keep myself from picking it up again. I'd grown to love that twitchy feeling in my hands.

I am here in the kink club watching because kink gives contour to moments like these. I am here at the play party because I want to study the edge, to understand whether I've got some Freudian repetition compulsion or something more specific. Moments where I set myself up for punishment and wonder why I do it—or wonder less now. I apologize to Michael both because I'm used to it, and because I am into it, manipulating someone under known conditions to get what I want.

"More than a cumulative effect of traumatic and/or insidious power relations, the body in S&M ritual becomes a means of addressing history in an idiom of pleasure," writes theorist Elizabeth Freeman.[2] Freeman analyzes S/M as an "erotic time machine" that allows participants to meet oppressive histories on their own terms, and not exclusively via the agony proscribed.[3] In the club, the couple in the scene ignores my presence once they've agreed I will be a voyeur. They are only involved in what they are making together, closed off from the sounds of other people having sex and from the opinions of people like me. They seem out of time, un-interruptible.

Freeman calls this "the deviant pause," a perverted divergence from "the agony proscribed." I do not know if these two people experience this pause, and so I can only speak to how I experience it. I am not trying to harm myself when I reenact oppressions; I am taking the time machine back to a moment that I visit fleetingly. Freeman writes, "the deviant pause . . . adds a codicil of pleasure to a legacy of suffering."[4] A "codicil" is a supplement to a will that modifies or amends it. Oppression or racialization or trauma has been handed down as an inheritance. I visit and push back. The pair in front of me is un-interruptible also because of the codicil. Their play together modifies the labels that I am using to understand them. Their scene interrupts, but not only to pause—to register additional data. This new data acknowledges the preexisting inheritance (heritage, tradition, distribution of wealth) and reroutes the direction of this legacy with another possible course.

In my present, I engage with sources like Freeman's that are centered on Blackness and kink, not centered on me or my body. I engage with these sources because I want to learn, but I also want to be redirected, to be told what I don't know, and what I can't. Another of these texts that I hold closely is Margot Weiss's book *Techniques of Pleasure: BDSM and the Circuits of Sexuality*, in which Weiss uses ethnographic research in the San Francisco Bay Area's BDSM community to describe how kink practices sometimes pretend to be separate from social conditions. In the opening of the book, Weiss describes a contemporary "slave auction" in which submissives are auctioned off to raise money for charity. She notes palpable discomfort in the audience members when an African American female "slave" is displayed for the crowd to bid on. Weiss does not categorically shun these practices. In an interview, Weiss notes the subtle and nonbinary ways that they are enveloped in racial history: "it's not that charity slave auctions are simply terrible, politically suspect and clearly wrong, nor is it that they're transgressive and that they open up new radical possibilities."[5]

Weiss argues that kink is entangled with and contaminated by the very conditions that give it power. Kink doesn't fix the problems of racialization. Race and other power dynamics are what makes kink hot for people. "SM performance," Weiss writes, "is not a repetition of social power; it carries and produces the complexities of social relationships, relationships shot through with contradictions unresolved—indeed, erotically and politically powerful precisely because they remain in tension."[6] Kink is not outside of what else exists socially, as I appreciate from my own engagement with anti-Semitic tropes. The contradictions are included, tense as they may be. The tension may be what matters most.

Kink participants sometimes say that they can play nonviolently with treacherous topics—say, an incest scene—because they are working *only* in the realm of imagination. Weiss disagrees with this conviction. She reminds us that role-play is not exclusively imaginary, but meaningful because it takes place inside reproduced racial and gender norms and their standard power dynamics. An erotic BDSM scene depends on the fact that it has connotations outside of BDSM play.

In Weiss's setup, I lower myself in front of a man because I believe that I am already socially lowered, and I want to cavort with the circumstances that exist. Or, I am a white woman watching a white man flog a Black woman, and I am inserting my own white lady savior programming into the dynamic. Having worked for many years in the nonprofit industry serving primarily BIPOC communities as a representative of mostly white, female staff, I am encoded with the racist programming that I have some capacity to save or rescue Black and Brown people from oppression. I have learned enough now to disabuse myself of this notion, and yet the notion still flickers up when I witness racialized dynamics. The racism has not died back entirely in me, but one thing I can do is notice what roles it assigns me and potentially destabilize them.

To play with "known conditions" here means something different than it means with Michael. My whiteness offers me many appointed positions. I could be the schoolteacher making sure punishment is meted out. I could be the white wife watching the master beat a slave from the plantation house window. These are not roles I desire, even as I slip back against the leather and check to make sure. I do not want these roles, but they are part of my indoctrination. I hope to contaminate or recontaminate them by investing them with the context of role-play.

The scene receives new layers as I meet it, as I take up space in the scene. No matter how vetted the participants, no matter how private the club. My own conventions and prejudices interact with the situation, even if I do not speak them aloud. I recall Dan Savage reminding a submissive that they are the one in control, "regardless of how things might appear to a casual or misinformed observer."[7] I am the misinformed here, the misaligned protector who can't presume what others need. I remember scholar Saidiya Hartman warning of the "difficulty and slipperiness of empathy" when overidentification with another obliterates that other person's divergence from the empathic viewer.[8] The twinge of empathy: a viewer like me wishes to behave ethically but in so doing perpetuates violence by projecting.

"Often this speech about the 'other' annihilates, erases," writes bell hooks. "No need to hear your voice when I can talk about you better than you can speak about yourself. No need to hear your voice. Only tell me about your pain. I want to know your story. And then I will tell it back to you in a new way. I am still author, authority."[9] And I am the author here, in this book. I maintain authority over what is being described. From this position, I want to recognize that I have habitually attempted hooks's erasure. Only once I recognize this can I turn back and try again, destabilizing the programming that encourages me to erase. If I can apprehend my white lady roles as play or costume, then I have not earned them, and they are not automatic.

The more I write, the more the selves I have inhabited appear gauzy, easily ripped apart. I write and edit the story of a person I am no longer, reflecting on what she slowly learned. Even in constructing a narrative, it falters and flips, nonlinear in its arc.

In the club, I turn toward what remains unauthored. I don't know what the participants bring to the scene I am watching, what it means to them. I can choose to interfere as little as possible, to inhabit a role that asserts I am on the outside of their exchange. I watch, and the scene interrupts my own thinking. The woman standing along the wall raises one hand. The man pauses and steps closer to her. She speaks quietly over one shoulder and gestures to him that she wants more on her thighs.

"Like this," I can just hear her murmur, one hand patting above the backs of her knees. The man bows to the woman and steps back into his place. I don't know what she needs, but he may.

What if the utmost ease is in permission to decenter myself? This might be precisely my point, my own infinite unsettling. I'm not sure yet where I fit in the kink club, which room I belong in most. When I first entered the club through the front door, a person with a moustache in a princess costume took my money, smiling. "The slave will give you your wristband," they said. They pointed to the corner, where another person kneeled inside a cage. A metal chain around their neck attached them to a hook on the wall and restricted their movement. I approached the cage. "My wristband?"

The slave bowed deeply and reached their hands out between the bars of their cage to affix a strand of pink plastic around my forearm. I have been in this position before, of someone attaching something to my wrist as an indicator of entry. In other clubs, it hasn't been all that different—someone was expected to serve me and not bother me otherwise. But here that character was being performed.

"Thank you," I said. I felt markedly moved by the slave's exaggeration of service. They lowered their chin and returned to a crouch. It seemed maybe that they were not supposed to speak. Their abjection was familiar if exaggerated, a hyperreal version of so many service jobs, a person approaching a boot as a shoeshine, or carrying food to a restaurant table. This was always already happening. As the theorist Julia Kristeva writes, "abjection acknowledges [the subject] to be in perpetual danger."[10]

Intentional, chosen abjection acknowledges a level of danger we can't defeat. We can't defeat it, but we are still not defeated either, because we keep going, living and acting even within its inescapable frame. I think of the writer and performer Johanna Hedva, who I once heard describe their political stance with the phrase: "we are going to lose."[11] Hedva has worked for years in activist and organizing communities. "If our enemy is capitalism," Hedva shrugged and repeated, "we are going to lose." They clarified that this attitude does not mean giving up our fight for what we believe in. No: this attitude situates itself conscientiously from abjection, from perpetual danger, generations of injury, oppression, and suppression of labor power. If we are going to lose, Hedva implies, burnout is less likely because we are not fighting on the condition that we will win. If we are going to lose, we have nothing to prove, and every single tool to try.

If no one is going to win, we can organize more horizontally. If no one can save anyone, we can offer mutual aid with the generosity made possible by giving without goals. If my chronic illness means I can't labor as is expected, I can invent other ways to work. If my body is never going to be completely right with whiteness, I can stop wasting energy there.

The slave wrapping wristbands playacts our existing reality. We are perpetually in danger of domination by others, some of us more than others, depending on our positions of oppression and privilege. The slave is white or white-passing, and so maybe for them it feels safe enough to play what they are playing, to be in that cage. I don't know, I'm not them. But I was around them, touched by their genuflection in my presence, maybe also made productively uncomfortable with the intensity of their servitude. It points at the places someone is already serving me that I haven't been willing to acknowledge: the Lyft ride I took to the club, the hands that dropped a package on my doorstop last week. I was *fascinated* by the slave: my attention was drawn and held. My fascination with kink gives me more capacity to look. To note the labors my privilege has sheltered me from having to see.

Chris Kraus's 2016 film *Die Blumen von gestern* (Bloom of Yesterday) is the closest thing I've seen to a Holocaust romantic comedy. Zazie, one of our main characters, is the granddaughter of a woman killed by Nazis. She is having some problems with repetition compulsions. When she meets the character Totila, grandson of an infamous Nazi war criminal, she complains about how attracted she is to him. Zazie, who often speaks in manic spurts, tells Totila that she has "certain visions" of him, meaning that she pictures him naked.[12]

"It's psychologically understandable," she says. She brings up the theory that the children of victims often want to sleep with the children of perpetrators "to force a reconciliation with their own superego."[13] Totila is very uncomfortable. A cartoonishly uptight and humorless Holocaust researcher, he insists that if the two of them are to talk about their grandparents, he and Zazie do so "seriously." For him, to be serious means to operate through archival information, and not involving their own physicality. Zazie argues that they must address trauma interpersonally: "We're people. People kill people. People love people." As Zazie grows increasingly agitated, Totila is forced to concede that he, too, has fantasies of seeing her—he can barely spit out the words—"naked?" Zazie finishes his sentence.

"Finally," she says, "a completely normal reaction from you." There's relief in the scene, even though Totila is still stiff, holding a pen aloft above the restaurant table, shifting papers around in the binders of research that he's brought to discuss.

The relationship between these two remains strained throughout the film, even as it resolves somewhat toward a romance. The film is billed as a comedy, though critics have complained[14] of its "uneven tone" and how it jerks between slapstick and drama. But this is where the film does its best work—this twitchy tonal jerking is the most real thing it can portray. It is addressing the cumbersome experience of not being able to grasp someone else fully, but still trying to interact.

"Think of experiences of moving along a street with another. It is not going smoothly; you keep bumping into each other. You might experience the other person as being out of time; as being too slow or too fast, as being awkward or clumsy," writes theorist Sara Ahmed in *Living a Feminist Life*. "Or we might turn toward each other in frustration, as we bump into each other yet again." Totila and Zazie do not get along easily. They are constantly activating unexpected feelings in one another. "Or you might experience yourself as being clumsy," Ahmed continues, "as the one who is too slow, or too fast, whose job it is to pick up the pieces of a shattered intimacy. Bumping into each other is a sign that we have not resolved our differences."[15]

Zazie points at this bumping again and again. She only succeeds in wrangling Totila into a frank conversation when she shocks him by screaming and pouring a can of red paint over her head, a clunky overdramatization of the mass murder of her ancestors. Only then, with kitsch and the threat of toxic substances in the paint, do the two of them begin to move clumsily toward an intimacy. I am taken with the red paint, not just because of the bloody vision it provides, but also because of how it implies the fluid. Beneath the paint, Zazie is a body with its own sticky fluids that leach from pores and membranes. The paint goes in where other things could—and do—come out.

Maybe in fluids we can unfasten ourselves from what history has told us we are, or what history has told us we deserve. For Zazie and Totila the fluids are literal, literalizing, and for some of us sex is this way too, involving an exchange of fluids. Not for all. Like the flogging scene I watch, much sex involves firm sheaths of gloves, ropes, purposeful untouching. In these cases, the role itself is the fluid, circuiting over, in and out, attempts at participation. We slide across one another where our experiences are not shared.

In the fluid it is harder to be good, or to prove one's goodness. I remember Georges Bataille, a granddaddy of sorts of the mystical erotic. Bataille famously declared that literature was never innocent, and in fact was always guilty and should take a stand as such, defining itself as unlike action, differentiated from it by its inability to clear itself of blame.[16] If I love the paint pouring over Zazie, noxious, clumsy, can I admit to loving these qualities in story, too? It's less an admission than a confession, a submission. I tried to be good, but gave in.

Once the flogging scene is over, I sit for a while in my corner against the wall. I need to try something, but I can't get myself interested in dominating someone else, so I lie down on a padded bondage table and ask my partner to try ropes. He says he would love to, but when he picks up his first rope, he droops it across my collarbone, over my shoulder, and then pauses, hesitant. He has never done it before.

"Is that okay?" He asks. I am a little annoyed by the question, wanting him already to charge forward. "It's a start," I say. "Let's ask for help."

The couple next to us is friendly and demonstrates to my partner how and where to make knots. I am absorbed by the intricacies of their knowledge of restraints, the details of Shibari knotting and the friction now of the rope on my skin. I am interested but not turned on, exactly, or maybe it's a turn on that I don't know how to feel for yet. One of Papadopoulos's new joys that I am inventing my way toward. What I do feel is the possibility of rest, an acceptance of the fumbling that happens as I feel my limbs posed by someone else's hands.

"You have to let your wrists go," my partner whispers into my ear. I consciously soften my hands, wrists, and forearms so that he can loop the rope between them and attach them to the knots he's now made at my lower back.

I roll from side to side on the table, testing, then tense up slightly when I feel as though I might fall off one side.

"It's OK," my partner says, "I'm holding on." I cannot see him, but I can feel the constriction and pressure. I reach the edge of the table and he tugs me back.

"Clumsiness might provide us with a queer ethics. Such an ethics attends to the bumpiness of living with difference," Ahmed writes.[17] My partner and I are both doing something we have not done before, and, queerly, in one sense, there's no expectation of how this experiment will end.

My partner asks me if I want to sit up. I try, but it's impossible with my hands and feet tied, and I ask him to pull me upright. I am not sure how exactly he will do this, and we both request instruction. The couple next to us gathers behind me with my partner, and I feel the strong tug backward, multiple people grabbing at the system of knots holding my pose. I breathe out and they pull me harder, so that I begin to rise off the table. My chest juts forward, my breasts exposed and exaggerated by the loops of rope. I've never displayed this part of my body exactly like this. I relax into the force behind me, and I feel graceful for one moment, poised like a mermaid emerging from water.

Suddenly something goes slack behind me, and I slump to one side of the table, one arm twisted awkwardly under my hip. I laugh, muffled, my mouth smushed. I think briefly of a time in my future when I may be too aged or disabled to pick up my own limbs, and hope there will be laughter then, too.

"You okay?" My partner asks.

"Totally," I mutter. He laughs, then, too, and unties me. We are relieved, disoriented by this first time trying something on, and it is no major failure to have fallen partway. It's not that different in my body from the feeling I have after penetrative sex, when all my muscles have gone limp and a piece of someone or something else is still inside me. It is similar because I feel both the pleasantness and the threat of intrusion. I can tolerate these together without one blocking the other out.

"All sexuality is destructive," writes Anna Mollow, "not in the sense of effecting literal death, but in the threat it poses to the integrity of the subject and thus to the social order."[18] Here Mollow discusses how sex ruptures the self, interconnects our individualities, and make us less able to function as boundaried individuals in a social world that demands these boundaries so that we can exchange commodities, conversation, and so on. By having sex, Mollow implies, we momentarily jeopardize our capacity to function individually. It reminds me again of crip-ness, sickness, and how being chronically ill has demanded I let others in, both painfully and fruitfully challenging my individuality. Instead of a fortress, I build a moat intended for others who are willing to swim across. The moat is its own social order. Sex is its own social ordering, in which membranes are open to things like clumsiness, bacteria, falling, and faltering emotions. Momentarily, we reside in a more porous, vulnerable interhuman field.

In a kink scene, aftercare is built into the process, so that when the ropes don't work out perfectly and there's a burn on my bicep when my partner undoes the knots, the couple next to us reminds us to sit together by the bar downstairs and debrief. What worked, what didn't work, what would we like to try differently next time? My partner apologizes too much. "I'm such an idiot," he says, and I put my hand over his mouth.

"No," I say, "that's not what we're doing right now." He doesn't need to lower himself to care right now, or to be cared for by me. His intelligence or value to me isn't determined by whether he held a firm hand on the ropes. We are both allowed to be here as we play, unsettled and slipping. My partner sticks his tongue out and licks between two of my fingers that are covering his mouth, teasing.

"Fine," I say. I move my hand from his mouth and realize on the way that maybe I liked that, the slick prod of saliva between my knuckles. Something subtle to revisit.

I used to think pleasure took place in a void-space where I needed to assimilate to certain prevailing modes and their standards and then get everything right, or I'd be dumped. Here I've gotten dumped off a table, almost, and we can laugh about it. What's different now from when I first began to consider Nazi kink is a more buoyant sense of humor, a humor that assumes we are going to lose, as Hedva teaches me, because we are already operating in the territory of the purposefully weird, fringe. My body is less concerned now with being correct on one particular front, knowing there are endless other benchmarks and touchstones to visit—what pleasure means, what others like, what might surprise me as meaningful or hot. Here I am now in the murky sphere of touch, rubbing my middle finger and ring finger together, observing an unexpectedly interesting wetness. More interest, more places to look. There's so much more to gain when we are going to lose.

In the same bell hooks essay in which hooks condemns authorial erasure of the "other," she presents an alternative, a relationship to marginality in which the margin is the access point to wholeness.

"I was not speaking of a marginality one wishes to lose, to give up, or surrender as part of moving into the center, but rather as a site one stays in, clings to even, because it nourishes one's capacity to resist," hooks writes. "It offers the possibility of radical perspectives from which to see and create, to imagine alternatives, new worlds."[19] The margin should not surrender to the established center of power, but nurture that which makes it marginal.

Thankfully, *Die Blumen von gestern* doesn't have a proper romantic comedy ending. The descendants of the doomed do not fall into everlasting love that instantly resolves their inherited trauma. The end of the film finds Zazie partnered with a woman and mother to a child whose gender other characters in the film struggle to read. Zazie has interrupted her self-reported pattern of dating German men along with a patterned heteronormative happy ending, and desire to categorize with gender. Zazie and Totila bump into each other in the perfume section of a New York department store, surrounded by unsexy bright lighting, both out of the places and times we knew them in before. What's hopeful about this film is its unevenness, its refusal to level out.

"Our work should be not to 'cure' difference but to recognize the multiple subjectivities difference brings into being," writes Sarah E. Chinn.[20] Every time I read one of these theorists on touch or sex or kink, I try on what they say, not to make things more about me, but to begin from my own body instead of requiring others do that labor.

"The power of a politically conscious, socially ethical hope is to readjust the balance among the senses," Chinn writes, "rework the relationship between body and consciousness, and reforge the links shattered by fear of difference." I hope I can reforge, wrapping words around myself until I am held differently. Held so strangely, maybe, that there is less to fear.

Fascias, meaning "bandages." I was held together.

What kind of cure does fascination offer? A bandage, a wrap. Fascination is a bind, a predicament I never fully find my way out of, but also a bind as in a union. Fascination takes care of me in discomfort and makes me stronger for it as it binds, as we are bound up together.

Fasciantur: they were bandaged.

And what cure is best left only to others? A bandage is honest about bumpiness, rather than letting systems of privilege persuade me that the surface is smooth.

Fasci bandages back. It constructs a new surface showing injury is inside.

Downstairs from where I watch the flogging, there is a couple having sex in a corner covered in pillows. Nothing is particularly kinky about the scene, except for the fact that other people are in the room with the couple, too. This happens sometimes—swingers or exhibitionists overlapping with kinksters at the same party. It's not always a match, erotically, but usually accepted as live and let live. Or live and let watch. This couple is in the missionary position, and from my seat across the room I can see the man's bare back and butt and his pants around his ankles, the ribbing of his white crew socks.

"Oh my love!" The woman shouts. It is quiet in the room otherwise. Each time the man drives into the woman she yells the same phrase loudly: "oh my love!" Again and again, so plainly affectionate. They are not the first words I would expect to be produced by sex at a play party. I think because they feel so centered on the private love between two.

"Oh my love." His small white butt squeezing. Back. Forward. "My love."

"The equivalence between the beloved and the world is confirmed by sex," writes John Berger.[21] Sex with another body can confirm one's sociality, one's nonisolation. "To make love with the beloved is, subjectively, to possess and be possessed by the world." In the dark room the beloved is named, the outside is welcomed, the primary kink the desire to bring it all in. "Death of course is within it," Berger continues. "This provokes the imagination to its very depths." The depths, the pits, the death of millions. They've provoked me toward imagination, toward a realm where identity is always opaque and evolving in context.

"Oh! My! Love!" The woman does not seem shy, and I hope she wants us to be looking at her. I peer toward them, and I can make out a tussle of hair to one side of her head, and one scabby knee. I touch my own hair without thinking, and then I notice that my partner touches my hair, too.

"You good?" He whispers. I barely nod. He rubs a circle with his thumb just under my right ear. I think he is trying to kiss me, but he realizes soon enough that I am occupied watching the thrusting couple. He moves his face a bit further from mine and turns his head, so we are both looking in their direction. "Do you like that?" he asks.

"Um, I think so," I mumble back. I bring my cheek to his so I can feel the roughness of his beard bristling against the edge of my mouth. We watch the couple together, and I feel the coarse friction of his face against mine, one of the first things I ever loved about touching him. He doesn't push me to say more. We breathe together and lean back against some velvety pillows. He lets me watch and rub my jaw against his. It's a friction that has made it possible for me to love him, because it's one he never attempts to fully resolve. If I don't have a full answer for him, he doesn't force me.

In her discussions of totalitarianism, Arendt states that power is only gener-ated relationally, that totalitarianism functions by taking away people's capacity to interact with one another. She emphasizes that it is relationships that con-stitute the free political person, insisting: "Politics arises in what lies *between men* and is established as relationships"[22] (emphasis in original), and, later: "Wherever people come together, the world thrusts itself between them, and it is in this in-between space that all human affairs are conducted."[23] There's a sexual aggression to "thrust," an interactive quality that continually represents itself and refuses to be erased. I doubt I'll ever be fully free of the internalized fatphobia, racisms, and classism that shapes the bodies I desire and desire to be, but when these coercions appear I can understand them as thrust, an insertion that can also retreat. History thrusts in and carries with it menaces, patterns of oppression. The thrust moves through a shared space that contains both pleasure and pain, but this thrusting is more than a victim Olympics. It's Weiss's circuitry that integrates and reintegrates reality—not to be frozen or infiltrated by it, but to remain permeable in its presence.

I am not the first to enter this circuitry from a Jewish perspective, or to thrust toward something that is half fantasy, half nightmare. Nazi kink has been circling for generations, beginning with the first details of the Holocaust, though often cloaked in purported fact or reportage. Yehiel Dinur's 1961 novel *House of Dolls* famously detailed concentration camp brothels filled with Jewish women and claimed to be based on a true story, though historians conclusively agree that these kinds of brothels did not exist under the Third Reich. Still the book has been lauded as bravely truth-telling, perhaps because it fuses the worst we can imagine with what is historically true.

"Sadomasochism can also aim for a certain visceral fusion, a point of somatic contact between a single erotic body in the present tense and an experience coded as both public and past." That's Elizabeth Freeman again, leading me through a perversion of time. Jews were lost, murdered horrifically, and that loss cannot be forgotten. I will never see myself as a winner, but I get to engage creatively with this loss, which is a much more connective stance than I can imagine winning could be.

"For instance, a modern-day Jew might participate in a reenactment of some horror from the Holocaust, experiencing anti-Semitism in more scripted and overt ways than she does in her everyday life, testing her limits, feeling a corporeal, painful, and/or even pleasurable link to her ancestors," Freeman continues. "Here, the aim is not displacement, but a certain condensation of public and private, collective and individual subjectivities."[24]

When I read this section of the Freeman, it's the first time I see a contemporary scholar including a Jew alongside an analysis of slave play, in this case in Isaac Julien's film *The Attendant*. Freeman's text includes and encircles me in its "condensation" of the "collective and individual." While not trying to make Blackness and Jewishness the same, I hope to condense our kinks in the moments when that condensation can empower pleasure and suspend separateness. A potent political trespass. It's about feeling apart but also a part, unseparated even from what I can't know.

Fascinavi, I was fascinated.

Fascino, let them be fascinated.

Marianne Hirsch would call unseparation the work of postmemory; Berger would call it possession; and I settle it here, with the edging of kink, the fumbling a real body always includes. I settle here, in the circumstance of writing, inviting a reader to play along, to join me in explorations that open and open again, conclusions that do not conclude. Like the Matrix, once I see an identity as a shapeshifter, I can't unsee it. And not only that, but I am beckoned to keep revisiting, letting in. What Jewishness means, yes, what sex means, yes, but more than either of these: what it's like to encounter a self with a self, both equally in flux, both equally jumbled in our relationship to here.

Sarah Schulman asks: "Can we be happy with the uncomfortable awareness that other people are real?"[25] It's another way of putting a concern Arendt tackled much of her life: how to exercise free will without domination. How to care without imposing your own vision or needs upon someone else. How to sit on the marble bench at the sauna or the leather one at the sex club and relate to the scene, hold yourself ethically there.

There's no way to hold someone else without intruding in some way. Even so, I seek to hold and be held. Only admitting intrusion can I hold and be held.

Fast, I held on fast.

Fasten, I wrote in my native language but clutched at the Latin roots of the words.

Fastened, I was tied up. In knots I fell, in knots I felt partial, unfinished, material.

"Sexual deviants, now seen as creatures whose very minds had gone temporally awry, were unimaginable before the modern regime of 'progress,'" Freeman writes. This statement concludes her analysis of how some sexual practices came to be categorized as "foreplay" or "places to visit on the way to reproductive, genital heterosexuality, but not places to stay for long." Freeman argues that "perverts" refuse the imposition of capitalism's product-oriented "commodity-time" by repeating bodily behaviors that are "unproductive" in how much procreative sex they can achieve.[26] Though we may not breed new human bodies, I see a distinct and separate procreative motion in kinky sex and kinky imagination. We are generative; generating possible communalities, solidarities, even because we refuse to produce, progress, advance.

I'll never be able to prove that what I am doing here is right, exactly, even if I lean in hard to the antiproductive. Writing, like kink, doesn't get us off like we were told it should. Writing does not make something productive, even for the reader. Even if you've bought this book, you are not acting industriously—reading encourages you to sit or lie down and "waste" time. Literature is inefficient, futile in the sense of production, as Bataille describes. What makes *re*-writing vital, meaning the squirm between and away from what I already understand—is that it won't ever prove I'm correct. I can't make myself good by writing, but I can untether from some existing binds. I can destabilize my relationship to role and resolution.

I lose. I am going to lose. As a writer, I fail to find the resolute end. As a Jew, I fail at getting better or over, but this makes possible an unremittingly reproductive self, meaning there is always more information to be incorporated, more association to be had—and meaning, most, that I am alive, making life. What proves they haven't killed us all more than our own multiplying invention?

Fascination allows me to make because it humbles me. Unlike the austerity of victimhood, it takes me down to the fecund *humus*, the ground, the matter that makes. I go down not to erase my whiteness or privilege, but to erase the conceit that I know. When I can't know what I'll desire next or make next, I am animate, current. I go on, I spawn.

Acknowledgments

Some names and identifying details in this book have been changed to protect the innocent, the guilty, and the neither.

Thank you to Tess Weitzner for believing in this endeavor in the early shapes. Thank you to Sandra Korn, Dawn Hall, and everyone at Wayne State for imagining it into a home. Thank you to my peer reviewers, who alleged there was a *why*.

Thank you to the editors of publications in which prior versions and fragments of this work appeared: Claudia La Rocco and Gordon Faylor at Open Space, Robert Yerachmiel Sniderman at PRTCLS, Wallace Ludel at Triangle House, and Penina Eilberg-Schwartz at Ayin Press.

Thank you to my friends, without whom my thoughts are unwoven. Everyone's voice goes in the pot, but thank you especially to Ayden Leroux, the original reader, Maia Ipp, the parallel heart, and Max Neely-Cohen, who picked up a chapter mid-pandemic and made eyes at it when I needed a revival. Thank you to Justin Carder, co-gatherer, co-reader, co-Berger. To Liat Berdugo, for not being afraid to say "victim Olympics." To Kim Upstill for soul glitter food. To Katie Loncke for kinky body laughs. To Mónica Gomery for the queer rabbinical seal of approval. To NJCF and to the reading group, who sharpened my slate—especially Danielle Durchslag, Micah Salkind, Ellie Lobovits, and Avery Trufelman. To Alexis Almeida for the generous host at the finish line.

Thank you to Somos in Neukölln, where I started this inquiry and slept the sleep of the undead. Thank you to the Santa Fe Art Institute, where I almost finished. Thank you to David Shields for saying one hand was tied behind the back. Thank you to Marius, Berivan, Nils, Jonas, Diana, Sam, and Lasse, for finding me at my most open approach.

And boundlessly to Josh Finn, for loving every new kind/ness, pointing out the rough and loving it, too.

Notes

Epigraph

Eli Clare, *Exile and Pride* (Cambridge, MA: South End Press, 1999), 118.

Anne Carson, "Just for the Thrill: An Essay on the Differences between Women and Men," in *Plainwater: Essays and Poetry* (New York: Vintage Books, 1995), 232.

On Beasting

1 "No Body Talk," *Eden Village Camp*, November 4, 2020, edenvillagecamp.org/bodytalk/.

2 Philip Lopate, "Resistance to the Holocaust," in *Portrait of My Body* (New York: Anchor Books, 1996).

3 Susan Sontag, "Fascinating Fascism" *New York Review of Books*, February 6, 1975, www.nybooks.com/articles/1975/02/06/fascinating-fascism/.

4 Sontag, "Fascinating Fascism."

5 Elizabeth Alexander, "'Coming Out Blackened and Whole': Fragmentation and Reintegration in Audre Lorde's *Zami* and *The Cancer Journals*," *American Literary History* 6, no. 4 (1994): 695–715. *JSTOR*, www.jstor.org/stable/489961.

6 Hannah Arendt, *Crises of the Republic: Lying in Politics; Civil Disobedience; On Violence; Thoughts on Politics and Revolution* (New York: Harcourt Brace Jovanovich, 1972), 24.

7 William Shakespeare, *The Merchant of Venice* (New York: Simon and Schuster, 2010), 99.

8 Melissa Broder, *Milk Fed* (New York: Scribner, 2021), 199.

9 Daniel Maier-Katkin, "The Reception of Hannah Arendt's *Eichmann in Jerusalem* in the United States, 1963–2011." HannahArendt.Net, Bd. 6, Nr. 1/2, March 2012, doi:10.57773/hanet.v6i1/2.64.

10 Adam Kirsch, "Beware of Pity: Hannah Arendt and the Power of the Impersonal," *New Yorker*, January 12, 2009, www.newyorker.com/magazine/2009/01/12/beware-of-pity-Hannah-Arendt#ixzz0XszqFzRI.

11 Dan Savage, "SL Letter of the Day: The Sub's Paradox," *The Stranger*, January 20, 2014, www.thestranger.com/blogs/2014/01/20/18683456/sl-letter-of-the-day-the-subs-paradox.

12 Leo Ferguson, Dove Kent, and Keren Soffer-Sharon, "Understanding Antisemitism: An Offering to Our Movement," Jews for Racial and Economic Justice, November 15, 2017, www.jfrej.org/assets/uploads/JFREJ-Understanding-Antisemitism-November-2017-v1-3-2.pdf. Accessed June 15, 2023, 9.

13 Ferguson, Kent, and Soffer-Sharon, "Understanding Antisemitism," 6.
14 Ferguson, Kent, and Soffer-Sharon, "Understanding Antisemitism," 11.
15 Ferguson, Kent, and Soffer-Sharon, "Understanding Antisemitism," 26.
16 Ferguson, Kent, and Soffer-Sharon, "Understanding Antisemitism," 23.
17 Ferguson, Kent, and Soffer-Sharon, "Understanding Antisemitism," 26–28.
18 Ferguson, Kent, and Soffer-Sharon, "Understanding Antisemitism," 17.
19 Ferguson, Kent, and Soffer-Sharon, "Understanding Antisemitism," 19.

Dark Night of the Species

1 Melanie Kaye/Kantrowitz, "The Issue Is Power: Some Notes on Jewish Women
and Therapy," in *Jewish Women in Therapy: Seen But Not Heard*, ed. Rachel Siegel and
Ellen Cole (London: Harrington Park Press, 1991). Reprinted in *The Issue Is Power:
Essays on Women, Jews, Violence, and Resistance* (San Francisco: Aunt Lute Books,
1992).
2 Len Gilbert, *The Furred Reich* (Self-published, 2017), 28.
3 Gilbert, *Furred Reich*, 27.
4 Gilbert, *Furred Reich*, 34.
5 Gilbert, *Furred Reich*, 35.
6 Gilbert, *Furred Reich*, 41.
7 Amelia Tait, "The Furred Reich: The Truth about Nazi Furries and the Alt-Right,"
New Statesman, February 2, 2017, www.newstatesman.com/science-tech/2017/02/
furred-reich-truth-about-nazi-furries-and-alt-right.
8 Tait, "Furred Reich."
9 Tait, "Furred Reich."
10 Gilbert, *Furred Reich*, 463.
11 John Berger, "Why Look at Animals?" in *About Looking* (New York: Pantheon
Books, 1980), 1–26.
12 Sarah Schulman, *Conflict Is Not Abuse: Overstating Harm, Community Responsibility,
and the Duty of Repair* (Vancouver, BC: Arsenal Pulp Press, 2016), 66.

Fascinatrix

1 Leora Fridman, "Get It Together: On the Art of Care and Shaky Unification,"
Temporary Art Review, December 13, 2018, temporaryartreview.com/get-it-together
-on-the-art-of-care-and-shaky-unification/.
2 *Feminist Health Care Group*, www.feministische-recherchegruppe.org/. Accessed
June 15, 2023.
3 "About," *Sickness Affinity Group*, www.sicknessaffinity.org/. Accessed June 15, 2023.
4 Marianne Hirsch, *The Generation of Postmemory: Writing and Visual Culture after the
Holocaust* (New York: Columbia University Press, 2012), 33.
5 Marie-Louise Paulesc, "Four Questions or More for Marianne Hirsch," *Journal of
Research in Gender Studies* 1, no. 2 (2011): 174–77. https://blogs.cuit.columbia.edu/
mh2349/files/2019/07/Four_Questions_or_More_for_Mar-1.pdf.

6 "Stella: One Woman's True Tale of Evil, Betrayal, and Survival in Hitler's Germany," Goodreads, accessed June 15, 2023, www.goodreads.com/en/book/show/521670.

7 Julie, "With all that I have known and have read about the war, I gained a new perspective through this book," Goodreads, January 24, 2016, www.goodreads.com/en/book/show/521670.

8 Julie Cohen, "This book, more than any other I've read, gives a clear and fascinating picture of what it was like to be a German in pre–World War II Germany," Goodreads, July 10, 2012, www.goodreads.com/en/book/show/521670.

9 "Bewitch," Merriam-Webster.com, June 15, 2023.

10 Veronique Dasen, "Pobaskania: Amulets and Magic in Antiquity," in *The Materiality of Magic*, ed. Jan N. Bremner and Dietrich Boschung (Munich: Morphomata, 2015), 177–203.

11 Pliny, *Natural History Volume VIII, LIBRI XXVIII–XXXII*, trans. W. H. S. Jones (Cambridge, MA: Harvard University Press, 1963), 28.

12 Daniel Ogden, *Magic, Witchcraft, and Ghosts in the Greek and Roman Worlds: A Sourcebook* (Oxford: Oxford University Press, 2002), 225.

13 Craig Arthur Williams, *Roman Homosexuality: Ideologies of Masculinity in Classical Antiquity* (Oxford: Oxford University Press, 1999), 92.

14 Nathan Rabin, "The Producers," *The AV Club*, December 14, 2015, www.avclub.com/the-producers-1798201346. Accessed June 15, 2023.

15 Max Czollek, *De-Integrate! A Jewish Survival Guide for the 21st Century*, trans. Jon Cho-Polizzi (Brooklyn: Restless Books, 2023).

16 Pascal Quignard, *Sex and Terror*, trans. Chris Turner (Kolkata, India: Seagull Books, 2011), introduction, x.

17 Stardust seeker, "Beckoning and exciting in spite of everything!," Goodreads, February 8, 2019, www.goodreads.com/book/show/42379527-stella.

18 aiyanaurora, "I have never read such an authentic book about World War II. It is very interesting and because it is so well written it is easy and fast to read," Goodreads, February 18, 2019, www.goodreads.com/book/show/42379527-stella.

19 Scherzkeks, "First of all: I would like to congratulate the publisher for the beautiful design of the cover. A great metallic effect," Goodreads, January 27, 2019, www.goodreads.com/book/show/42379527-stella.

20 Leselissi, "What a story! What a woman! Fierce! Of course I could not resist it, and immediately googled Stella Goldschlag," Goodreads, November 29, 2018, www.goodreads.com/book/show/42379527-stella.

On Diasporic Speech

1 Rosie Lerner, "Fascinating Fasciation." *Indiana Yard and Garden—Purdue Consumer Horticulture*, www.purdue.edu/hla/sites/yardandgarden/fascinating-fasciation/. Accessed June 15, 2023.

2 "Fasciation," *American Dictionary of the English Language*, http://webstersdictionary1828.com/Dictionary/fasciation. Accessed June 15, 2023.

3 "Beyond the Museum: Diaspora Garden," Jüdisches Museum Berlin, www.jmberlin.de/en/beyond-museum-diaspora-garden. Accessed June 15, 2023.

4 "The WANDERING JEW; / Or, The Shoemaker of JERUSALEM. / Who Lived When Our Saviour JESUS CHRIST Was Crucified, and by Him Appointed to /

Wander till His Coming Again." Ebba 33904—UCSB English Broadside Ballad Archive, ebba.english.ucsb.edu/ballad/33904/xml. Accessed June 21, 2023.

5 George K. Anderson, "The Beginnings of the Legend," in *The Legend of the Wandering Jew* (Providence, RI: Brown University Press, 1965), 11–37.

6 Riaz Hassan, "Interrupting a History of Tolerance: Anti-Semitism and the Arabs," *Asian Journal of Social Science* 37, no. 3 (2009): 452–62. *JSTOR*, www.jstor.org/stable/23655209. Accessed June 21, 2023.

7 Leo Ferguson, Dove Kent, and Keren Soffer-Sharon, "Understanding Antisemitism: An Offering to Our Movement," Jews for Racial and Economic Justice, November 15, 2017, www.jfrej.org/assets/uploads/JFREJ-Understanding-Antisemitism-November-2017-v1-3-2.pdf. Accessed June 15, 2023, 14.

8 RA Walden, "Crip Ecologies (2022)." *Crip Ecologies (2022)—RA Walden*, rawalden.com/Crip-Ecologies-2022. Accessed June 15, 2023.

9 John Berger, *Ways of Seeing: Based on the BBC Television Series* (London: British Broadcasting Corporation and Penguin Books, 1990), 11.

10 "Building a Stairway to Get Us Closer to Something beyond This Place," Millennials Are Killing Capitalism, May 13, 2021, https://millennialsarekillingcapitalism.libsyn.com/hanif-abdurraqib-fred-moten-building-a-stairway-to-get-us-closer-to-something-beyond-this-place.

11 "How to Dress for a Riot," *Triple Canopy*, canopycanopycanopy.com/contents/how-to-dress-for-a-riot. Accessed July 5, 2023.

12 Anne Boyer, *The Undying: Pain, Vulnerability, Mortality, Medicine, Art, Time, Dreams, Data, Exhaustion, Cancer, and Care* (New York: Farrar, Straus and Giroux, 2019), 261.

13 John Berger, *And Our Faces, My Heart, Brief as Photos* (New York: Pantheon Books, 1984), 95.

Monumental

1 bell hooks, "Marginality as Site of Resistance," in *Out There: Marginalization and Contemporary Cultures* Ed. Russell Ferguson, Martha Gever, Trinh T. Minh-ha, and Cornel West (New York: MIT Press. 1992), 341–43.

2 Melanie Kaye/Kantrowitz, "To Be a Radical Jew in the Late 20th Century," in *The Tribe of Diana: A Jewish Women's Anthology*, ed. Melanie Kaye/Kantrowitz and Irene Klepfisz, 2nd exp. ed. (Boston: Beacon Press, 1989), 312.

3 Sam Holleran, "Shoahtecture," *Jewish Currents*, November 26, 2018, jewishcurrents.org/shoahtecture. Accessed June 15, 2023.

4 "Stalags—Holocaust and Pornography in Israel," *Jewish Film Festival*, jfi.org/year-round/jfi-on-demand/stalags-holocaust-and-pornography-in-israel. Accessed June 15, 2023.

5 Roy Brand and Amit Pinchevski, "Holocaust Perversions: The Stalags Pulp Fiction and the Eichmann Trial," *Critical Studies in Media Communication* 24, no. 5 (December 2007): 387–407.

6 "An Interview with Marianne Hirsch," Columbia University Press, cup.columbia.edu/author-interviews/hirsch-generation-postmemory. Accessed June 16, 2023.

7 Alexandros Papadopoulos, "How to Use Gay Nazis in Job Interviews: Queer Media, Striptease-Lectures, and the Art of Existential Sodomism," *Journal for Artistic Research*, April 10, 2018, www.researchcatalogue.net/view/351358/351371.

8 Lauren Berlant and Lee Edelman, *Sex, or the Unbearable* (Durham, NC: Duke University Press, 2011), 63.

9 Berlant and Edelman, *Sex, or the Unbearable*, xvii.

10 Elizabeth V. Spelman, *Repair: The Impulse to Restore in a Fragile World* (Boston: Beacon Press, 2002), 134.

Chaotic Neutral

1 "Fragen aus dem Leserkreis," in *Figaro*, Heft 15 (not numbered), 1927.

2 "Fragen aus dem Leserkreis."

3 Chad Ross, *Naked Germany: Health, Race, and the Nation* (New York: Berg Publishers, 2005), 73.

4 Ross, *Naked Germany*, 75.

5 Elizabeth V. Spelman, *Repair: The Impulse to Restore in a Fragile World* (Boston: Beacon Press, 2002), 37.

6 Spelman, *Repair*, 133.

Pure Love

1 Naturist Society, "Uncover Your Natural State,'" *Naturist Society Foundation*, April 18, 2020, naturistsociety.com/. Accessed June 15, 2023.

2 "Lupin Lodge Naturist Retreat Los Gatos: Silicon Valley Nudist Resort," *Lupin Lodge*, September 24, 2020, www.lupinlodge.com/welcome-to-lupin-lodge/. Accessed June 15, 2023.

3 "Lupin History," Lupin Lodge, May 12, 2019, www.lupinlodge.com/lupin-history/. Accessed June 15, 2023.

4 Bouke de Vries, "The Right to Be Publicly Naked: A Defence of Nudism," *Res Publica* 25 (2019): 407–24, https://doi.org/10.1007/s11158-018-09406-z.

5 Chad Ross, *Naked Germany: Health, Race, and the Nation* (New York: Berg Publishers, 2005), 1.

6 Ross, *Naked Germany*, 3.

7 Richard Cleminson, "Making Sense of the Body: Anarchism, Nudism, and Subjective Experience," *Bulletin of Spanish Studies* 81, no. 6 (2004), https://doi.org/10.1080/1475382042000272256.

8 Ellen E. Woodall, "The American Nudist Movement: From Cooperative to Capital, the Song Remains the Same," *Journal of Popular Culture* 36, no. 2 (April 2003): 264–284, at 264. https://doi.org/10.1111/1540-5931.00006.

9 Glyn Stout, "A Tribute to Lupin Women," *Lupin Lodge*, January 26, 2019, www.lupinlodge.com/a-tribute-to-lupin-women/. Accessed June 15, 2023.

10 Jason Green, "San Jose: Lupin Lodge Owner Sentenced in Water Theft Case," *Mercury News*, August 12, 2016, www.mercurynews.com/2016/02/01/san-jose-lupin-lodge-owner-sentenced-in-water-theft-case/.

11 Jennifer Wadsworth, "Bad Nudes Bared: Lupin Lodge's Idyllic Clothing-Free Lifestyle Unravels in Alarming Fashion," *San Jose Inside*, October 27, 2019, www

.sanjoseinside.com/news/investigative-reports/bad-nudes-bared-lupin-lodges-idyllic
-clothing-free-lifestyle-unravels-in-alarming-fashion/?all=1.

12 Jennifer Wadsworth, "Lawsuit: Lupin Lodge Nudist Resort Exploited Workers,"
San Jose Inside, October 21, 2015. www.sanjoseinside.com/news/lawsuit-lupin-lodge
-nudist-resort-exploited-workers/.

13 Wadsworth, "Lawsuit: Lupin Lodge."

14 Stout, "A Tribute to Lupin Women."

15 Benfell, "Killing People," *Not Housebroken*, December 14, 2013, disunitedstates.org/
2013/12/14/killing-people/. Accessed June 15, 2023.

16 "Lupin History," *Lupin Lodge*, www.lupinlodge.com/welcome-to-lupin/lupin-history
-75th-n-magazine/. Accessed December 30, 2016.

17 Nathan Heller, "Private Dreams and Public Ideals in San Francisco," *New Yorker*,
July 30, 2018, www.newyorker.com/magazine/2018/08/06/private-dreams-and
-public-ideals-in-san-francisco.

Name It to Tame It

1 Maggie Nelson, "In Conversation with Julia Bryan-Wilson," City Arts and Lectures,
January 19, 2018, Nourse Theater, San Francisco. Public Talk.

2 Lawrence Abu Hamdan, *Walled Unwalled*, video installation essay, http://
lawrenceabuhamdan.com/walled-unwalled.

3 "The Whole-Brain Child," Dr. Dan Siegel, December 10, 2020, drdansiegel.com/
book/the-whole-brain-child/. Accessed June 15, 2023.

4 Katherine McKittrick, *Dear Science and Other Stories* (Durham, NC: Duke
University Press, 2021), 16.

5 Leo Ferguson, Dove Kent, and Keren Soffer-Sharon, "Understanding
Antisemitism: An Offering to Our Movement," Jews for Racial and Economic
Justice, November 15, 2017, www.jfrej.org/assets/uploads/JFREJ-Understanding
-Antisemitism-November-2017-v1-3-2.pdf. Accessed June 15, 2023, 24.

6 Ana Cecilia Alvarez, "Natural Processes," *Real Life*, January 22, 2019, reallifemag
.com/natural-processes/.

How to Ride

1 "What to Wear to the Kentucky Derby," *Kentucky Derby*, www.kentuckyderby.com/
visit/what-to-wear. Accessed June 16, 2023.

2 Aubrey Almanza, "Here's Why Guests Will Be Wearing Fascinators to the Royal
Wedding," *Allure*, May 20, 2017, www.allure.com/story/history-of-fascinators.

3 Susan Sontag, *Notes on "Camp"* (New York: Penguin Classics, 2018), 24.

4 Laura Jacobs, "A Brief History of Fascinators," *Vanity Fair*, May 9, 2018, www
.vanityfair.com/style/2018/05/a-brief-history-of-fascinators.

5 Billy Ray Belcourt, George Dust, and Kay Gabriel, "Top or Bottom: How Do We
Desire?" *New Inquiry*, October 10, 2018, thenewinquiry.com/top-or-bottom-how-do
-we-desire/.

6 Peter Wyden, *Stella: One Woman's True Tale of Evil, Betrayal, and Survival in Hitler's Germany* (New York: Simon and Schuster, 1992), 285.
7 Sontag, *Notes on "Camp,"* 12.
8 Almanza, "Here's Why Guests."
9 Ellie Pithers, "Princesses Beatrice and Eugenie on Keeping It Real." *British Vogue*, October 8, 2018, www.vogue.co.uk/article/princesses-beatrice-eugenie-of-york -interview.
10 Antonio Marco Martínez, "The Fascinating Source of the Word 'Fascinating,'" *History of Greece and Rome*, October 31, 2013, www.antiquitatem.com/en/fascinating -evil-eye-apotropaic-phallus/. Accessed June 16, 2023.
11 "Witchcraft," *Encyclopedia of Diderot and d'Alembert Collaborative Translation Project*, trans. Steve Harris (Ann Arbor: Michigan Publishing, University of Michigan Library, 2007). Web, June 16, 2023, http://hdl.handle.net/2027/spo.did2222.0000.729.
12 Matt Diehl, "Music Single Review: 'Pony,'" *Entertainment Weekly*, November 8, 1996, https://web.archive.org/web/20180707094704/ew.com/article/1996/11/08/music -single-review-pony/. Accessed July 7, 2018.
13 Max Czollek, "Gegenwartsbewältigung [Overcoming the Present]," trans. Jon Cho-Polizzi, *TRANSIT* 12, no. 2 (2023), https://transit.berkeley.edu/2020/czollekcho -polizzi/#_ftnl.
14 Leo Ferguson, Dove Kent, and Keren Soffer-Sharon, "Understanding Antisemitism: An Offering to Our Movement," Jews for Racial and Economic Justice, November 15, 2017, www.jfrej.org/assets/uploads/JFREJ-Understanding -Antisemitism-November-2017-v1-3-2.pdf. Accessed June 15, 2023, 11.
15 Ferguson, Kent, and Soffer-Sharon, "Understanding Antisemitism," 11.

Testing Testing

1 Harry Dodge, "The River of the Mother of God: Notes on Indeterminacy, V. 2 (2014)," Harry Dodge, June 2014, harrydodge.com/portfolio/the-river-of-the -mother-of-god-v-2-notes-on-indeterminacy/, 34.
2 *The Elephant in the Room: Sculptures of the Marx Collection and of the Nationalgalerie Collection*, November 1–September 29, 2019, Hamburger Bahnhof—Nationalgalerie der Gegenwart, Berlin.
3 "Matthew Barney's Cremaster Cycle: Nine Hours of 'Challenging' Art on Film," *The Guardian*, July 14, 2015, www.theguardian.com/artanddesign/2015/jul/14/matthew -barney-cremaster-cycle-art-film.
4 Alexandra Keller and Frazer Ward, "Matthew Barney and the Paradox of the Neo-Avant-Garde Blockbuster," *Cinema Journal* 45, no. 2 (Winter 2006): 3–16.
5 Dodge, "River of the Mother of God," 34.

On Fascia

1 Elaine N. Marieb and Katja Hoehn, *Human Anatomy and Physiology* (Hoboken, NJ: Pearson Education, 2007), 133.

2 Marieb and Hoehn, *Human Anatomy and Physiology.*
3 Gabrielle Kassel, "10 Ways to Keep Your Fascia Healthy So Your Body Moves Pain-Free," *Healthline*, January 10, 2020, www.healthline.com/health/fascia.
4 Dodge, "River of the Mother of God," 81.
5 Elaine Scarry, *On Beauty and Being Just* (Princeton, NJ: Princeton University Press, 1999), 50.
6 Adolf Faller and Michael Schünke. *The Human Body: An Introduction to Structure and Function* (Stuttgart: Thieme Medical Publishers, 2004), 127.
7 Yasser El Miedany, ed., *Pediatric Musculoskeletal Ultrasonography* (New York: Springer, 2020), 22.
8 "Fascia," *Wikipedia*, web.archive.org/web/20190410043442/https://en.wikipedia.org/wiki/Fascia. Accessed April 10, 2019.
9 Scarry, *On Beauty and Being Just*, 111.
10 Simone Weil, "Love of the Order of the World," in *Waiting for God* (New York: Harper and Row, 1951), 159.
11 For more on the role of Jewish contemporary art in cultural reproduction, see: Leora Fridman, "A Birth of One's Own: On Inheritance, Curation, and Production," *Ayin Press*, May 18, 2023, ayinpress.org/a-birth-of-ones-own-on-inheritance-curation-and-production/.
12 Leo Ferguson, Dove Kent, and Keren Soffer-Sharon, "Understanding Antisemitism: An Offering to Our Movement," Jews for Racial and Economic Justice, November 15, 2017, www.jfrej.org/assets/uploads/JFREJ-Understanding-Antisemitism-November-2017-v1-3-2.pdf. Accessed June 15, 2023, 19.
13 Ferguson, Kent, and Soffer-Sharon, "Understanding Antisemitism," 17.
14 Tirzah Firestone, *Wounds into Wisdom: Healing Intergenerational Jewish Trauma* (Rhinebeck, NY: Adam Kadmon Books, 2019), 52.
15 Elizabeth V. Spelman, *Repair: The Impulse to Restore in a Fragile World* (Boston: Beacon Press, 2002), 124.

Formula One

1 Neville Thurlbeck, "Undress: Maybe a Few More Beatings . . . Zey Need More of Ze Punishment: Secret Tape Reveals Vile Max Mosley's True Depravity," *News of the World*, April 6, 2008, web.archive.org/web/20080409210551/www.newsoftheworld.co.uk/0604_mosley2.shtml.
2 Laura Oliver, "News of the World Wins Right to Show Max Mosley Video," Journalism.Co.Uk, April 9, 2008, www.journalism.co.uk/news/news-of-the-world-wins-right-to-show-max-mosley-video/s2/a531322/.
3 "F1 Chief Mosley Loses Sex Tape Court Battle," *France 24*, April 9, 2008, www.france24.com/en/20080409-f1-chief-mosley-loses-sex-tape-court-battle-formula-one.
4 "Eye Pop," *TV Tropes*, tvtropes.org/pmwiki/pmwiki.php/Main/EyePop. Accessed June 23, 2023.
5 "Ahooga," Urban Dictionary, www.urbandictionary.com/define.php?term=ahooga. Accessed June 23, 2023.
6 "How Tipping Point Is Easing the Burden on Low-Income Drivers," *Medium*, July 3, 2018, medium.com/tipping-point/how-tipping-point-is-easing-the-burden-on-low-income-drivers-9d58eeabbbd5.

7 "Brich Rachamana (Now: With Sheet Music!)," Velveteen Rabbi, velveteenrabbi
.blogs.com/blog/2012/09/brich-rachamana-now-with-sheet-music.html. Accessed
June 23, 2023.
8 Judith Butler, *Precarious Life: The Powers of Mourning and Violence* (New York: Verso
Books, 2004), 49.
9 Butler, *Precarious Life*, 49.
10 "Fasces," Wikipedia, June 1, 2023, en.wikipedia.org/wiki/Fasces.
11 Pascal Bruckner, *The Temptation of Innocence: Living in the Age of Entitlement* (New
York: Algora Publishing, 2000), 134.
12 Antonio Marco Martínez, "The Fascinating Source of the Word 'Fascinating,'"
History of Greece and Rome, October 31, 2013, www.antiquitatem.com/en/fascinating
-evil-eye-apotropaic-phallus/.
13 Butler, *Precarious Life*, 20.
14 Bruckner, *Temptation of Innocence*, 293.
15 Joan Ringelheim, "Women and the Holocaust: A Reconsideration of Research,"
Communities of Women 10, no. 4 (1985): 741–61.
16 "Building a Stairway to Get Us Closer to Something beyond This Place," Millennials
Are Killing Capitalism, May 13, 2021, https://millennialsarekillingcapitalism
.libsyn.com/hanif-abdurraqib-fred-moten-building-a-stairway-to-get-us-closer-to
-something-beyond-this-place.
17 Édouard Glissant, *Poetics of Relation*, trans. Betsy Wing (Ann Arbor: University of
Michigan Press, 1997).
18 Butler, *Precarious Life*, 44.

Oh My Love

1 Lisa Robertson, "Time in the Codex," in *Nilling: Prose Essays on Noise, Pornography,
The Codex, Melancholy, Lucretius, Folds, Cities, and Related Aporias* (Ontario, CA:
Bookthug, 2012), 12.
2 Elizabeth Freeman, "Turn the Beat Around: Sadomasochism, Temporality, History,"
Differences 19, no. 1 (2008): 34–35.
3 Freeman, "Turn the Beat Around," 34.
4 Freeman, "Turn the Beat Around," 63.
5 Tracy Clark-Flory, "BDSM: It's Less Transgressive Than You Think," *Salon*,
January 12, 2012, www.salon.com/2012/01/12/bdsm_its_less_transgressive_than
_you_think/.
6 Margot Weiss, *Techniques of Pleasure: BDSM and the Circuits of Sexuality* (Durham,
NC: Duke University Press, 2011), 230.
7 Dan Savage, "SL Letter of the Day: The Sub's Paradox," *The Stranger*, January 20,
2014, www.thestranger.com/blogs/2014/01/20/18683456/sl-letter-of-the-day-the
-subs-paradox.
8 Saidiya V. Hartman, *Scenes of Subjection: Terror, Slavery, and Self-Making in
Nineteenth-Century America* (Oxford: Oxford University Press, 1997), 18–19.
9 bell hooks, "Marginality as Site of Resistance," in *Out There: Marginalization and
Contemporary Cultures* Ed. Russell Ferguson, Martha Gever, Trinh T. Minh-ha, and
Cornel West (New York: MIT Press. 1992), 341–43.
10 Julia Kristeva, *Powers of Horror: An Essay on Abjection* (New York: Columbia
University Press, 1982): 9–10.

11 Johanna Hedva, "Your Love Is Not Good: Johanna Hedva and Legacy Russell," *Dear Reader*, June 6, 2023, Amant, New York. Public Talk.

12 *Die Blumen von gestern*. Directed by Chris Kraus, Dor Film Produktionsgesellschaft, 2016.

13 "THE BLOOM OF YESTERDAY (2016)—FULL TRANSCRIPT." *SUBSLIKESCRIPT*, https://subslikescript.com/movie/The_Bloom_of_Yesterday -3756046. Accessed October 13, 2023.

14 Jessica Kiang, "Film Review: 'The Bloom of Yesterday,'" *Variety*, November 21, 2016, variety.com/2016/film/reviews/the-bloom-of-yesterday-tokyo-film-review -1201903706/.

15 Sara Ahmed, *Living a Feminist Life* (Durham, NC: Duke University Press, 2017), 166.

16 Georges Bataille, *Literature and Evil*, trans. Alastair Hamilton (London: Marion Boyars Publishers, 1997), 10.

17 Ahmed, *Living a Feminist Life*, 166.

18 Anna Mollow, "Is Sex Disability?: Queer Theory and the Disability Drive," in *Sex and Disability*, ed. Robert McRuer and Anna Mollow (Durham, NC: Duke University Press, 2012), 285–312.

19 hooks, "Marginality as Site of Resistance," 341–43.

20 Sarah E. Chinn, "Feeling Her Way: Audre Lorde and the Power of Touch," *GLQ: A Journal of Lesbian and Gay Studies* 9, no. 1–2 (2003): 181–204.

21 John Berger, "Ernst Fischer: A Philosopher and Death," in *Why Look at Animals* (New York: Penguin Books, 2009), 94.

22 Hannah Arendt, *The Promise of Politics* (New York: Schocken Books, 2005), 95.

23 Arendt, *Promise of Politics*, 106.

24 Freeman, "Turn the Beat Around," 40.

25 Sarah Schulman, *The Gentrification of the Mind: Witness to a Lost Imagination* (Berkeley: University of California Press, 2012), 161.

26 Freeman, "Turn the Beat Around," 34.

About the Author

Leora Fridman is a writer, educator, and curator whose work is concerned with identity, care, collectivity, and embodiment. She teaches at the Eugene Lang College of Liberal Arts at the New School and is Director of the New Jewish Culture Fellowship. She lives in Brooklyn, New York.